ALSO BY FREDERIC WEHREY

Sectarian Politics in the Gulf:
From the Iraq War to the Arab Uprisings

THE BURNING SHORES

THE BURNING SHORES

INSIDE THE

BATTLE

FOR THE

NEW LIBYA

Frederic Wehrey

FARRAR, STRAUS AND GIROUX ▪ NEW YORK

Farrar, Straus and Giroux
175 Varick Street, New York 10014

Copyright © 2018 by Frederic Wehrey
Maps copyright © 2018 by Jeffrey L. Ward
All rights reserved
Printed in the United States of America
First edition, 2018

Library of Congress Cataloging-in-Publication Data
Names: Wehrey, Frederic M., author.
Title: The burning shores : inside the battle for the new Libya /
    Frederic Wehrey.
Description: First edition. | New York : Farrar, Straus and Giroux, 2018. |
    Includes bibliographical references and index.
Identifiers: LCCN 2017049275 | ISBN 9780374278243 (hardcover)
Subjects: LCSH: Libya—History—Civil War, 2011– | Libya—
    History—Civil War, 2011– —Participation, American. | Libya—
    Politics and government—21st century. | Libya—Economic
    conditions—21st century.
Classification: LCC DT236 .W44 2018 | DDC 961.205—dc23
LC record available at https://lccn.loc.gov/2017049275

Designed by Richard Oriolo

Our books may be purchased in bulk for promotional, educational, or
business use. Please contact your local bookseller or the Macmillan
Corporate and Premium Sales Department at 1-800-221-7945, extension
5442, or by e-mail at MacmillanSpecialMarkets@macmillan.com.

www.fsgbooks.com
www.twitter.com/fsgbooks • www.facebook.com/fsgbooks

1 3 5 7 9 10 8 6 4 2

FOR MY PARENTS

What *fury*, citizens, what anarchy of iron?
—LUCAN, *CIVIL WAR*

CONTENTS

DRAMATIS PERSONAE

QADHAFI FAMILY

MUAMMAR AL-QADHAFI—ruler of Libya, 1969 to 2011.

SAIF AL-ISLAM AL-QADHAFI—Western-educated second son of Muammar Qadhafi; captured in 2011.

KHAMIS AL-QADHAFI—youngest son of Muammar Qadhafi; commander of an elite military unit; killed in 2011.

AMERICANS

BRIAN LINVILL—U.S. military attaché in Libya, 2008 to 2012.

J. CHRISTOPHER STEVENS—U.S. special envoy to the Libyan opposition, 2011; U.S. ambassador to Libya, 2012. Killed on September 11, 2012, during an attack on the U.S. diplomatic mission in Benghazi, along with three other Americans: Sean Smith, Tyrone Woods, and Glen Doherty.

DEBORAH JONES—U.S. ambassador to Libya, 2013 to 2015.

GENE CRETZ—U.S. ambassador to Libya, 2008 to 2012.

UNITED NATIONS

BERNARDINO LEÓN—head of the United Nations Support Mission in Libya (UNSMIL), 2014 to 2015.

LIBYAN POLITICIANS

MAHMUD JIBRIL—U.S.-educated technocrat under Qadhafi; interim prime minister under the National Transitional Council; head of the National Forces Alliance political gathering.

ALI ZEIDAN—prime minister of Libya, 2013 to 2014.

MUSTAFA ABD AL-JALIL—former judge under Qadhafi; chairman of the National Transitional Council.

LIBYAN ACTIVISTS

SALWA BUGAIGHIS—human rights lawyer; murdered in Benghazi on June 25, 2014.

WAIL GHERIANI—Salwa's son.

IMAN BUGAIGHIS—Salwa's sister; professor of orthodontics; former spokesperson for the National Transitional Council.

LAILA BUGAIGHIS—chief medical officer at the Benghazi Medical Center; Salwa's cousin.

FATHI TERBIL—lawyer representing the families of prisoners killed in the 1996 massacre at Abu Salim prison; his detention helps spark the 2011 uprising.

ABD AL-SALAM AL-MISMARI—lawyer and activist; assassinated in 2013.

ABU BAKER HABIB—English school owner in Benghazi and confidant of Ambassador J. Christopher Stevens.

"MARYAM"—activist in Derna.

LIBYAN ISLAMISTS IN TRIPOLI

ABD AL-RAUF KARA—Salafist militia leader in Tripoli who heads the capital's de facto police and antiterrorism squad.

ABD AL-HAKIM BELHAJ—former leader in the Libyan Islamic Fighting Group (LIFG) turned businessman and politician.

MISRATANS

SALIM JOHA—former army officer and revolutionary leader during the 2011 siege of Misrata.

ABD AL-RAHMAN AL-SUWAYHLI—Misratan political leader; supporter of the Political Isolation Law and of Libya Dawn.

SALAH BADI—hard-line militia leader in Misrata; a commander of the military forces attacking Tripoli during Libya Dawn.

ZINTANIS

UTHMAN MLEQTA—former caterer and head of a Zintani militia allied with Hiftar.

LIBYAN NATIONAL ARMY AND OPERATION DIGNITY

KHALIFA HIFTAR—former army officer under Qadhafi and dissident, residing in the United States. Returns to Libya in 2011 in an unsuccessful bid for military leadership of the anti-Qadhafi rebels. Launches Operation Dignity in Benghazi in 2014.

WANIS BU KHAMADA—commander of the Benghazi-based "Thunderbolt" Special Forces; joins Operation Dignity in 2014.

ABD AL-SALAM AL-HASI—Special Forces general who serves as a longtime liaison to the Americans during and after the 2011 revolution.

"ISSAM"—leader of a pro-Dignity militia in Benghazi's Majuri neighborhood.

LIBYAN FEDERALISTS

IBRAHIM JADHRAN—federalist militia leader and head of the Petroleum Facilities Guard who blockades oil facilities in the Gulf of Sirt from 2013 to 2016.

ABU BAKR BAIRA—U.S.-educated federalist politician.

LIBYAN ISLAMISTS IN BENGHAZI AND THE EAST

WISSAM BIN HAMID—former car mechanic; head of the Benghazi Libya Shield One militia; later leads the Benghazi Revolutionaries' Shura Council against General Hiftar's campaign.

FAWZI BU KATIF—U.S.-educated engineer; Muslim Brotherhood member. His February 17 Brigade militia was contracted to protect the American diplomatic facility in Benghazi.

MUHAMMAD AL-GHARABI—Islamist and leader of the Rafallah al-Sahati Companies militia in Benghazi.

FATHI AL-OBEIDI—deputy to Wissam bin Hamid who assists the Americans during the 2012 attack in Benghazi.

"Tariq"—Islamist militia fighter in the Benghazi Revolutionaries' Shura Council.

Salim Darbi—former jihadist and cofounder of the Abu Salim Martyrs Brigade in Derna; killed fighting the Islamic State.

Abd al-Hakim al-Hasadi—former jihadist and cofounder of the Abu Salim Martyrs Brigade.

LIBYAN JIHADISTS

Ahmed Abu Khattala—former mechanic and Abu Salim prisoner who leads a jihadist militia in Benghazi; key suspect in the 2012 Benghazi attack; apprehended by the Americans in 2014; tried and convicted in 2017.

Muhammad al-Zahawi—leader of the jihadist Ansar al-Sharia militia; killed in 2015.

"Ahmed"—Libyan jihadist in Syria turned Islamic State fighter.

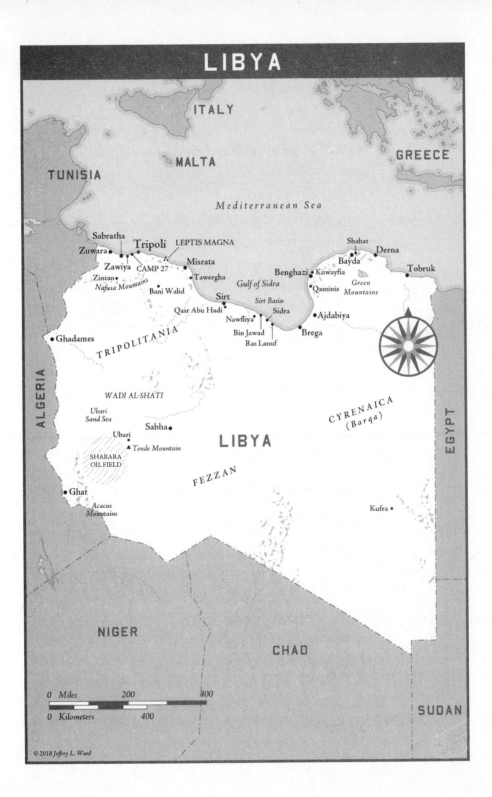

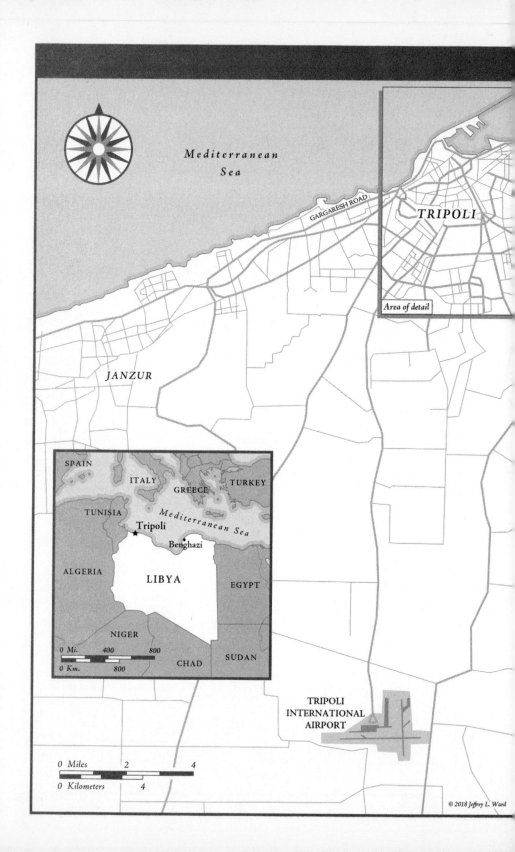

Mediterranean
Sea

GARGARESH ROAD

TRIPOLI

Area of detail

JANZUR

SPAIN

ITALY

GREECE

TURKEY

TUNISIA

Mediterranean Sea

Tripoli

Benghazi

ALGERIA

LIBYA

EGYPT

NIGER

0 Mi.   400   800

0 Km.   800

CHAD   SUDAN

TRIPOLI
INTERNATIONAL
AIRPORT

0 Miles   2   4

0 Kilometers   4

© 2018 Jeffrey L. Ward

TRIPOLI, LIBYA

MITIGA
INTERNATIONAL
AIRPORT

SUQ-AL-JUMAA

Mediterranean Sea

Corinthia hotel

*OLD
CITY*

Green Square/
Martyrs' Square

Radisson Blu hotel

OMAR-AL-MUKHTAR STREET

Algeria Square

Qadhafi compound
at Bab al-Aziziya

GHARGHUR

Rixos hotel

University of Tripoli

U.S. embassy

0 Miles 1 2

0 Kilometers 2

Abu Salim prison

BENGHAZI, LIBYA

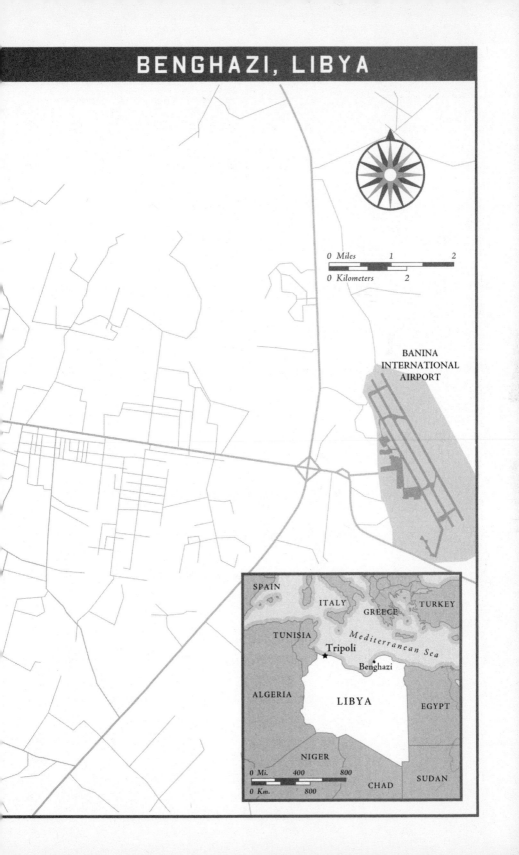

THE BURNING SHORES

PROLOGUE

FROM THE ROCKING BOAT, they could see the coast of Qaminis town. They were a few hours out of Benghazi when the motor died, somewhere on the eastern rim of the Gulf of Sidra. It was the onset of dusk. The crew set about repairs, while the dying and wounded waited. Now, in the moonless dark around them, they heard the boom and splash of artillery fired from the shore. And with each lurch and roll, Tariq felt an unbearable pain from his shattered femur.

He could hardly believe it'd come to this. He was thirty-six years old and had been born into privilege in England, where his father had been a professor. He'd come back to Benghazi, studying law at the university and entering private practice. In 2011, he was among the first to revolt, joining a group of lawyers, doctors, and academics protesting at the city's courthouse. Then came the fighting against the dictator. Nostalgia had suffused those heady months with more unity than had actually existed among the rebels. But at least they shared a goal. In the years that followed, many of the protestors would be murdered or exiled. Those who remained would join the opposing sides of a war that ravaged the city of the revolution's birth.

It was nearly three years to the day after the dictator's death when that war came to Tariq's home in Benghazi. He lived in a neighborhood called Tabalino, just north of the university, a well-to-do quarter of cubist villas, iron balustrades, and leafy streets. It was known for private schools and a reputable clinic, all since shuttered. The university was now the front line. One night, a militia made up of young men he'd grown up with and gone to school with attacked Tariq's house. He fled into the desert with his wife and newborn. And then he returned to Benghazi to join the battle.

Salvos of artillery and mortars crashed into shops, cafés, and homes; snipers dueled from windows and balconies. Civilians died in the cross fire. Close-quarter combat happened mostly at night, when infiltration teams tried to slip past sentries. They shouted across the lines at night, "*Khawarij!*"—an Islamic term denoting deviants from the faith.

How did this happen, Tariq wondered, this dissolution, this unstitching? Benghazi had once been home to all of Libya's outlooks and tribes. The nurse-mother to us all, people called it. That was what he was really fighting for, the right to remain and to belong.

I'd gone to Benghazi in the fall of 2015. By this time, the civil war between former comrades-in-arms had lasted longer than the 2011 war to unseat Muammar Qadhafi. A period of hope had followed his death, marked by the first national elections in decades. Then came the fracturing and descent into civil war. The resulting vacuum allowed the Islamic State to establish its strongest branch outside Iraq and Syria. It enabled a surge of migrants from Africa, with thousands perishing before they ever reached the sea or suffering horrific abuses at the hands of smugglers. And it drew in competing Arab powers whose supply of weapons to Libya's warring militias only prolonged the misery. Meanwhile, the Americans and Westerners had fled.

One evening at a cluster of apartments just before sunset, Tariq got caught in a hail of gunfire coming from the north. He scrambled for cover. One of his friends was hit in the leg and the chest with large-caliber rounds. The young man died quickly. Moments later Tariq felt a stabbing pain in his upper thigh and fell to the ground.

The femur bone that joins the leg to the hip is wrapped in a bundle of arteries, nerves, and muscle. Even a normal fracture, from a fall for instance, can cause bleeding, clotting, and death. A wound from a high-velocity bullet is catastrophic. If the bullet severs or even nicks the femoral artery, a person will lose enough blood to die within minutes. In Tariq's case the bullet was smaller than those that had killed his friend—it missed the artery but smashed the bone and lodged in his thigh.

At a field clinic, they set his leg with plastic cartons and moved him to a port south of Benghazi where they planned to evacuate him to Misrata, a city to the west. But shelling had forced a delay. Tariq waited all through the night, with no anesthetic. The next day, they loaded him on a small wooden boat along with the other wounded.

When the motor failed, they waited through the interminable night as shells fell around them. Dawn crept slowly over the horizon. The waves pushed the powerless boat closer and closer to shore.

■

LIKE TARIQ, I wondered: How did this happen? How does a country reach such a point? This book is an attempt to find an answer.

It traces the arc of Libya's post-Qadhafi journey from euphoria and hope to despair and war. Based on years of travel and reporting across the country, from the revolution's end to the present, it narrates the experiences of Libyans who sought to bend the new order to their will—and were irrevocably changed in the process. It tries to find the turning points and missteps that caused the splintering of Libya—which I believe was not preordained after the fall of Qadhafi. Ultimately, I want to understand what it was that caused revolutionaries like Tariq and countless others to turn against one another.

The harrowing of Libya today is part of a larger drama unfolding in the Arab world, the struggle of a region trying to remake its politics through violence and other forms of contention. It is too easy to dismiss the current chaos as inevitable, as the bitter proof of a revolution's dashed hopes. In fact, the battle for the new Libya is far from over.

The battle is also a distinctly American saga, the tale of an intervention by a superpower chastened by its adventures in Iraq and Afghanistan, which this time acted from afar and absolved itself from the follow-up. Then came the attack on the U.S. diplomatic outpost in Benghazi, which killed four Americans and triggered endless partisan attacks at home. The Libya that exists in the American mind is ineluctably linked to that night—and the Obama administration's response. The ensuing war within the Beltway is not a concern of this book, though I account for its impact on America's policy in Libya—and on Libyan lives.

I also believe that the histories and fates of Libya and America are more intertwined than many realize. Libya was once home to the largest overseas American military base in the world. More distantly, the opening verses of "The Marines' Hymn"—"From the halls of Montezuma / To the shores of Tripoli"—reference an 1805 invasion by American marines to unseat a troublesome Muslim ruler in what is now Libya and replace him with one more amenable to American interests. It was the young republic's first deployment of its military forces in foreign lands.

A little more than two hundred years later, America returned to the shores of Tripoli, this time from the air, intent on avoiding the sort of ground expedition recorded in the hymn of its marines.

What follows, then, is partly the story of that return, and its consequences.

PART I

"NO OWNERSHIP"

1

"THE TENT CONQUERED
THE CASTLE"

L ATE AUGUST IN TRIPOLI is a time of forbearance. It is still a
month before the easterly winds will start their slow assault on the
dulling heat. Flowering bougainvilleas have long since bloomed and
now dangle down the sides of white-walled villas. At night, families
emerge to stroll on a seaside promenade; backgammon players crowd
the porticoed cafés of Algeria Square. It is Ramadan 2009. And in just
a few weeks it will be forty years since Muammar Qadhafi came to
power.

In preparation, louvered shutters across the city are freshly painted
green—the official color of the dictator's "state of the masses." In Green
Square, in the shadow of an ancient citadel, workers sweep parade
grounds and erect scaffolding on vast stages. A Jumbotron video screen

looms overhead, ready to broadcast the coming pageantry. Troops of Boy Scouts practice marching.

Qadhafi's visage is everywhere on billboards. In one, a gallery of revolutionary icons—Mandela, Guevara, Nehru, and Nasser—flanks the smiling dictator in Bedouin headgear. In another, a crowd gathers before a green tent, emanating rays of light. The crowd is waving their hands, as if in gratitude or supplication.

THE TENT CONQUERED THE CASTLE, reads the wording above.

■

MUAMMAR AL-QADHAFI was born in a tent, a woven goat-hair dwelling that is typical among roaming Bedouin, on June 7, 1942, near a village called Qasr Abu Hadi. He grew up in a sparse country: the village sits on the Gulf of Sidra on a rocky plain flecked with acacia and thorn scrub. Libya then was one of the poorest countries in the world, a nation of mostly illiterate farmers, fishermen, and pastoralists, like his father. The tribe at the time was the dominant unit of social and political organization. And in his final years, after flirting with assorted ideologies, Qadhafi returned to this tribal milieu, ending his rule with an ethos of the desert and leaving a legacy of desertlike desolation.

Libya has always been a place on the margins. The name itself is borrowed from a term first used by the ancient Egyptians to describe the inhabitants on their western borders. In the classical imagination, it denoted all of Africa, a realm of wonders and terrors. "Libya is the world's third part," wrote the Roman poet Lucan. "Serpents, thirst, the heat of the sand . . . Libya is the only thing that can put forth such a swarm of suffering."

The Greeks, Carthaginians, and Romans passed through, settling mostly on a sliver of fertile coast where they built cities linking the Saharan south with the Mediterranean basin. The Arabs arrived in the seventh century, displacing the remnants of the Byzantine empire and Christianity and starting a long process of Islamization. During the nearly four centuries of Ottoman rule, Libya remained a backwater:

the Ottomans and their principalities never fully controlled it but rather governed through pacts with local notables.

The Italians arrived in 1911, latecomers to European imperialism, and wrested the territory from the Turks. Resurrecting the ancient term "Libia" to stress the region's Roman antecedents, they set about colonizing it, luring Italian settlers to emigrate with exaggerated promises of empty farmland. They joined the historic provinces of Tripolitania (the west), Cyrenaica or Barqa (the east), and Fezzan (the south) under a single governor.

With the rise of the Fascists in Italy came a decade of unrelenting military conquest, marked by aerial bombardment and poison gas. The trauma of that period remains today. To be sure, the Italians imprinted Libya with asphalt highways and buildings, but they did little for Libyans themselves, shutting them out of education or any role in governance. Their farming projects subverted the economy of pastoralism. Their brutal counterinsurgency imprisoned two-thirds of the population in eastern Libya in concentration camps; by some estimates, one out of every five persons in the country perished as a result of Italian rule.

But the colonial era also gave rise to one of Libya's great legends: the Sufi teacher turned guerrilla leader Omar al-Mukhtar. For nearly two decades, before his capture and execution at the age of seventy-three, Omar al-Mukhtar fought the Italians across the eastern Green Mountains with a band of fighters numbering no more than a thousand.

A lesser-known Libyan combatant in that struggle was the father of Muammar Qadhafi, whose exploits later hagiographies would laud and embellish. The Libya that his only son, Muammar, grew up in stood on the cusp of great change. After World War II, the country was administered by the victorious British and French militaries, remaining bereft of any political institutions, with the exception of a Sufi revivalist movement under the Sanusi dynasty. The Sanusi protostate gave way to the monarchy after independence: on December 24, 1951, Muhammad Idris, the diffident, scholarly grandson of the Sanusi order's founder, became the ruler of the United Kingdom of Libya.

His reign was relatively peaceful, but far from successful. Infrastructure and education were underdeveloped and the country was mired in poverty. Years of famine killed and displaced thousands. The literacy rate barely rose above 10 percent. The discovery of oil in the 1950s—Libya has the largest reserves in Africa and the ninth largest in the world—did little to improve things. "I wish your people had discovered water," Idris reportedly told an American diplomat. "Water makes men work; oil makes men dream." Idris also opened Libya to American and British military bases, yet these allies looked uneasily on his rule—and his staying power.

"The king offers Libya no inspiring leadership," a 1953 CIA assessment noted. "In fact he seems more interested in retiring to his ancestral hills and allowing the infant state to disintegrate."

As is often the case, the first steps toward modernization taken by a sclerotic king are his last. Urbanization and education exposed young Libyans to the seductions of Arab nationalism. On September 1, 1969, a group of such Libyans, army officers who'd been cadets together at Benghazi's military college, overthrew King Idris in a bloodless coup. Like Muammar Qadhafi, the captain who became their leader, many hailed from rural backgrounds and lesser tribes, shut out from the cronyism of the monarchy.

What followed in the months ahead was an attempt by Qadhafi to replicate the rule of his idol, Gamal Abd al-Nasser, in neighboring Egypt. The recipe would involve a mix of socialism and pan-Arabism with the nationalization of foreign banks and oil companies and the closure of foreign military bases (negotiations for the departure of the Americans had already been under way during King Idris's rule). The new regime set about purging the last vestiges of the monarchy, especially the Sanusi endowments. But the putschist officers lacked the administrative and economic skills to run the country.

In 1973, buoyed by the quadrupling of oil prices and an infusion of sudden wealth, Qadhafi embarked on a decades-long political experiment at home and militant adventurism abroad. The dictator first turned inward, codifying his musings into a multivolume tract called the Green Book. Breathtaking in scope and incoherence, the Green Book was a farrago of socialism, democracy, and capitalism. Put into practice, it resulted in the deinstitutionalization of Libya and the dismantling of the professional bureaucracy, to be replaced by various popular committees and people's militias. Libya was proclaimed in 1977 to be a "state of the masses," or a *Jamahiriya*, an Arabic neologism coined by Qadhafi himself.

A series of drastic reforms accompanied the new experiment. Some had a positive impact: literacy rose to 82 percent and a free health-care system expanded across the country. Women's status improved as well: laws forbidding polygamy and child brides were implemented, and women were afforded access to higher education. Yet other, more radical initiatives proved catastrophic. Believing that renting was a form of tyranny, Qadhafi allowed tenants to claim ownership of land and dwellings. He exhorted workers to seize businesses and turn them into collectives, banned private land ownership, and created state supermarkets. The result was the gutting of the entrepreneurial class and its flight abroad.

Radicalism at home was matched by radicalism abroad. Anti-imperialism, anti-Westernism, and anti-Zionism had long been hallmarks of Qadhafi's worldview. Now, buttressed by newfound oil wealth, he used Libya to project that ideology, training a wide array of militants, including Palestinian groups, the Irish Republican Army, European and Latin American leftists, African insurgents, and even South Pacific separatists. By one count, more than thirty organizations passed through Libyan camps. It wasn't just unconventional warfare that defined Libya's bellicosity abroad: Qadhafi embroiled Libya in a disastrous nine-year war with neighboring Chad over a uranium-rich piece of border territory called the Aouzou Strip.

By the early 1980s, this militancy had brought Libya into confrontation with America, especially the administration of Ronald Reagan, who famously called the dictator the "mad dog of the Middle East." In 1986, citing evidence of Qadhafi's complicity in the bombing of a West Berlin disco that killed American soldiers, Reagan sent fighter-bombers to strike Libya's terrorist training facilities. Dubbed Operation El Dorado Canyon, the raid destroyed a number of camps and military targets, killing roughly forty soldiers and civilians, with the loss of one American aircraft and its two-person crew. The attack also resulted in a gradual diminution of Qadhafi's anti-American statements and support for terrorism, but only after a bloody uptick: the bombing in 1988 of Pan Am Flight 103 over Lockerbie, Scotland, that killed 270, and a French airliner over Niger in 1989 that killed 156. Qadhafi's refusal to hand over suspects in the bombings resulted in a UN embargo against the country in 1992. The United States added its own sanctions in 1996.

By the 1990s, Libya was in ruins. Falling oil prices, combined with the effects of ill-conceived policies and now sanctions, had inflicted untold suffering on the population. The mask of egalitarianism fell away: a kleptocratic elite centered on Qadhafi's family enriched themselves at the expense of the masses. The Revolutionary Committees became little more than thugs and enforcers. Unemployment was rising, inflation had soared to 50 percent, and Libyans faced shortages of basic foodstuffs, with fistfights arising over loaves of bread at state-run bakeries. And despite his pretensions of doing away with tribalism, Qadhafi leaned on tribes even more to maintain control.

Then, at the turn of the millennium, Qadhafi came in from the cold. In 1999 he surrendered the suspects in the Pan Am Lockerbie bombing and positioned himself as a useful counterterror partner for the West, especially after the September 11, 2001, attacks on the United States. The dictator had faced an Islamist insurgency of his own starting in the mid-1990s, led by Libyan jihadists returning from Afghanistan, and he was quick to frame his campaign against these local militants as part of America's "global war on terrorism." His government, he liked to point out, was the first in the world to issue an Interpol arrest warrant for Osama bin Laden, as early as 1998.

On top of this, in December 2003, Qadhafi announced Libya would dismantle its nascent nuclear weapons program and surrender its stocks of biological and chemical weapons—a decision the Bush administration claimed had been accelerated by its invasion of Iraq. In fact, the Libyan ruler had entered into secret negotiations with Washington well before this, under Clinton, and his choice to disarm resulted less from coercion and more from the prospect of reintegration into the global economy. In 2003, the United Nations lifted its sanctions, followed soon after by the United States.

In 2006, after thirty years of enmity, America and Libya restored full diplomatic relations, marked by the reopening of an embassy in Tripoli and agreements on trade, science, and education. The oil companies returned, and the Pentagon began a modest effort to assist the Libyan military. Yet a seeming tug-of-war between reactionary and reform-oriented factions in Tripoli threatened to upend the diplomatic gains. Where Qadhafi stood was always unclear. Some hoped that limited engagement with Libyan moderates could influence the domestic power balance in favor of a supposedly progressive camp led by Qadhafi's London-educated son, Saif al-Islam.

But how much power did Saif and his reformers really have? And was the seeming perestroika genuine?

■

I FIRST WENT to Libya in the summer of 2009 as a military officer working at the U.S. embassy. I was no stranger to the Arab world and its discontents—and to the paradoxes of U.S. policy in the region. I'd studied at Cairo University at the peak of an Islamist insurgency against Egypt's dictatorial president Hosni Mubarak. I'd lived with Palestinian families during the Israeli occupation of Gaza and with Bedouin Arab tribes in Israel's Negev Desert. During military service in Iraq, I'd met with dozens of former regime henchmen, Ba'athists, and soon-to-be insurgents. Leaving active duty, I'd interviewed the spiritual guide of Hizballah in southern Beirut and sat on the floor of his mosque listening to his sermon on American abuses in Iraq. In Saudi Arabia's restive Eastern Province, I'd met with wanted dissidents from the kingdom's minority Shi'a sect.

Still, nothing could prepare me for Libya. It had been an enigmatic place ever since my youth, when one of my first political memories was

Ronald Reagan's bombing of the country. For most of the intervening years, the idea of going to work in the country on behalf of the U.S. government would have seemed far-fetched.

The Libya I encountered was a place of enchantment. You could choose to insulate yourself completely in its culture and history. Wander at night in the warrens of Tripoli's Old City, past the Gurgi mosque with its glazed tiles, the clock tower, and the cavernous baths. Travel west or east for a day to the Roman ruins at Sabratha and Leptis Magna, resplendent with colonnaded streets, amphitheaters, and views of the sea. Pause for a moment on the manicured lawn of a war cemetery, where the fallen of Britain and its empire rested after fighting the Axis. Journey south to the white-terraced town of Ghadames, the "pearl of the Sahara."

The postcard sheen quickly wore off. The modern city of Tripoli seemed stricken and tired. True, you did not find the soul-crushing poverty of Cairo's slums. But an aura of dread pervaded the place; people still disappeared in prisons. You were never without a minder from the *mukhabarat* or secret police. Libyans looked at the potted roads, the shabby housing in short supply, and the threadbare clinics, and they saw little benefit from the country's staggering oil wealth.

They started to wonder where it was all going.

■

MY OWN VIEW of Libya's decay was focused on its military. I was working at the embassy's defense attaché office, shepherding the limited American effort to assist the Libyan army.

The American defense attaché was a lieutenant colonel in the U.S. Army named Brian Linvill. Born in South Carolina to a family of educators, Linvill chose a military career. He was commissioned as an artillery officer after graduation from Ohio State University and then became a foreign area officer: a soldier-diplomat who specializes in a particular region and speaks a local language. To prepare him for the job, the army sent him to Princeton University to earn a master's degree in Middle Eastern studies and a year-plus of Arabic training in Monterey, California, where he met a fellow military student named Anna whom he would marry.

He rushed headlong into his Libya assignment, inhaling the country's culture and lore. Libya soon became a family affair. His wife, a fluent Arabic speaker and accomplished opera singer, taught music at an international school. They took their children on weekend trips to archaeological sites. His brother, Darren, a professor at Clemson University, would later conduct research on Libya's educational system. Linvill had an easy smile that disarmed his Libyan hosts.

The Libyan army we dealt with was shockingly decrepit, the result of decades of deliberate neglect by Qadhafi, who had feared the army might try to overthrow him. After he toppled the monarchy in 1969 with his fellow army officers, Qadhafi faced a succession of counter-coups, linked to his comrades-in-arms. And so by the late 1980s, he started depriving the army of funds and equipment and stopped training new officers. In its place, he set up the Revolutionary Committees and other popular militias—lightly armed rabble. And in the 1990s, he built up his ultraloyal palace guard—elite brigades commanded by his sons and staffed by favored tribes, whose main purpose was to put down revolts. All the while, the regular army withered away. Linvill and I met officers who wore civilian clothes at work because they lacked funds to maintain their uniforms and did not want to wear them out. Soldiers who reported for duty would show up for just a few hours and then vanish to work second jobs.

Undoing the ruin of the military was a challenge. We started with the basics, focusing first on teaching English to a small cadre of Libyan recruits, which would allow them to receive more advanced schooling abroad. But even that effort was stymied by incompetence. Students wouldn't report for their courses, and those who did make it overseas were often ill prepared. In one case, a Libyan student showed up for frogman training in Italy, only to "sink like a stone when he jumped in a training pool," according to U.S. diplomatic cables released by WikiLeaks. After his instructors fished him out and resuscitated him, he divulged that he'd obtained the training slot through family connections and "wanted a vacation in Rome."

Still, there were pockets of competence in the Libyan military that America and its allies hoped to cultivate. The idea was that by bolstering the capacity of a few key army units, we might be able to get the Libyan government to do more policing of the Saharan desert, where al-Qaeda was taking root. One unit in particular grabbed our attention: the 32nd Reinforced Brigade, comprising ten thousand soldiers and plentiful armor and transport. The brigade recruited from loyal tribes who swore an oath of personal fealty to Qadhafi, and its high-walled bases ringed the capital to defend against aggressors, or to quash dissent from within. It was the most powerful of the dictator's elite security formations, and its commander was Khamis al-Qadhafi, Qadhafi's youngest son.

Tall, with a clean-shaven jaw, the twenty-six-year-old Khamis looked the part of the princely captain. As a child, he had been wounded in the U.S. airstrikes of 1986. Now, as a young man, he seemed the more responsible of Qadhafi's offspring, or at least he eschewed the philistine lifestyle of his brothers: Hannibal, the most notorious of the siblings, had repeated run-ins with European police; Muatassim had hired the pop singers Beyoncé and Usher to perform at parties; soccer-crazed Saadi had been suspended from an Italian team for failing a drug test.

But Khamis seemed different. Linvill said he was "smart, intelligent, and conversant in English . . . earnestly interested in how to professionalize the Libyan military." His trim khaki uniform stood in sharp contrast to the double-vented suits of his brothers. He was studying business management in Spain. And he held the key to Libya's future: his 32nd Brigade was the one military unit that would be decisive in the succession to Qadhafi. "Anyone intent on assuming power would try to align himself with Khamis," a State Department diplomatic cable asserted.

The 32nd Brigade was also a potential source for lucrative defense contracts. The British subsidiary of General Dynamics signed an £85 million deal to revamp the brigade's command and control systems. For its part, the United States rebuffed several requests to sell Khamis sophisticated weaponry, including "Little Bird" helicopters—agile craft ideally suited for special operations. But Washington continued to entertain other forms of assistance in the hopes of wooing the young commander. Linvill was among the foreign military attachés who attended the brigade's parades and exercises. It was all part of a broader, burgeoning courtship that would reach its consummation in America's cooperation with Libya against al-Qaeda.

For several years, the Central Intelligence Agency (CIA) and Britain's Secret Intelligence Service (colloquially known as MI6) had routinely turned over al-Qaeda suspects to the Qadhafi regime, where they disappeared into prison. American and British intelligence officers visited Libyan jails to conduct interrogations—or they let the Libyans extract the information themselves, using torture. By March 2010, though, Qadhafi had freed many jihadists as part of a multiyear rehabilitation spearheaded by his son Saif al-Islam. Though the United States looked to Libya as a partner against jihadism, the program was seen as a sign of a new, more progressive approach to fighting terrorism that was gaining sway across the Muslim world, especially in Saudi Arabia. This so-called strategy of deradicalization entailed pro-regime clerics persuading their militant counterparts that violent struggle was theologically invalid. In the case of Libya, the Libyan Islamic Fighting Group (LIFG), which had waged a campaign against Qadhafi in the 1990s, formally renounced its use of violence and reiterated its opposition to al-Qaeda. American academics and counterterrorism specialists were invited to witness the release of the recanted jihadists and were treated to a gala dinner hosted by Saif.

The spectacle built upon an earlier Libyan blitz to woo American intellectuals. Qadhafi had hired the Monitor Group, the Washington-based PR firm, to improve Libya's image in the world and burnish his credentials as a sort of philosopher-king. Respected American and Western thinkers accepted paid junkets to Tripoli to chat with the dictator; some took consulting fees. Back home, they penned supportive op-eds. "A laid-back autocrat" and "a complex and adaptive thinker," wrote the democracy theorist Benjamin Barber in *The Washington Post*. "If Gadafy is sincere about reform, as I think he is," asserted the sociologist Anthony Giddens in *The Guardian*, "Libya could end up as the Norway of North Africa."

But behind this rehabilitation, behind the counterterrorism cooperation, Libyan-American relations remained stuck in mutual enmity. The country was still a place of fear. The regime had not improved its human rights record—a fact that partially implicated the West. Desperate for outside investment and recognition, Qadhafi had handed the Americans and the Europeans enormous leverage, but, seduced by his promise of petrodollars, they'd not fully harnessed it.

Moreover, Libya was still culpable for the greatest act of mass murder against American citizens before September 11, 2001, the 1988 bombing of Pan Am Flight 103 over Lockerbie, Scotland. True, reparations had been paid. But for the families of the victims, America's opening of diplomatic ties was an affront. And the release of the convicted bomber, a Libyan intelligence officer named Abd al-Basit al-Megrahi, from a Scottish prison because of a terminal cancer diagnosis further strained relations. Though American diplomats had implored Qadhafi to keep the welcome reception low-key, al-Megrahi was accompanied by Saif al-Islam on a private jet to Tripoli and received on the tarmac by a crowd waving flags. He later appeared on state television with the dictator himself. That week, I saw banners in Green Square proclaiming THE BROTHER LEADER AL-QADHAFI KEPT HIS PROMISE OF DELIVERING THE INTERNATIONAL PAWN ABD AL-BASIT AL-MEGRAHI and THE RETURN OF AL-MEGRAHI IS A VICTORY FOR THE HONOR OF THE LIBYAN PEOPLE.

It was a welcome that infuriated Washington.

∎

IN EARLY 2011, I returned to Libya for another short military tour. Winter rains raked the capital, flooding its ill-planned alleys. The air on my predawn run along the harbor was biting and cold; great thunderclouds barreled in from the north.

The mood at the embassy was glum. The so-called reform project under Saif al-Islam had slowed to a halt, and with it the pace of American diplomatic engagement. The U.S. ambassador, an affable but blunt diplomat named Gene Cretz, had fallen afoul of Qadhafi after one of his cables leaked by WikiLeaks disclosed an unflattering portrait of the dictator and what one source called his "voluptuous" Ukrainian nurse. On running tracks and tennis courts Cretz was harassed by crowds of Libyans, sent by the intelligence service—"rent-a-mobs," one diplomat called them. Then Qadhafi's intelligence chief Abdullah al-Sanusi sent a warning that Cretz "could get killed for saying things like this in my country." It was too much. Fearing for his safety, the State Department sent the ambassador home the next day.

The U.S. military's program of outreach had also collapsed with Qadhafi rebuffing several training initiatives. But then in January 2011, an opportunity emerged. Captain Khamis al-Qadhafi accepted an offer to tour the United States as part of a graduate school internship sponsored by an American engineering company, which had hundreds of contracts inside Libya. The intent of the visit, a company spokesperson said, was to educate Khamis on "how business is conducted" by having him visit American firms. Yet there was a diplomatic angle too. During the trip, Khamis would tour the United States Air Force Academy, the National Defense University, and West Point to see how the United States educated its military officers. The State Department did not pay for the visit. But Lieutenant Colonel Linvill was assigned to accompany the young captain during his trip. He would later write that the Khamis visit to the States was an "engagement breakthrough."

It happened at just the moment that popular protests were roiling Tunisia and Egypt. Huddled in cafés before screens broadcasting Al Jazeera, Libyans in Tripoli watched as Tunisians celebrated the ouster of their despised president and Egyptian crowds flooded into Tahrir

Square. I started seeing flyers circulating on Libyan social media calling for a "Day of Rage" on Thursday, February 17, the anniversary of a 2006 Benghazi protest against Danish cartoons depicting the Prophet Muhammad where ten people had died at the hands of Libyan police. "No tranquility after today," a Facebook page announced.

Each day brought new reports of the Libyan regime trying to preempt any unrest. Qadhafi promised more free housing and subsidies. He closed border traffic between Libya and Tunisia and Egypt, released prisoners, and canceled soccer matches. He paraded tribal leaders on state television who proclaimed their devotion to the dictator. One night in Green Square I watched a car rally of shouting youths who screeched and skidded in circles, waving green flags. Still, Khamis al-Qadhafi, the commander of Libya's most feared military unit, the one that could be counted on to quash an uprising, was thousands of miles away, touring Wall Street and American military schools.

At the embassy, American diplomats dismissed the possibility that the Arab revolts would reach Libya. Linvill told me reliable political reporting was sparse in the restive east since few embassy officers visited the region. At the embassy's country team meetings in February, according to U.S. diplomats, the CIA representative, concerned with preserving his agency's counterterrorism relationship with the regime, was the most forceful in arguing against the likelihood of serious unrest.

■

THEN ONE NIGHT, February 16, everything changed. A light rain fell across Tripoli. The phone rang inside the attaché's office in the American embassy. It was Linvill, calling from the States: Khamis Qadhafi had cut short his trip and was coming back to Libya. The regime was preparing to fight for its life.

2

UPRISING

ON FEBRUARY 17, 2011, a human rights lawyer in the eastern city of Benghazi named Salwa Bugaighis drove with her eldest son to join a protest at a courthouse by the sea. It was just before noon when she left her home in the farmlands. She would not return until after midnight.

An attractive woman of medium height, Salwa had high cheekbones framed by mahogany hair in a chin-length bob. She favored ample lipstick and eyeliner and bright-colored clothing—floral-print scarves and silk blouses. When protesting, she would often wear aviator sunglasses while carrying signs—an alluring look that naturally drew the lenses of photographers. Other Libyans—Islamists and conservatives—objected to this appearance, but for Salwa—and her sister and cousins—their opinions didn't matter: dress was a personal choice. Her mother, after all, wore the headscarf and her father never had much say on women's clothes.

She was born in 1963 and had grown up comfortably just a five-minute walk from the city's most modern thoroughfare, Dubai Street, lined with glass-paned boutiques and electronics outlets. Hailing from a family with long roots in the east, she was proud of its accomplishments: her grandfather founded the first library in Benghazi, and her father was the head of Benghazi's municipal council. In the 1980s, though, the family's fortunes fell. Her father ran afoul of Qadhafi and fled abroad after the dictator started confiscating private holdings across the country.

Her older sister, Iman, thinks his extended absence explains much about Salwa's outspokenness and independence: with her father and elder brothers gone for long periods, it was just Salwa and her sister, along with her mother and a younger brother. The mental toughness that resulted was matched by verbal eloquence, evident even in high school. "She always knew the right word," her sister recalls.

At the University of Benghazi, Salwa studied law. Years later she would tell her eldest son, Wail, about a brush with fate she had in her student days. This was during the time of Qadhafi's hanging of dissident students, horrid televised spectacles with sobbing confessions by the condemned. Shortly after one of the executions, someone from the regime had warned her on campus that she would be next if she didn't keep her mouth shut.

She refused to be cowed. In the years before the revolution she joined a group of lawyers who set up a weekly salon to debate current affairs in rented hotel conference rooms. A risky undertaking, it barely skirted the boundary of what was permissible in Libya by focusing on global topics such as Palestine and Iraq and not domestic ones. One evening she brought her son Wail to the group when he was not yet in his teens. A man he'd never seen before entered the room uninvited and interrupted the discussion to confer with the attendees. "It didn't seem quite right," Wail recalls, "but the adults tried to protect us." Wail realizes now who the intruder was and why Salwa had told him nothing afterward: the man was an intelligence officer.

Now, on February 17, Wail drove his mother to join that same group of lawyers at the courthouse. He was twenty-one years old and in his third year of university, and he knew that this time the regime would not respond with verbal warnings. As he dropped her off at the courthouse, he saw police and vehicles on the seaside road. He saw men in yellow construction hats carrying truncheons just blocks away.

Wail's father was already at the courthouse and tried to protect him once again. "You shouldn't be here," he told him. "We don't know what's going to happen." Nobody did. But they knew *why* it was happening in Benghazi: the city had been the engine of change in Libya for nearly a century, whether in the struggle against the Italians or in demanding independence.

It began in the fifth century B.C. as a Greek colony called Euesperides and then Berenice, after a Ptolemaic princess. Built over salt lagoons and underground springs, it inspired countless legends down through the years: there is today in Benghazi a neighborhood called al-Laythi, named for a nearby spring said to be the source of Greek mythology's famed River Lethe, "the river of forgetfulness." Dead souls in Hades were required to drink its waters before they were allowed to return to earth.

The city passed under Roman, Byzantine, and Arab rule. By the time of the Ottomans it had emerged as a trading hub between the coast and the desert. The Italians came next, building it up with lilting rooflines in the neo-Moorish style, arcaded plazas, and an imposing cathedral. But Benghazi's residents—Benghazinos, the Italians called them, a name that has stuck today—proved defiant. "The Italian authorities would never manage to do away with the customs that had held that society and its individuals in equilibrium," wrote the Benghazi resident and novelist Alessandro Spina.

During World War II, Benghazi changed hands between the British and the Germans five times, becoming the most bombed city in North

Africa. After Libya's independence in 1951, it flourished as a center of culture and education, and the seat of political power. All that changed after Qadhafi's coup in 1969 when the dictator shifted resources and institutions west. Benghazi saw little of Libya's petroleum wealth and its infrastructure fell into disrepair. With a surge of labor from the country-side, it expanded into ill-planned suburbs. The architecture turned shoddy and brutalist, sprouting up blocks of poured concrete with jutting rebar.

By the turn of the millennium, it was a wreck, its institutions gutted and its storied cosmopolitanism just a memory. Inside its derelict, dual-domed cathedral, birds fluttered amid beams of sunlight. Stinking sewage had filled its lake. How was this possible, people asked, in the second-largest city in one of Africa's richest countries? The ruin stood in marked contrast to the capital.

Blessed with means, the Bugaighis family had it better than many in Benghazi. They took trips to Dubai and Europe. Wail excelled in sports and by 2010 had been drafted onto Libya's national basketball team. Still, the strictures of life in Qadhafi's "state of the masses" stifled him. "Libya was boring," he said, "so you had to make stuff up."

Salwa thrived in her legal practice. She took on human rights cases, a delicate business in Qadhafi's Libya. Among her clients were political prisoners. Some were Islamists; others were simply dissidents or critics of the regime. She did not agree with them but she wanted to defend their rights nonetheless.

Many of those she defended were incarcerated in a notorious prison in Tripoli called Abu Salim. Indeed, what happened there fifteen years before played a large role in bringing her—and many others—to protest at the courthouse in February 2011.

■

ABU SALIM TODAY is a treeless place in one of Tripoli's poorest neighborhoods. A mural on an outside wall hints at the horrors within: an ogre-faced guard aims a rifle at the head of an orange-clad prisoner. This was Qadhafi's most feared dungeon, reserved for political prisoners.

Violent militants went there, but so too did those whose only crime was to question Qadhafi's rule. Most never had a trial.

Conditions were horrendous. "It was fifteen men to a room, sleeping head to foot," a former inmate told me. And then there was the torture. "Dogs that tore at your flesh," he continued. Guards sliced open kneecaps with razor blades and poured salt on the wounds. They plucked out teeth and fingernails.

A reckoning was inevitable.

On June 28, 1996, at around four-thirty in the afternoon, a group of prisoners overpowered unarmed guards serving dinner, wresting the keys from them. They flung open the gates of the high-security wing and flooded into an open, inner courtyard. The guards on the catwalk above opened fire, killing six and wounding twenty. A short time later, Qadhafi's intelligence chief, Abdullah al-Sanusi, arrived at the prison and asked for negotiators. The inmates demanded fresh air, better medical care, and food, time outdoors, visitors, and proper trials, to which al-Sanusi agreed, except for the trials.

Al-Sanusi's offer was a ploy. Outside the prison, his security men executed the wounded prisoners, and the next day, shortly before dawn, the remaining prisoners were marched out of their cells and forced to lie facedown in the courtyard. At around eleven o'clock, it started: grenades and bursts of automatic gunfire until around one-thirty, when guards walked among the dying, dispatching them with pistol rounds to the head. A prison cook tallied the deaths at twelve hundred using a grim arithmetic: the number of meals he served before the twenty-ninth and the number he served after. Forced to sweep up the aftermath, a former inmate told me he found teeth and bits of brain on the sandy floor.

The carnage escaped the glare of media, but word of the horror trickled out. Qadhafi finally acknowledged the killings in 2004, yet the families of the victims would not forget, especially in Benghazi. Many of the dead hailed from the eastern city, and nearly everyone seemed to have a relative or knew someone who'd been imprisoned there. They wanted answers, and starting in 2007, the families of the victims held protests in Benghazi every Saturday, rallying around one of Salwa's colleagues, a fellow lawyer named Fathi Terbil. For Terbil, the Abu Salim cause was deeply personal: his brother, cousin, and brother-in-law died in the massacre. He now demanded reparations, an independent investigation, and punishment for those responsible.

In those tense, electric days of February 2011, the regime knew that Terbil had the power to mobilize, and so they acted. At three-thirty in the afternoon on Tuesday, February 15, two days before the planned Day of Rage protests, security officers raided Terbil's Benghazi home and arrested him. It would prove a fatal miscalculation. By nine o'clock that night, protestors, many of them women, gathered outside the security headquarters demanding his release. The crowd swelled. "Wake up, wake up, Benghazi," they chanted.

The next three days changed everything. "In Abu Salim, I found the opportunity, the key," Terbil would say, "to attack the regime."

On the afternoon of the sixteenth, hundreds of protestors marched from iconic Tree Square down to Nasser Street to be met by rubber bullets and water cannons. Scores were injured. That night at her house, Salwa had a meeting with her family.

"Listen, there's still a chance this guy might go to extremes over just a small protest," Wail said.

"We're not doing anything wrong," Salwa replied, "we're just asking for our rights, things we should've had a long time ago."

At that time, their demands were for greater social justice, freedom, and a constitution, not the removal of Qadhafi. They'd chosen the court because it was a symbol of justice. But those demands changed quickly. Enraged by the killing of protestors the day before, the youths had adopted the slogan of Tahrir Square: The People Want the Fall of the Regime. The older lawyers tried to calm them down. "But after ten minutes we joined them," Salwa's sister said. There was no going back now; protests were erupting in other eastern cities and across the country. The courthouse gathering formed a coalition that would become the rebels' governing body, demanding a democratic, civil state. Salwa's sister, Iman, emerged as its spokesperson.

The next day, the eighteenth, the protestors converged on the head-quarters of a security brigade in Benghazi, the despised Fadil Brigade. Its soldiers opened fire on a funeral procession passing across its entrance, killing dozens. Two days later something unexpected happened. One of the protestors, a diabetic middle-aged manager at an oil company named Mehdi Muhammad Zeyo, packed fuel cylinders into his black Kia sedan and drove headlong toward the entrance of the Fadil Brigade base, flashing a V sign with his fingers to the youths outside. The guards fired off bursts of bullets that punctured the car's engine and sent the fiery wreck hurtling through the gates. Bulldozers and protestors rushed in, some falling wounded or dead in the gunfire. The compound's soldiers shed their uniforms and fled, while others retreated to the rear, trapped by the surging crowds.

The next tipping point came in an unlikely form: a hulking army officer with a silvery coiffure and a reputation for quashing dissent. Major General Abd al-Fattah Younis, the minister of interior, was a confidant of Qadhafi's who'd helped him topple the Libyan monarchy in 1969 and crushed Islamist militants in the 1990s, sending thousands to Abu Salim. Now, as the commander of a Benghazi special forces unit, he was charged with relieving the besieged Fadil Brigade.

Late on the night of the nineteenth, Benghazi's elders, lawyers, and some defected officers met him at his headquarters, trying to per-suade him to switch sides. It was a fraught, hushed meeting, held in an antechamber in his office to escape the gaze of lurking security men. "Please don't push me," he begged them, according to one attendee. He was torn, pointing to a red telephone, the hotline to Qadhafi, and then to his sidearm. "One bullet in the head will solve my problems," he said.

The following day, Younis arrived at the Fadil base, but instead of obeying orders, he promised the soldiers inside safe passage out of the city and ordered the police not to fire on the demonstrators. Cheers and honking horns greeted the decision. The regime had lost Benghazi.

The rebels formed the National Transitional Council (NTC), appointing a mild-mannered judge named Mustafa Abd al-Jalil as its chairman. They voted Younis as their military commander. But not everyone hailed the NTC and, especially, the gray-haired general. Many of Benghazi's Islamists distrusted Younis as a former henchman who'd come late to the revolution. This was the man, after all, who had repressed them decades before, sent his special forces into their homes, and bombed their villages.

The Islamists came from diverse origins. Some were students, doctors, or engineers. Others, though, came from Benghazi's margins, a world away from the comfort of Salwa's villa. They were mechanics, appliance repairmen, or building contractors. They lived in dusty, cheerless neighborhoods such as al-Laythi, famous for "jihadists, drug dealers, and footballers," a friend once quipped, or in Sabri, for decades a beachfront shanty of tight alleys and open sewage. Some had fled abroad and now returned.

Salwa knew these young men and knew the Islamists; her own brother was a member of the Muslim Brotherhood. And now several Islamists had joined her in front of the courthouse, including Tariq, the young British-born lawyer. In those first heady weeks and months he and other Islamists worked with the liberals toward what they said was their common goal of a civil democratic state. Yet tensions existed beneath the surface.

The Islamists' ranks included a radical fringe that looked dimly on the defected officers led by General Younis. They would grow stronger, forming their own militias and joining a diverse coalition led by a fellow Islamist and oil engineer named Fawzi Bu Katif.

A mustachioed middle-aged man with carefully parted hair, Bu Katif speaks in precise if heavily accented English. Like many rebel leaders he had not served in the military. He did, however, have experience as a manager in Libya's oil sector, one of the few functional sectors under Qadhafi's rule. And that proved useful for organizing men to fight.

As a young man, Fawzi Bu Katif had gone to America and relished the freedom he'd found, the loosening of ties to family and town. He studied at Ohio State and traveled the breadth of the country. He said he learned to think for himself and devoured philosophical writings, in addition to his engineering studies. He also grew more pious.

"Eventually, I realized this was not a life," he told me. "Girls, night-clubs, parties. So I had to come back."

It was a homecoming that was both spiritual and physical. Returning to Benghazi, he worked secretly for the banned Muslim Brother-hood. He was arrested and thrown in Abu Salim prison, serving a total of eighteen years. "My family didn't recognize me when I got out," he said.

The militia he formed during the revolution was called the Febru-ary 17 Brigade, and it enjoyed official sanction from the rebels' political authority. Moving to an old military camp, he started training young men to fight using captured tanks, mortars, and rockets. Some defected military officers helped them—an encouraging sign of unity. But in the coming months, that cooperation would be strained as Bu Katif's mili-tia and others grew in power, setting up their own chains of command and their own supplies of weapons.

■

ONE DAY IN early March, Bu Katif's cell phone rang. "There's some general driving in from Cairo," someone told him.

At the time, Abd al-Fattah Younis was the defected officer with the most clout in liberated Benghazi—but another such figure loomed on the horizon. For nearly two decades, a Libyan army general and onetime Qadhafi ally named Khalifa Hiftar lived with his family in Vienna, Virginia, near a golf course and country club. It was a quiet existence, marked by attendance at annual meetings of Libyan Ameri-cans, all of them dissidents, in locations across the States. These friends were never quite sure exactly where his income came from. Then one day, a few weeks after the start of the Libyan revolution, he packed his bags and went to Dulles International Airport. A fellow Libyan exile drove him, an Islamist, who would become his sworn enemy. It was the start of a remarkable homecoming and a fateful step in Libya's history.

Born in 1943 in Ajdabiya, Hiftar hailed from a prominent tribe; his father had won acclaim fighting the Italians and later joined the army under King Idris. Following this martial lineage, he graduated from what was then called the Royal Military College in Benghazi. There he met another cadet, Muammar Qadhafi, whom he would support in toppling the monarchy.

As a Libyan army officer, Hiftar reportedly led Libyan soldiers fighting in Egypt's 1973 war with Israel and then participated in Qadhafi's ill-fated conflict with Chad. In 1987, in a shallow escarpment called Wadi Dum, Chadian forces hit Hiftar with a predawn ambush, decimating his ranks and capturing the general along with hundreds of his men. For Libya, it was a humiliating rout: guerrillas in pickups had bested Qadhafi's heavy armor and artillery. Libya's Dien Bien Phu some called it.

As Hiftar languished in a Chadian prison, Qadhafi disowned him and his fellow prisoners. After seven months of captivity, he defected and the Chadian president released him to join the anti-Qadhafi opposition, along with hundreds of other Libyan army prisoners. American CIA officers soon arrived, providing weapons and training to Hiftar's dissident "Libyan National Army" (LNA) at camps outside the Chadian capital.

But then in 1990, his luck ran out: a Chadian army commander overthrew the Chadian government, reportedly with help from Libyan intelligence. The dissidents' haven was finished. "I am dead already," Hiftar told his troops, according to a witness. Salvation arrived in the form of an American plane that landed one morning to spirit Hiftar and his fighters out of the country. After an epic escape across Africa with CIA help, Hiftar settled in northern Virginia while his fellow conspirators scattered across the United States.

Now, decades later, he was returning to Libya. Yet the country of his birth had changed; some of the revolutionary youth did not know who he was. "We had heard him on television before he came, making speeches about weapons and strategy," a Benghazi friend told me. "But we had to Google the Chad war to see who he was."

Arriving in Benghazi, he met with Bu Katif, the leader of the February 17 Brigade, and others, demanding an official directive from the rebels' leadership to lead their military forces. He never got it: Abd al-Fattah Younis, his old classmate at the military college, had already been appointed. Moreover, some of the Islamists in the rebels' ranks cast a wary eye on him. "He drove to the front in a bunch of Infiniti cars," one of them said. But Hiftar wouldn't take no for an answer, and in the coming months, as the rebels pushed out of Benghazi, he would jostle and maneuver for leadership.

■

BACK IN TRIPOLI, Captain Khamis al-Qadhafi had returned from the United States, cutting short his tour of corporations and American military schools with Lieutenant Colonel Brian Linvill. The Arab Spring was no longer an abstraction or a tumult that only afflicted Libya's neighbors; it now threatened his father's rule. Oddly enough, in Washington, D.C., just days before, an American ambassador had asked him what he thought of developments in Tunisia and Egypt. "I think it's a positive thing," Khamis replied. "The room was stunned," Linvill recalled. Arriving in Tripoli, the Libyan captain took command of his 32nd Brigade and moved quickly to smash an uprising in Zawiya, a coastal town to the west.

Linvill returned to Tripoli on Saturday, February 19, the same day as Khamis, to find the city simmering. He began calling his contacts, mainly officers in the Libyan military, but many refused to answer their phones, and those who did sounded nervous. Still others assured him that the storm would blow over. After all, they said, the opposition was speaking about possible compromise and reforms with Saif al-Islam.

But then that changed. Late on the night of the twentieth, Saif gave an impromptu televised address to the Libyan people. Slouching and wagging his finger, he blamed the unrest on foreign agents and accused the protestors of wanting to set up an Islamic emirate in the east. They were risking a civil war, he warned, "worse than Iraq and Yugoslavia." Two days later, Qadhafi the father gave his now-famous diatribe threatening to "purify" Libya "house by house" and "alley by alley." Libyans who had held out for Saif lost all hope, but others were not surprised at the lecture. "We always knew that he had to follow his father," a friend told me.

After the address, protestors converged on Green Square. Security men and police sprang into action, determined to prevent the plaza from becoming a rallying point like Tahrir Square. By dawn, vehicles with antiaircraft guns arrived while gunmen bounded to the tops of adjacent buildings, for firing positions. The protestors scrambled and fell under the shooting.

The next day, Linvill drove to the Radisson Blu hotel, perched on a hill on Tripoli's eastern edge. Climbing to an observation deck, he peered across the convulsing landscape. Tendrils of smoke uncoiled from burning police stations and ransacked buildings. Naval ships in the harbor had pulled away from their piers for protection. In Green Square, men in orange overalls were scrubbing down the remnants of the night's carnage.

At the American embassy, the chargé d'affaires, a diplomat named Joan Polaschik, organized an evacuation. Two weeks earlier she'd put the embassy on alert and run drills for just such a possibility. It was a standard protocol; every American embassy has a plan of escape on the shelf, describing, down to the smallest details, assembly points and routes. The first option fell through when thousands of panicked travelers clogged up Tripoli International Airport, forcing the convoy of American diplomats to turn around and head back to the embassy.

Plan B. The State Department chartered a catamaran from Malta called the *Maria Dolores* to carry nonessential staff, family members, and as many American citizens as they could assemble. Take only what you can carry, they were told. But a withering storm delayed the crossing from Tripoli's harbor, forcing the passengers to stay on the docked vessel for two nerve-racking days. Finally, the weather relented, and after a seasick journey the evacuees reached the Mediterranean island.

There were now just nineteen Americans left at the embassy. Early Thursday morning Polaschik had told them they had just twenty-four hours to leave. President Obama was due to make a public announcement, she said, and "it won't be good if we're still here in Libya," a diplomat recalls her saying. They set about destroying the embassy's reams of classified material, finishing just before dawn the next day. That morning, they locked the compound gates, lowered the American flag, and left for Mitiga Airport, the capital's second airport on its eastern approach.

Somewhere on the way, the diplomats ran into security men firing at protestors. "Guys with weapons drawn, shooting off rounds at people dashing between buildings" Linvill remembers. The Americans did not know it then, but they were witnessing the last throes of active resistance in Tripoli. Soon the capital would be cowed into silence.

Arriving at the airport, the Americans met stranded foreign oil workers and invited them to join their flight. They boarded the plane and stowed their luggage. Until now, the diplomats' departure had been kept secret from the Libyan government. If it had known, it might've tried to obstruct them or, worse, take them hostage, as a form of insurance against America attacking. Then, just as they were fastening their seat belts, the CIA station chief got a cell phone call. It was Abdullah al-Sanusi, the head of Libyan intelligence.

He sounded worried. Was everything okay? Are you leaving?

No, no, Abdullah, everything is fine, the station chief replied. I'll see you tomorrow.

He hung up. The ruse seemed to work. As the plane took off, a diplomat called back to Washington. "We are wheels up," he said.

And within minutes of the plane's departure, the White House announced U.S. sanctions against Libya.

■

IN EASTERN LIBYA, the rebels' military campaign began to falter. By March, they had pushed west as far as the coastal oil terminals at Ajdabiya and Brega, but now they were overstretched. Some blamed their commander, General Younis, while others decried their lack of military experience. Whatever the reason, the fighters fell back to Benghazi, quarreling over leadership. They pleaded for help with the outside world and they readied themselves for the assault they knew Qadhafi was preparing.

On March 18 it came: a strung-out caravan of soldiers, tanks, long-barreled artillery, and pipe-organ rocket launchers. The first artillery rounds that hit the city came from the Palmaria, a formidable cannon with a range of twelve miles. At dawn the next day, young rebels rushed to hold the line, fighting with captured tanks, recoilless rifles, and whatever they could find. A few defected pilots, paunchy, gray-haired men in rickety MiGs, tried to bomb Qadhafi's columns; the rebels shot down one of the planes by mistake. As the attackers surged, people turned to hurling rocks or bricks from balconies, but by late morning all seemed lost. Qadhafi's troops had breached the suburbs. Benghazi seemed doomed to fall.

Salwa and her sister watched smoke rising from the university before joining the exodus out of the city, along the only open highway to the east.

INTERVENTION

THE FIRST TIME SAMANTHA POWER took note of Libya in
2011 was when Qadhafi called Egypt's president Hosni Mubarak
to advise him on dealing with the mounting unrest. Soon after, she
began receiving a stream of reports about protests in Benghazi.

"It started to stand out as a place where people were taking tremen-
dous risks," she told me. "It was an inspiring tale; people coming to the
square and reading poetry. It stood out because there was this place and
a set of images."

Power held a pivotal post in the Obama White House, as special
assistant to the president and senior director for multilateral affairs and
human rights—two portfolios that gave her a central role in coordinating

the administration's response. A former professor of human rights law at Harvard and a journalist who covered the wars in Yugoslavia, Power had long been a passionate advocate for atrocity prevention. She'd written a Pulitzer Prize–winning book on America's history of inaction during twentieth-century genocides. In 2004, she'd lambasted the international community over its failure to intervene in Darfur.

"Tens of thousands of Africans are herded onto death marches," she wrote, "and Western leaders are again sitting in offices. How sad it is that it doesn't even seem strange."

Just prior to the Arab uprisings, Power had cochaired a White House review of the Arab world, concluding that the region was ripe for political reform and that the old American policy of backing authoritarian regimes needed to change. The review finished just as a Tunisian street vendor named Muhammad Bouazizi set himself on fire, sparking an uprising that would lead to the downfall of the Tunisian president. Within a month that revolution had inspired massive protests in Egypt's Tahrir Square demanding the ouster of President Mubarak. Power's policy review assumed a sudden immediacy, thrusting a dilemma on the president: a longtime American ally was facing unprecedented public pressure and the risk of widespread violence. On January 29, Obama made the momentous decision of supporting a replacement for the Egyptian ruler. And on February 11, Mubarak agreed to step down, bringing to a close nearly three decades of rule after an eighteen-day revolution.

A week later, protests in Libya confronted the White House with a different sort of crisis: the prospect of violent repression on a scale unlike anything seen in other Arab states.

The media blackout in Libya made it difficult to get reliable information, and intelligence—both technical and human—was limited. Much of the reporting on the crackdown came from Libyan Americans in touch with relatives on the scene. Power received these visitors to the White House eagerly.

"We didn't have a lot of assets on the ground," she told me. "So this community of Libyan Americans, they could relay accounts of how many people died."

Were these reports and predications accurate? As Qadhafi's armed columns hurtled toward Benghazi, he warned the rebels on a radio show that "we will find you in your closets." But he also offered amnesty to those who disarmed and encouraged those who didn't to flee to Egypt. As the uprising unfolded, even normally proactive humanitarian groups were cautious, questioning claims of an imminent genocide or the use of rape as a weapon of war. And contrary to the assertions of Libyan exiles, the regime was not using armed helicopters or fixed-wing aircraft against protestors in Benghazi.

Still, Qadhafi had made his bloodcurdling threats, and he had a history of violent reprisals against his people, at Abu Salim prison and in his campaign against Islamist insurgents in the 1990s.

"We all believed the threat of an impending massacre," an administration official told me, adding, however, that "no sound analysis had been done about Qadhafi's actual capacity for carrying out his threats, especially in the face of armed resistance."

A major turning point for the administration was Saif al-Islam's public speech. Before this, the United States had hoped he might've exercised restraint on Qadhafi. But with his diatribe on February 20, Saif revealed himself to be every bit as hard-line as his father. The speech effectively dashed any hopes in Washington for a negotiated transition.

"They were announcing this was a battle to the death," Power says. "He was pursuing a military solution to a political problem, and it stood to reason that it would end very bloodily."

The initial American response focused on applying diplomatic pressure, led by the American ambassador at the United Nations, Susan Rice. Rice had served as senior director for African affairs and as director for international organizations and peacekeeping at the Clinton White House during the Rwandan genocide and shared Power's outlook on humanitarian intervention. Now, backed by Power, she worked for a quick response from the United Nations, one that they both hoped would avert a repeat of Rwanda. Rice was heartened by what she calls the "fortunate convergence of regional and international organizations": the UN, NATO, and the Arab League were moving toward a consensus that something had to be done against what she saw as a looming "humanitarian catastrophe," even if the African Union was "acting foolishly." All of this was in stark contrast to her experience dealing with Rwanda in the 1990s.

"In the way that the stars were not aligned in Rwanda," Rice told me, "they were aligned in Libya."

Samantha Power agrees.

"There was this sense of possibility in New York that never existed before," Power said, "to deal with killings as they were ramping up—and not waiting for a Rwanda."

On February 26, the United Nations Security Council passed Resolution 1970, which imposed sanctions on the Qadhafi regime and referred Libya to the jurisdiction of the International Criminal Court. It was the first time the Security Council had voted unanimously on such a referral and Power had hoped that it would serve as a restraining force on the Qadhafi regime—and on the rebels. She applauded its passing as a major victory.

But then, none of it worked. The international legal machinery had failed to deter a dictator. By the first week of March, as Qadhafi's forces turned the tide, the Europeans were pushing for military action, with the French and the British calling for a no-fly zone. Still, the administration was wary about this option.

"It didn't seem like a punishment that fit the crime," Power told me. It risked entangling America in a war with Qadhafi without actually removing his tools of repression: according to intelligence and reliable reporting, aircraft were not being used against civilians. But that was not the only issue. Having been elected on a platform to disengage from Iraq and Afghanistan, Obama didn't want to start another war in a Muslim country, especially one that did not directly threaten America's national security and about which the U.S. government knew little. It was an ignorance worsened by the fact that the White House at the time had a dearth of Middle East expertise, especially among those pushing for a response. "Everyone was viewing this through the lens of R2P, not the Middle East," said one White House official, using the shorthand for a doctrine for humanitarian intervention called the Responsibility to Protect, endorsed by UN member states in 2005.

The debate picked up. The Pentagon was the loudest voice against intervention. In the run-up to hostilities, Defense Secretary Robert Gates made no fewer than six public speeches against it. Intervention, he argued in congressional testimony on March 2, would sap an already strained military. Then there were questions about who exactly were the rebels. Gates also worried about the lack of postconflict planning. What would follow the dictator? The results from Iraq and Afghanistan were not encouraging.

Nevertheless, by mid-March the push for intervention gathered strength. Arab and international consensus was building. On March 10, Gates held a meeting with NATO's secretary-general, arguing that any American role was contingent on a United Nations Security Council resolution and regional participation. On March 12, the Arab League formally asked for intervention under a UN mandate. Yet in Washington, the White House was still divided. Proponents argued a victory by Qadhafi would further embolden other Arab leaders to choose violent repression. A protracted civil war, some pointed out, could spill over into Tunisia and Egypt. And if the French and other Europeans went ahead with a military operation, they feared that the United States would get dragged in anyway. But opponents of intervention held their ground. What was in it for the United States? And where would it lead?

It was Secretary of State Hillary Clinton who eventually mollified one of the remaining concerns: Who were the rebels, and what did they want?

On the morning of March 14, Clinton arrived in Paris. The French had long been out in front of Washington in demanding military action in Libya—a boldness that irked administration officials. "All flourish and no substance," one of them quipped to me. French motivations on Libya were both domestic and geopolitical: French president Nicolas

Sarkozy saw the Libyan intervention as a way to boost his public standing and the French elite worried that their country's relevance in the world was fading. And to bolster their case, they were hosting an important emissary from the Libyan rebels, whom Clinton intended to meet.

Worldly and fluent in English, Mahmud Jibril was a U.S.-educated political scientist who had worked on economic reforms under Saif al-Islam. He'd joined the revolution from Abu Dhabi, emerging as the NTC's de facto foreign minister. Jibril's doctoral dissertation at the University of Pittsburgh was a sweeping study of America's stormy relations with Libya. Now, on the night of March 14, he was charged with the burden of remaking those relations.

He arrived late at Clinton's suite at the Paris Westin, with its views of a luminous Eiffel Tower. As the conversation progressed, he found her "serious, sincere, and very detailed in her questions." She wanted to know about the rebels. Who are you? What are your plans? Suppose you took the regime down, she said to Jibril. Would there be reprisals? Jibril told me he did his best to reassure her in the forty-five-minute meeting. By his own account, he spoke of his goal of a civil democratic state, early elections, and the need to avoid a vacuum after the conflict. He left the meeting unsure of America's reaction but feeling fortified nonetheless: simply seeing the secretary of state, he believed, was a major victory for the revolution.

As Qadhafi's troops closed on Benghazi, the need for action acquired newfound urgency. It was up to Obama alone to make the call. At a fraught National Security Council (NSC) meeting on March 15, intelligence officials told President Obama that regime forces had pushed to the environs of Ajdabiya, a strategic town that supplied water and fuel to Benghazi. It would fall in twenty-four hours, they warned. Obama asked if a no-fly zone would stop the killing. The chairman of the Joint Chiefs of Staff, Admiral Michael Mullen, replied that no, it would have no effect.

The president was irritated. "I want real options," he told his cabinet. Dispatching aircraft, applying more sanctions, or inducing more defections was hardly commensurate with the crisis they faced. Before leaving for dinner, he directed aides to prepare other responses, including a broader United Nations resolution that would let the United States protect civilians by bombing government forces on the ground. When he returned, he asked once more for input on whether to intervene. And then he decided.

It was an exceedingly difficult call. In the end, what tipped the scales was not the appeals from his advisors—especially the triumvirate of so-called hawks, Rice, Power, and Clinton. Rather, it was a compromise that Obama had worked out for himself. America would use its unmatched capabilities in airpower and precision strike—what the military called a "comparative advantage"—on the front end of an intervention and then hand off responsibility to its European partners. The intervention would be collective, not unilateral, and Washington would exempt itself from any ownership of what came next.

All of this, Samantha Power told me, came "from a desire to help these people, but not a desire to do what we did in Afghanistan and Iraq, to *own* this to the point that it sucks the air out of our foreign policy and our domestic agenda."

Obama directed Susan Rice at the United Nations to take a French and British Security Council resolution and strengthen it. She worked frantically. And on March 17, Resolution 1973 passed: the sweeping measure authorized member states "to take all necessary measures, to protect civilians" short of a foreign occupation. The White House was shocked at the speed. Abstentions by China and Russia had been critical; Beijing and Moscow, eyeing their own restive provinces, looked warily on a resolution that validated outside intervention under humanitarian guises, but chose not to veto it nevertheless. For their part, the French were especially delighted at the outcome at the UN—and at the rapid turnaround in Washington's thinking.

On March 19, at 5:45 p.m., four French Rafale jets bombed Qadhafi forces outside Benghazi. At a meeting in Paris, Sarkozy surprised the assembled NATO officials with an announcement of the strikes.

Benghazi was saved. The military campaign the Americans had code-named Operation Odyssey Dawn had begun, three hours ahead of schedule. It was Sarkozy seeking "a little publicity," according to Defense Secretary Gates.

■

THE INITIAL AMERICAN, British, and French strikes pummeled Libya. Cruise missiles and air-dropped munitions all but eviscerated Qadhafi's air defense system across the country. "We were completely blind," a Libyan officer told me after the war.

Twelve days after the first strikes, the United States handed over leadership of the air campaign and naval blockade to NATO, under the moniker Operation Unified Protector. By any definition, it was a remarkably broad military coalition of NATO members, contributing aircraft and naval forces, along with non-NATO states: Sweden, the United Arab Emirates (UAE), Qatar, and Jordan. Yet the European and Arab forces depended on American logistical and intelligence support, frustrating Washington and highlighting shortcomings in the military capabilities of America's coalition partners. After the campaign, the Europeans in particular would come under scathing American criticism. "This whole thing was done on a shoestring," a White House official said. "How these guys were going to fight the Warsaw Pact is beyond me."

For the Libyan rebels on the front lines, the airstrikes were at once terrifying and mystical. They never saw the aircraft that would demolish the tank right in front of them. Yet the rebels also cursed NATO, demanding more strikes and closer support for their ground movements. "When it was the U.S. and France, their fire was accurate, they were supporting us," one rebel commander told me. "But NATO was too slow." Much of this was due to inflated expectations about what the coalition could provide. "They thought the sky would be black with aircraft," a NATO official said. A particular shortage was the intelligence, surveillance, and reconnaissance (ISR) assets needed to corroborate targets before an airstrike. The United States could provide only two Predator drones because its operations in Afghanistan and Iraq demanded the others.

Aside from the operational strain on the coalition, there were political fissures about NATO's mandate: Was it to protect civilians, or did it entail actively aiding the anti-Qadhafi rebels? Russia and China criticized the ongoing operation, charging that it aimed for regime change.

On March 28, Obama tried to put these rumors to rest. "If we tried to overthrow Qadhafi by force," he argued, "our coalition would splinter . . . to be blunt, we went down that road in Iraq." But in its April ministerial meeting, NATO revised its definition of "threat to civilians" to apply only to Qadhafi's armed forces, not to threats by the rebels. The implication was that NATO was tacitly taking sides. NATO officials I interviewed, however, were adamant about adhering strictly to the mandate: the coalition, they asserted, refrained from intervening on behalf of the rebels or pushing for regime change. "There was no coordination between NATO military forces and the anti-Qadhafi fighters," a NATO air commander told me. "Full stop. We were not their air force."

But as the campaign progressed, that changed: the logic of civilian protection eventually demanded that the regime had to go. The French, British, and Americans—along with the Qataris and Emiratis—took a decidedly partisan view toward the anti-Qadhafi rebels, shipping them arms, advising and training them, and coordinating airstrikes with them. It was an interference that would have far-reaching effects after the war.

■

WHEN LIEUTENANT COLONEL LINVILL landed in Istanbul following his knife-edge escape from Tripoli, a Defense Department official met him at the airport and handed him orders: report to AFRICOM headquarters in Germany, to the intelligence section, or J2. He was the only Defense Department official who had spent appreciable time in Libya, and his contacts on the ground were invaluable to the air campaign. Many of these contacts in the Libyan military had defected and were now leading the revolution. But Benghazi had gone dark; Qadhafi had cut the Internet. Once it got turned on, Linvill started receiving calls via Skype, routed through phone numbers in Michigan and California; the rebels were using U.S.-based numbers to evade Qadhafi's surveillance. He heard that the rebels were forming "operations rooms"—command centers—on the ground, and he told one of his contacts, "You need to get me in touch with someone inside an operations room."

It was one of the very first contacts the Americans had with anti-Qadhafi military forces. And from then on the rebels began pushing a valuable, round-the-clock stream of intelligence to Linvill.

One of Linvill's key interlocutors was a general in the Libyan Special Forces named Abd al-Salam al-Hasi, who'd defected early in the uprising. A compact man with a patrician's bearing and an officious jaw, al-Hasi takes evident pride in his early connections to the Americans; when I met him at his office after the revolution he showed me a photo on the wall of him shaking hands with then defense secretary Leon Panetta. In early 2011, al-Hasi opened a command center in Benghazi and set up a phone link to AFRICOM. The center was filled with tech-savvy Libyans who used Google Earth and computers, and al-Hasi passed AFRICOM the coordinates of Qadhafi's forces based on a network of informants that stretched across the country.

Gradually, though, it dawned on Linvill that al-Hasi's reach among the revolutionaries was limited: many other armed factions had similar operations rooms and separate chains of command. It raised the question of just who exactly the United States was dealing with.

This same question would plague the successive overtures to the Americans by regime officials seeking to negotiate. On March 20, Linvill received a phone call from one of his Libyan military contacts, a general who was the Libyan army's foreign liaison officer and who had remained loyal to Qadhafi: Would the United States be amenable to a seventy-two-hour cease-fire? Linvill ran it up the chain of command at AFRICOM. There was no response. Years later, this call would become the subject of intense scrutiny, with critics of the intervention seizing on it as evidence of the administration's reckless obsession with regime change. These voices claimed that the terms of the general's offer included Qadhafi stepping down, but Linvill, who spoke directly with the Libyan officer, insists that this was never the case. Moreover, he told me, "there were real questions about Qadhafi's span of control over the loyalists."

In the weeks and months ahead, there would be other attempts by the Libyan government to engage the Americans; none of the American diplomats involved in those talks believed they were genuine or conducted in good faith. Qadhafi himself refused to meet with several foreign intermediaries, including a UN envoy, suggesting he had no interest in any deal, especially one that included his removal from power.

■

BACK IN THE WHITE HOUSE, staffers were frustrated by the scant information on the rebels. True, the CIA had sent officers. But that effort struggled to keep up with the pace of the revolution in a country where the United States had made minimal intelligence investments.

"It was a scratch station," one White House official told me, referring to the CIA presence. "I was completely astonished at the disjuncture between the intelligence reporting traffic and what was happening on the ground."

The new men and women on the scene in the Libyan revolution were largely unknown, and the White House needed to find out who they were. But more important, it wanted to signal American commitment. By early March, the Europeans had appointed diplomatic envoys to Benghazi, and Washington wanted one too. And so when the State Department asked Ambassador Gene Cretz for a name he turned to a colleague and friend.

■

JOHN CHRISTOPHER STEVENS was born on April 18, 1960, in Northern California, in Grass Valley, a onetime gold rush town at the edge of the Sierras. When he turned fifteen, after his parents divorced, he went south to live with his mother in Piedmont, a hilly East Bay suburb. It was a comfortable upbringing, marked by early brushes with the world, such as a summer in Barcelona as a high school exchange student. It would also be defined by a family tradition of service. His father, Jan, worked on water and environmental issues for the California attorney general's office, his sister Anne became a pediatric rheumatologist; his brother, Tom, is a judge; and Hilary, a half sister from his father's second marriage, is a physician in a lower-income clinic.

His early years also included immersion in the performing arts. His mother, Mary, is an accomplished cellist with a local symphony; his late stepfather was a music critic with the *San Francisco Chronicle*. Stevens played the saxophone in a jazz band and sang in an a cappella choir at Piedmont High School. While he was there, he met another student named Austin Tichenor and the two became lifelong friends, attending the University of California, Berkeley, where they joined the same fraternity and shared an apartment.

Tichenor works today as a playwright, director, and actor in a traveling theater troupe called the Reduced Shakespeare Company. He performed with Stevens in a high school production of *The Music Man* and directed him in three college plays. He is convinced now that these early stage performances helped make Stevens an effective diplomat. "Theater teaches empathy," he told a group of students.

"Chris was never going to be a professional actor, but his instincts were lovely because they were all truthful," Tichenor said to me. "The best actors put on this mask to become other characters, but they don't become fake, they become true. And that's the thing that Chris absolutely had."

Tichenor and another friend have long pondered what it was exactly that sparked Stevens's passion for the Middle East in particular and can locate no other source. There was no college course, Tichenor told me, even though Chris was a history major who "double majored in everything," from geology to art history to logic. Chris's father, Jan, agreed, recalling that the family's only contact with the Middle East was a viewing of *Kismet*, a musical set in the Baghdad of *The Arabian Nights*.

While still at Berkeley, Stevens took the Foreign Service exam to become a diplomat but failed the famously subjective oral portion. After graduation, for what his friend Austin thinks is the not uncommon reason of delaying entry into adulthood, he joined the Peace Corps. He was selected to go to Morocco, to teach English for two years. The night before he departed, a noirishly foggy evening in the Bay Area, his father recalls, his family staged a skit of *Kismet* with his baby sister, Hilary, playing an Arabian princess and Chris the romantic warrior.

Stevens's time in the Peace Corps was a captivating experience and it's not hard to see why. The small Moroccan town where he taught, Ouaouizerth, is a place of isolated beauty, set against the verdant slopes of the Atlas Mountains next to a lake. It is a town inhabited by ethnic Imazighen, which perhaps for Stevens only added to the exoticism: the Imazighen (singular: Amazigh), also known as Berbers, are a highlands people whose spoken language is wholly different from Arabic. People in Ouaouizerth recalled the blond, lanky American as an effective, friendly, and curious teacher. He stayed after school to help students and often produced a small notebook from his pocket to jot down a new Amazigh word or phrase. He lived near the market and jogged every afternoon on a dirt path around town.

When Stevens returned home, he was hooked.

"From then on out, he always had an Arabic tutor," his sister Anne remembers.

He contemplated pursuing a doctorate in Arabic or Middle East studies. "But our practical father had insisted on law school," Anne said. Yet even at Hastings Law School in San Francisco, his heart was set on international service. He focused on international law, "as the next best thing to the Foreign Service," his father said, and after graduation worked on international trade cases at the D.C. office of a large law firm while preparing to take the test again. He passed this time, joining the State Department in 1991. Postings across the Middle East followed: Riyadh, Cairo, Damascus, and Jerusalem.

He was by all accounts a talented diplomat. In Jerusalem, a fellow

Foreign Service officer remembers him navigating with equal felicity the Arab-Israeli impasse and tensions among U.S. agencies, which she called "a microcosm of the Middle East conflict." "He was always the smartest in the room," the diplomat added, "but never let you know that," asking questions with a "childlike curiosity and enthusiasm." His friend Tichenor observed this quality even in college. When they'd rushed fraternities together, a ritual of blatant self-promotion, Stevens was always "asking about the other guy."

"Sometimes later on in life I thought it might've been a deflection," Tichenor told me. "'I don't have to talk about myself if I am asking about you.' But I think it was genuine."

He kept up a vigorous social life as a diplomat, playing tennis with locals, colleagues, and dignitaries alike. A bachelor in a peripatetic profession, he stayed single while having a number of serious but long-distance relationships with equally accomplished women. He lent dating advice to female friends. "Don't date that guy," he told one of them, "he's just like me, he'll never commit."

In 2007, he volunteered for a posting in Libya, where the United States had just reopened its embassy. I'd met him there briefly in 2009 when he was weeks away from finishing his tour as the deputy chief of mission; we'd conferred only once, about the upgrade of a classified facility. It is the sort of administrative chore that is the frequent bane of a midlevel diplomat and which detracts from interacting with locals. I imagine it bored him, but he handled it with efficiency and cheer.

By the time of the 2011 Arab uprisings he was in Washington, D.C., watching with awe the unfolding drama, especially in Libya. Even in those uncertain days he sensed that the regime was finished. "I can't resist commenting on Libya," he wrote to family and friends five days after the start of the Libyan revolution. The threatening speeches of Qadhafi and his son Saif, he told them, were "fatal missteps showing the Qadhafis for what they really are."

Then came the offer to return to Libya as America's envoy to the opposition. He said yes within minutes.

■

STEVENS WENT FIRST to Rome to wait until it was deemed safer to move to Libya and then to Malta. Here, he faced the problem of travel to Benghazi. There were no flights, so he negotiated with a Greek shipping company to secure passage on an old freighter. What followed was a crossing that has entered diplomatic lore.

On the night of April 5, Stevens and his team of diplomats and security officers rolled their sports-utility vehicles, computer gear, and weapons onto the gangway of the aging ship. Cramped into cabins on the swaying ship, they arrived in Benghazi, spending the first night in port before moving to the Tibesti Hotel, a cement monstrosity with a linoleum lobby that reeked of cigarette ashes. A car bomb in June later forced them to relocate to a complex of low-roofed villas in the wealthy Fwayhat neighborhood.

The American envoy quickly became a presence in the liberated city. "My mandate was to go out and meet as many members of the leadership as I could in the Transitional National Council," he would later say. He met with revolutionaries of all stripes: the defected officers, day laborers, Islamists, and tribal leaders, lingering and listening for hours. "He didn't so much as walk into a room as saunter or float," recalled one American diplomat who accompanied him. On May 2, when the United States killed Osama bin Laden, Libyans on the street flocked to congratulate Stevens. "As if I had something to do with it," he wrote in an email to his friend Austin. "Qadhafi is next," a Libyan assured him.

That same month, Stevens met Khalifa Hiftar at the general's headquarters. By then, the Hiftar's bitter rivalry with Abd al-Fattah Younis had reached its nadir. "They behaved like children," said an NTC member. It was hardly what the rebels needed, given the other splits within their ranks. In mid-April, Hiftar held a press conference, denouncing Younis as incompetent and asking for Western support. "When I lead, I want NATO to defend my front line so we can move forward," he stated. It was vintage Hiftar: self-assured, grandiose, and slightly messianic. Now, in the meeting with Stevens, he pressed his demands further. Accompanied by one of his sons, who would later serve as his aide and emissary, the general bragged about a network of sleeper cells in Tripoli waiting to rise up. Could the United States supply him with weapons?

He closed the meeting with Stevens with a warning of an even greater threat than his rival Abd al-Fattah Younis: the Islamists, whom he claimed were undercutting his authority.

■

BY EARLY APRIL, revolutionaries in eastern Libya, including Islamists, had amassed an impressive number of fighters and were pushing Qadhafi's forces west. Weapons and training from a powerful ally in the Persian Gulf, the tiny emirate of Qatar, contributed to the advance. It was just the start of Qatar's meddling in Libyan affairs, and it prompted a strong counterreaction from Qatar's Gulf rival, the United Arab Emirates.

The two ambitious monarchies saw the 2011 Arab uprisings as opportunities to project influence beyond their borders, to refashion the shifting political landscape to their will. But they had opposing visions. The Emirates leadership evinced a fear of the Muslim Brotherhood or any form of Islamist participation in politics that bordered on obsessive. Qatari rulers had no such worries: the Qatari branch of the Brotherhood was never as politically active as other affiliates and focused mostly on education. Free from concerns about an Islamist challenge to their rule, Doha hosted and supported Brotherhood figures from across the region. More broadly, though, it cultivated ties with a diverse cast of Islamist actors across the Middle East—some of them extremist— as a form of hedging and to amplify its power amid its larger Gulf neighbors.

Contrary to its critics, Doha backed Islamist rebels in Libya not because it was committed to a covert Islamist project but rather because it saw them as the most capable fighters. For their part, the Emirates started supporting the faction of ex-officers and technocrats linked to Younis and Mahmud Jibril, the NTC member who'd impressed Secretary of State Clinton. The ensuing competition between these two loose factions would widen as the revolution progressed; shared opposition to Qadhafi barely concealed the distrust, which would burst to the fore after his toppling.

As the summer wore on, the Islamists enjoyed the increasing attention from Westerners like the French, British, and Americans. By many accounts the Islamist leaders were more accessible and more organized than older uniformed defectors from the Qadhafi regime. Linvill remarked that the February 17 Brigade's Fawzi Bu Katif and his deputy, a wealthy Hewlett-Packard manager, were the "most polished," with fluent English from their time in the States. The deputy had attended a private high school in Northern California just twenty minutes away from Chris Stevens's high school, and the two men quickly bonded.

But could this faction of rebels be trusted?

Certainly, there were jihadists and ex-jihadists within the movement, including members of the Libyan Islamic Fighting Group. Some were veterans of wars in Afghanistan, Algeria, and Chechnya; many had done time in Abu Salim prison. In spite of their past—or rather because of it—Bu Katif welcomed them.

"We didn't know how to fight," he told me, "and the Iraq and Afghanistan veterans were the only ones who did."

■

SOME THOUGHT the revolution wouldn't reach Libya's third-largest city at all. Located some five hundred miles west of Benghazi, Misrata was Libya's industrial hub, and its inhabitants were better off than most. But they also had deep social ties with Benghazi and the east, and when they saw the shootings in those first bloody days, they too marched. During one of the protests, the security forces responded with gunfire, hitting a young man named Khalid Bu Shama who later died from his wounds. That was the catalyst. Thousands of mourners attended his funeral, eliciting an even harsher response from the regime, with even heavier weaponry. Enraged protestors ransacked police stations, raided armories, and seized a military airport, destroying helicopters on the tarmac.

On the second day of the uprising, the commander of a nearby military base, a fifty-one-year-old colonel from Misrata named Salim Joha, defected, walking alone to the protests. He found a town primed for rebellion but utterly lacking in leadership and organization: they were students, the unemployed, and engineers, bound together by blood or friendship. Joha quickly formed a committee with other defected officers to bring order to the multitude of militias that had formed. A misstep by the regime gave him the time and space to do this: Qadhafi's forces temporarily withdrew, enabling the rebels to organize. "Qadhafi thought maybe he could deal with Misrata differently," he told me. "He gave priority to the east. This was his mistake."

The reprieve didn't last. Two weeks later, a heavily armed brigade arrived to mete out punishment. But the rebels were ready: at a roundabout near the courthouse, flanked by high-rise office buildings, they pre-staged Molotov cocktails. With the clanking and groan of approaching tanks, the rebels dispatched trucks hastily fitted with guns like the "Dushka"—Russian for "sweetie"—to meet them. Fire short, controlled bursts, the defected officers told the youth; the drum barrel magazine holds only thirty rounds. The Misratans beat a hasty retreat, luring the attackers to the ambush zone downtown where they destroyed a personnel carrier with a rocket and felled a commander with sniper fire.

Spooked by these losses, Qadhafi's forces withdrew. By any measure, it was a miraculous victory for Misrata. "Angels were with us in those early days," said Joha.

But the war wasn't finished, and the city steeled itself for more fighting. Liberated Benghazi sent arms to Misrata by boat while rebels set up barricades of shipping containers, sandbags, bulldozers, anything they could find. They guarded against spies and saboteurs. The counterattack finally came on March 12, when an even larger column of tanks rumbled toward the city: the vaunted 32nd Brigade, led by Khamis al-Qadhafi. Misratan commanders pleaded for help from NATO, yet for weeks it looked like the city would be left to its own devices. "Tanks were moving everywhere, shelling us," Joha told me. "I thought, 'What the hell are these people [NATO] doing?'" Fighting in the dense urban quarters made it difficult for NATO to strike for fear of causing casualties. Still, the Misratans cursed the coalition, demanding that it send attack helicopters like the Apache to provide close-in support.

Then came teams of Western special operations forces that enabled the airstrikes to be more precise. They saved the city, according to Joha. "It was a life jacket thrown to a drowning man," he said. The French were first; four special operations officers arrived at the end of April, followed by the British and Americans. The commandos told the rebels to paint a large Z or N on the top of their vehicles so that aircraft and drones overhead could distinguish them from Qadhafi's forces. But most important, they helped the Misratan forces plan their breakout from the siege in July, calling in airstrikes to support the offensive.

Misrata was not the war's only new front. Just as the battle was turning in the rebels' favor there, another offensive in the Nafusa Mountains was starting to chip away at Qadhafi's defenses. The Nafusa Mountains arc around Tripoli like a crescent moon, from the Mediterranean coast to a southern plateau. It is a natural haven for dissidents: remote villages sit atop its bluffs, each one accessible only by narrow roads that snake through ravines. Whoever controls the Nafusa commands the western approaches to the capital.

Among the first Nafusa towns to break with the regime was Zintan, the largest community in the region. Qadhafi tried to talk them down with emissaries, and when that didn't work, he tried to buy them off. The youth of Zintan would have none of it.

In quick succession, the rest of the mountains revolted, storming army barracks and police stations, some rebels carrying only Italian-era carbines. Qadhafi's brigades rained down rockets in response, striking farms, homes, and mosques. But for the first two months, NATO barely touched the area; its shortage of planes and surveillance drones meant that it had to focus first on the eastern front and then on Misrata.

The Nafusa forces hunkered down and fortified their lines. Foreign advisors arrived—from France, America, the Emirates, and Qatar—bringing with them weapons and, crucially, training. Yet, as in Benghazi, the foreigners did not coordinate and sometimes competed, each country running its own supply lines to disparate rebel factions. The Emirates supported Zintan, while the Qataris sent weapons to Islamist fighters hostile to Zintan. By early July, though, the shaky coalition was edging to the gates of Tripoli.

Meanwhile, in the desert to the south, the oasis town of Sabha had risen up. Home to an Italian-era military fortress, Sabha was long an important conduit for Qadhafi to Mali and Niger, the Sahelian states to the south. But economic and social grievances had festered, especially among the town's dark-skinned Tabu people, whom Qadhafi had confined to ramshackle slums while handing control of lucrative smuggling routes to favored Arab tribes. Farther to the east, the isolated town of Kufra, another smuggling entrepôt near the Chadian-Sudanese border, revolted as well.

As the summer commenced and the revolution spread, the regime appeared hemmed in, controlling only the capital and the so-called oil crescent of the Sirt Basin, a historic zone of pro-Qadhafi sentiment.

It already seemed appropriate to ask: What would follow the dictator?

■

IT IS EASY to be charmed by Dr. Aref Ali Nayed when you meet him. A Sufi theologian, he is also a devotee of Western philosophy, according to one of his aides, partial to Montesquieu and John Stuart Mill—though in Libya's later chaos he will shift to darker, postwar writers:

Frankl, Fromm, and Arendt. For some in the West, Nayed was a reassuring figure. They projected onto the man their aspirations for a new Libya, one whose Sufi sensibilities they hoped would reconcile Muslim identity with modernity and pluralism. "A man of god and technology," gushed one *New York Times* profile.

The scion of a wealthy Benghazi merchant family, Nayed had earned degrees in engineering and philosophy. He taught Islamic thought in Italy and Malaysia before heading back to Libya to take over his father's construction and telecommunications company. Soon after the start of the revolution, he joined the NTC, working closely with Mahmud Jibril, and secured backing for the rebels from the United Arab Emirates, using his business links. Within months, he was leading the NTC's "Tripoli Task Force," charged with developing a plan for the restoration of services, security, and governance after the liberation of the capital.

That summer, U.S. diplomats got to know the plan in meetings in Qatar and the United Arab Emirates. "He was incredibly polished, with a PowerPoint presentation; we hadn't seen that from anybody," recalls one American diplomat who attended. He'd anticipated seemingly every need for Libya's postconflict recovery, from sanitation to medical care to cell phone coverage. Still, the Americans had questions about Nayed's credibility and influence inside Libya: Did his task force really represent the rebels on the ground? The doubts were heightened by Nayed's predilection for self-promotion. "We called him 'The Spin Doctor,'" a senior State Department official working on Libya later told me, a crude reference to the Sufis' practice of devotional whirling.

Then, at a meeting in Dubai in late July, Nayed asked the Americans for weapons. "We are creating a contingent of forces called the 'Tripoli Guards,'" his briefing stated. An American diplomat in attendance blanched: the specter of Iraqi dissident Ahmed Chalabi and his personal militia, the Iraqi National Congress, leapt to mind. In the run-up to the 2003 American invasion of Iraq, the exiled Chalabi had maneuvered Washington, D.C.'s halls of power, skillfully exaggerating his popularity in Iraq. The last thing Washington wanted was to repeat that fiasco by supporting a takeover of Tripoli by a Libyan faction with uncertain backing on the ground.

Lieutenant Colonel Linvill, attending the Dubai meeting, saw through the charade quickly. Contrary to common assumptions, Nayed didn't speak for the NTC. "He didn't have the *wasta*," Linvill concluded, using the Arabic slang for personal clout. "It was clear to us that he and his merry band had played out." And as the summer wore on, that clout grew even shakier as a competing rebel faction emerged with plans of its own for the liberation of Tripoli.

In many respects, the ex-jihadist named Abd al-Hakim Belhaj is the alter ego of Aref Nayed. Both men profess piety, both are intensely political creatures and businessmen, and both attempted to steer the course of the revolution. But their paths could not have been more different. If Nayed enjoyed family wealth, advanced degrees, and easy entrée to Western diplomats, Belhaj came from modest means; his family had lost its wealth in Qadhafi's collectivization. As a young man, he acquired hard-won skills in combat, evading foreign intelligence, and surviving torture in prison. The West now viewed him with suspicion.

I met him in late 2016, in Istanbul, where he now spends much of his time. Seated in an overstuffed chair in a gold-leafed café, he wore a Tissot watch and an untucked Izod shirt. We were a world removed from the life he'd known for decades.

Belhaj was born in 1966 in Tripoli in the eastern neighborhood of Suq al-Jumaa—long a bastion of anti-Qadhafi and Islamist sentiment. After studying civil engineering, he joined the anti-Soviet jihad in Afghanistan in the late 1980s. Upon returning to Libya, he founded a militant organization—the Libyan Islamic Fighting Group (LIFG)—with the goal of toppling Qadhafi and installing a new government run by Islamic law or *sharia*. When Qadhafi crushed the LIFG in 1998 he fled back to Afghanistan, finding a haven with the Taliban until their collapse in 2001.

A life on the run ensued. Though he'd met bin Laden and some

LIFG fighters did join al-Qaeda, the organization as a whole did not, and Belhaj condemned the terrorist attacks on America. That didn't matter for the Americans. In 2004, acting on a tip from British intelligence, the CIA detained him and his pregnant wife in Bangkok, then sent him back to Libya, where he was tortured in prison. He was finally released in 2010 after renouncing violence as part of the theological "revisions" facilitated by Saif al-Islam.

Just after the first Benghazi protests in February 2011, Qadhafi's intelligence chief, Abdullah al-Sanusi, summoned Belhaj to his headquarters, where an officer confronted him with text messages proving his dissident activity. Feigning cooperation, Belhaj said he would join him after midday prayers. Then he vanished, sneaking out through the garden and escaping to Tunisia, where he vowed to finish the struggle he'd begun decades before.

He quickly established himself as a commander on the Nafusa mountain front, partially due to Qatari weapons. With Qatari support, Belhaj formulated his own plan for the liberation of Tripoli, ignoring the work of Aref Nayed, whom he dismissed as being out of touch and spending too much time in the Gulf. "I saw his plans," he scoffed, tracing a cloud in the air with his hands. "Some Indian guy in Dubai wrote them," he told me, referring to one of Nayed's assistants. Moreover, Belhaj emphasized, it was his men, not Nayed's, who were the ones actually fighting on the ground.

As the summer wore on, the weak NTC, epitomized by its indecisive chairman, Mustafa Abd al-Jalil, failed to reconcile these differences and tilted toward Qatar and the Islamists. Frustrated by this shift, Nayed leaned even more on the Emirates for armed support, preparing with Emirati assistance yet another, more secret plan for securing Tripoli. The stage was set for chaos after Qadhafi.

Developments in the east only added to the rebels' disarray. By the summer, General Younis's command of the rebel campaign was failing. He rarely visited the front, preferring instead to stay in Benghazi and bicker with his rival, Khalifa Hiftar. His Special Forces soldiers often appeared to be no more than a rabble. In mid-July, he launched a three-pronged offensive on the oil port of Brega but was beaten back, losing several hundred men. On July 27 the NTC sent a delegation to retrieve Younis from the front and bring him back to Benghazi for consultations. The official reason for the summons was to discuss his mismanagement of the war and possible misappropriation of funds, though many suspected him of trying to broker a cease-fire with the regime.

Younis never made it to Benghazi, and what happened next remains a mystery.

The NTC's Ministry of Defense questioned and then released him. A hard-line jihadist militia took him next, possibly with the connivance of NTC officials, as payback for Younis's crackdown on Islamists decades earlier. His badly burned body was found on a road outside Benghazi. Whatever the motive, the murder of Younis stunned the rebels. Chris Stevens was shocked as well, believing that the revolution had lost one of its leading lights, though other Westerners who met him were not so sure, citing his inability to command. Libyans themselves were also divided—about his checkered past and his eleventh-hour defection—and his death widened the distrust between the Islamists and ex-regime factions.

The revolutionaries were without a head for the rest of the war.

■

"LISTEN, WE CAN'T support you forever," Mahmoud Jibril remembers an agitated Nicolas Sarkozy saying. "We can't keep paying for this."

It was June 15. By this time, the rebel campaign had stalled, and both Paris and Washington were worried about the endurance and commitment of the NATO coalition. The White House in particular worried that European parliaments would not vote on an extension of the military campaign. Now, in the hall of the Élysée Palace in Paris, Jibril had arrived with what the French had hoped was an answer: a plan for liberating Tripoli. Rather than push solely from the east, the rebels would rely on an uprising from within the capital, along with an assault from the Nafusa Mountains. Already, acts of sabotage in Tripoli were under way: an underground network conducted hit-and-run attacks with smuggled rifles and so-called *gelatina*—homemade explosives normally used for fishing. The cells also had a list of security facilities secretly compiled by the owner of a food catering company that had serviced the regime before the revolution.

Jibril handed Sarkozy a list of those targets. He was impressed, but still had questions.

"Can you carry out the uprising on the fourteenth of July?" Sarkozy queried him. The date was the anniversary of the fall of the Bastille, which triggered the French Revolution.

"Yes," Jibril replied, "as long as you supply the weapons."

"Don't worry about that," Jibril remembers Sarkozy saying. "Our friends in Qatar and the Emirates will do that."

Within weeks, the secret plan to take Tripoli had a name, Mermaid Dawn, riffing on the historic nickname for the city, the Bride of the Sea or Mermaid. The rebels got help as Sarkozy had promised, even though they missed his target date of Bastille Day. French and British commandos smuggled in antitank missiles and radios and trained saboteurs. The UAE and Qatar sent weapons as well. By mid-August, NATO was pounding military targets in the capital using intelligence supplied by the food caterer and verified by Western intelligence operatives.

On Saturday, August 20, just after sunset and the breaking of the Ramadan fast, Mustafa Abd al-Jalil delivered a televised speech, closing with the words "The noose is tightening." The clandestine cells took this as their cue and sprang into action, seizing a mosque and using its loudspeakers to call for revolt. Defying fears of bloody house-to-house combat, Qadhafi's Praetorian units melted away: the rebels had secretly recruited the army commander charged with guarding Tripoli's southern gates.

But whatever hopes existed for an orderly seizure of the capital quickly fell apart. Emboldened by the lack of resistance in their path, fighters from Zintan and Misrata as well as Belhaj's men rushed in. A scramble ensued; commanders lost control over the exultant youths in their ranks who executed loyalists and looted. In all of this, the political leadership of the NTC was caught unprepared. Its leaders were scattered geographically, often out of the country, and not talking to one another or to the armed groups on the ground. And as shown by the competing road maps put forth by Nayed and Belhaj, they'd failed to advance a unified plan for the day after.

On August 23, the rebels started their final assault on Qadhafi's fortified compound at Bab al-Aziziya. But just as they breached the palace walls, Abd al-Hakim Belhaj drove in with an Al Jazeera camera crew, stopping at the iconic statue of a fist clenching a U.S. fighter plane. It was ground zero of the revolution, and now, on live TV, Belhaj posed next to it, proclaiming to the world that he was the leader of the liberating forces.

The interview jolted the rebels. Salim Joha and the Misratans were livid at the upstaging, and the Nafusa fighters who'd sheltered and supported Belhaj felt betrayed. But no one was more outraged than Nayed and Jibril: the ex-jihadists' Al Jazeera interview was the clearest confirmation yet that the Islamist rebels and their Qatari backers had eclipsed them.

The United States was also caught off guard by the speed of Tripoli's fall. White House officials had expected a drawn-out battle and had only learned of the assault when Twitter accounts they were monitoring lit up with news of the fighting. Mindful of the danger that Tripoli could fall into chaos, the United States was eager to make sure that the rebels' political authority was present. "We wanted to get the NTC's leadership in Tripoli as soon as possible on TV, to be the face of the liberation," Linvill told me. And soon after the fall of Qadhafi's compound, the Western states rushed their diplomatic personnel from Benghazi to Tripoli, eager to show support for the NTC.

But beneath the euphoria some worried—prophetically, it turned out—that Benghazi, the seat of the revolution, was being abandoned. It was a concern voiced repeatedly by Chris Stevens.

■

THE REVOLUTION was not finished. Loyalists still held out in towns like Bani Walid in the west, Sabha in the south, and, most important, Qadhafi's birthplace of Sirt on the central coast. An intense hunt began for the dictator and his family, who had fled the capital before the final assault. On August 29, Khamis al-Qadhafi, Qadhafi's youngest son and most capable commander—and onetime object of lavish Western attention—set out from Tripoli for Bani Walid in a sixty-vehicle convoy. He never made it. Competing accounts describe his end at the hands of a rebel ambush or an Apache helicopter strike. All that remained was the smoldering wreck of his Land Cruiser.

On September 21, NATO agreed to extend its sea and air campaign for ninety days in support of the new government. But the clock was ticking. The revolutionaries, led by the battle-hardened fighters from Misrata and the east, launched a ferocious assault on Sirt, facing a dug-in foe. Withering artillery fire pushed the rebels back three times; they responded with artillery barrages of their own, oblivious to civilian casualties. NATO aircraft dropped propaganda leaflets on the town's defenders emblazoned with a skull and crossbones and an Arabic message that translated to "The previous regime no longer rules Libya; there are two choices before you—death or surrender." Western advisors on the ground called in airstrikes.

And then came what one White House official called the "lucky shot."

Muammar Qadhafi, the quixotic despot who had once crowned himself the king of kings, met his end after being pulled from a drainage pipe just outside Sirt. An American Predator drone and French jets had attacked his escaping convoy. Cell phone video shows the jubilant rebels dragging him from the tunnel, taunting him and sodomizing him with a stick. Blood mats his bedraggled hair and streams down his face, soaking his shirt. He appears by turns confused and taken aback. He scolds his captors: "What is this? What are you doing?" A rebel yells back in his face, "Misrata, Misrata!"

What happened next is a matter of dispute. Off camera, one of the fighters approached the wounded dictator and shot him in the chest and temple with a pistol. The Misratans' spokesperson denied the execution to Western reporters, saying instead that Qadhafi had died from wounds suffered in the airstrike en route to Misrata's hospital. But the NTC later admitted he had been shot after capture. Rebels laid the corpse in a meat freezer in Misrata for days, where Libyans queued in the hot sun for a macabre but satisfying glimpse of the "Brother Leader."

Under international law, the killing was a war crime, an embarrassment for Libya's transitional leadership, and an omen of things to come. For now, though, the spell had been broken. The Libyans who waited to view his corpse sought closure. They needed to see for themselves that the outsized figure they had known only from a distance through posters, televised speeches, and his reign of fear was really gone.

Hillary Clinton learned of his death during a TV interview in Kabul, Afghanistan. Upon hearing the news, she chuckled on camera and pumped her fists: "We came, we saw, he died."

Years later, a Libyan friend in Tripoli had a different take.

"We thought it was the last bullet," he told me. "But it was just the first."

4

FALSE HOPES

I RETURNED TO LIBYA in February 2012, this time not as a military officer but as a civilian, doing research for a think tank. I'd spent most of 2011 focused not on Libya but on the Gulf Arab states, completing a book on the Arab Spring protests in Saudi Arabia and Bahrain and how the ruling dynasties there had quickly silenced them. Libya by comparison looked more hopeful, though it already bore the scars of the Gulf monarchies' divisive meddling, an interference that would worsen in the coming years.

My first impression was of color, splashed everywhere. Yards of graffiti with garish cartoons of the deposed tyrant—frizzy-haired and ratlike—now adorned Tripoli's walls. The bold tricolor of the Libyan flag flapped from balconies, along with the rainbow banner of the ethnic Imazighen, long forbidden under Qadhafi. Handbills stuck to lampposts announced the formation of this or that political club while vendors hawked revolutionary memorabilia alongside knockoff watches and cologne on Omar al-Mukhtar Street. Even women's dresses seemed brighter.

I stood under the floodlights at Martyrs' Square, formerly Green Square, watching a rally. Carrying scrawled placards and waving flags, people marched and leaned out of cars in a wild circumambulation. They posed for pictures, eager to talk. I loitered for hours.

But early signs of dissolution were everywhere, greeting you first thing in the baggage claim of Tripoli International Airport, where a memo plastered to a glass door bore the seal not of a customs authority or a national government but of the Zintani militia that controlled the airport. Throngs of militiamen milled about in the waiting lounge. On the way to Tripoli, detritus from the vanquished regime lined the highway: collapsed concrete from Qadhafi's palace, the husks of crippled tanks, and bullet-pocked barracks. Gone were the white uniformed traffic cops at the palm-ringed plazas. Trash had piled up.

Young militiamen in ski caps careened in mud-coated trucks, swiveling the twin barrels of their antiaircraft guns. Nights erupted in a cacophony of screeching drag races and the rat-tat-tat of gunfire, mostly celebratory, but sometimes not: a militia fracas, payback for some past crime or the commission of a new one.

■

CONTRARY TO SOME assumptions, the United States did try to anticipate what would follow the dictator. Washington and its allies had churned out volumes of assessments, estimates, and plans. Lots of them. "The size of a Manhattan phone book," said one White House staffer.

What was lacking was the will to act on them.

As early as March 6, 2011, the NSC set up an interagency team to plan for post-Qadhafi Libya. Over the next few months, the working group gathered input from agencies such as Treasury, State, Defense, and the CIA. Weighing the chances of Libya falling into a protracted civil war, they debated whether the country would need peacekeepers or a stabilization force and how to jump-start the economy and disarm revolutionary fighters. Other planning efforts began as well. The evacuated staff of the American embassy in Tripoli set up an "embassy in exile" in Washington that ran a parallel project, and the Pentagon conducted a war game called Island Breeze to simulate scenarios after Qadhafi. Forecasting about what would happen after regime change was hardly new territory after Iraq and Afghanistan. "This was not our first rodeo," quipped a diplomat involved in the State Department effort.

Fearing revolutionary Libya's potential draw as a terrorist haven, the NSC set up an interagency working group to track Libyan jihadists. "These were the guys that escaped Qadhafi's maw and returned exultant during the revolution," the group's cochair told me. Filled with intelligence officers and special operators, the group knew from experience that when governments collapse, jihadists can fill the void.

Once Benghazi fell to the rebels, an international team of post-conflict experts drawn from the UK, France, Italy, and other countries began applying the lessons of Afghanistan and Iraq. They canvassed revolutionary governance in Benghazi, releasing a detailed report that seems in some areas prophetic. The most pressing challenge for the country's new leadership, they wrote, would be "ensuring anti-Qadhafi militia do not evolve into armed wings of political factions but are merged into new, democratically accountable national security organisations."

Yet these voluminous plans dissolved on first contact with Libyan realities. First, there was the uncertain authority of the fragile transitional government, whose leadership was always leery about how much foreign assistance they wanted after liberation. On top of this, some of the more radical Islamists in the revolution were fearful of a foreign occupation. But the suspicion ran broader than that: even less dogmatic

Libyans had been weaned on Qadhafi's propaganda that painted the West as imperialistic and predatory. Then there was the outsized influence of the Gulf states, the United Arab Emirates, and Qatar, which had played a crucial role in the liberation of Tripoli and whose Libyan allies were dominating the new scene.

Far more important, though, was President Obama's reluctance about getting entangled in post-Qadhafi Libya, which consigned the planning efforts to irrelevance. Libya seemed all but forgotten: the number of NSC principals' meetings after the death of the dictator fell off drastically and the working group to track jihadists disbanded because of a "lack of interest from the West Wing," its cochair told me. "There was less interest in keeping Libya front and center of the principals' agenda," a senior administration official acknowledged, "particularly because it had consumed so much time for [the past] six or seven months." According to some lower-level staffers, a mind-set of "we did our part" and "no ownership" seemed to take hold across the NSC, enforced by Obama's chief of staff.

"I was glad to finally leave them," said one White House staffer about the residual Libya meetings after the revolution. "It was all an elaborate kabuki."

Much of the neglect sprang from Obama's insistence that the Europeans take the lead for Libya's postconflict recovery. And the Europeans assured the Americans that this would be the case. "The Europeans told us, 'We got this, don't worry about it,'" said Derek Chollet, a White House advisor who led the Libya planning. But that support never materialized, partly because the Europeans believed that the UN should play a central role, an emphasis that Washington supported.

The UN started planning for post-Qadhafi Libya as early as April 2011, issuing a report on its anticipated needs. But there were always questions about its capacity, with the Pentagon in particular raising concerns about how well the UN and supporting states could stabilize the country without troops to ensure security. Even so, the directive from the White House was clear: no boots on the ground. And the UN itself had decided against any peacekeeping troops or military observers, partly for bureaucratic reasons—which UN member states would contribute soldiers, especially in the wake of fatigue from Afghanistan and Iraq?

The assumption all along was that ground troops would not be involved," Chollet told me. "So that meant that the protective tissue, the spinal cord needed to ensure the success of the international stabilization efforts was not there."

Much of the planning, though, offered optimistic assessments of Libya's reconstruction. The NATO campaign had left the country's infrastructure intact and the country had petroleum wealth. True, it might be some time before oil production reached prewar levels. Yet the country's new leaders had access to tens of billions of dollars of overseas frozen assets, which the United States had worked hard to unlock. "We believed that this would not be a strictly bottom-up affair, that Libya had a lot going for it," Chollet said.

I agreed at the time. Lacking deep sectarian or ethnic fault lines, Libya's society was not as divided as Syria's or Iraq's. Its population of six million was overwhelmingly Sunni and Arabic speaking, and its ethno-linguistic minorities were small in number and dispersed on the periphery. And contrary to some assumptions, modern Libya was not an entirely artificial creation born of European machinations. To be sure, it had distinct subregions with their own identity: Cyrenaica in the east, Tripolitania in the west, and Fezzan in the south. But after World War II, Libyan elites from these regions had collaborated, sometimes uneasily, to build the independent state within its contemporary borders.

Still, for more than four decades, Libya had been synonymous with just one man. What would happen now that he was gone?

■

I FINALLY CAUGHT UP with Lieutenant Colonel Linvill at the makeshift American embassy in Ambassador Cretz's residence, an elegant villa with patios and a well-tended lawn. Pro-regime looters had trashed the old compound during the revolution, and the new arrangement exemplified what the State Department called "expeditionary diplomacy": the garage was now the visa section, the kitchen a conference room, and bedrooms offices. To enter the embassy you had to pass through a security gauntlet that started with a heavy iron gate; that summer, it became unhinged and crashed down on a Libyan guard, killing him.

The return of American diplomats to Tripoli in the fall of 2012 was a bittersweet homecoming, for none more so than Ambassador Gene Cretz, who'd left the country in late 2010. In speeches, he'd sounded notes of triumph, urging American businesses to return to Libya. But he was also cautious.

"Nobody knows now what the political fabric of this country is going to look like after forty-two years in which there was no political fabric," he told a reporter, referring to Qadhafi's long reign. "So I think there is a genuine cause to be concerned that things could go wrong."

Linvill poured us glasses of scotch under a patio awning. By Libyan custom and law, alcohol was verboten outside the embassy gates. But the embassy had cases of it shipped in from a Dutch company that specialized in catering to diplomats. More than once, though, the militias that controlled Tripoli's port intercepted the shipments.

It turned out he almost never made it back to Libya at all when his presence at the embassy became the object of a bureaucratic tussle over how much military presence the administration would permit. If "no boots on the ground" was the guiding mantra, some in Washington were questioning whether Linvill—a serving military officer—counted as a "boot" or a "shoe." As an attaché, he fit squarely into the latter camp, effectively acting as a Department of Defense diplomat on the embassy's "country team." He wore a suit and tie most of the time, not fatigues, and he never carried a gun. But the State Department was skittish.

"State was worried about the optics of having too many U.S. military folks running around," Derek Chollet told me. "Though to be fair," he continued, "so too were the Libyans, and the Pentagon often made some exorbitant requests about the number of people it needed in the country."

The problem of limited space at the embassy complicated matters further—there simply weren't enough beds or offices in the villas to house more personnel from the military. Then there were Libyan sensibilities. Though the traditional leadership was divided, the one thing they agreed upon was rejecting foreign military troops on their soil. Even a minimal military footprint at the embassy—U.S. special operations forces who helped with security—required constant reassurances to nervous Libyan officials that they were not a prelude to a larger occupation. The same anxieties delayed the arrival of the United Nations' security detail. In Linvill's case, the month-and-a-half-long debate over his return ultimately required authorization from President Obama himself.

When he finally arrived on the ground in October, he found that American diplomats were focused on supporting Libya's nascent civil society and, especially, its upcoming parliamentary elections, the country's first national elections in over half a century.

■

IT WAS ALL happening so fast. Perhaps too fast.

Some Western observers cautioned against holding national elections so soon after the war, before the demobilization of militias. Past experiences showed that doing so rewarded the strongest factions and those with the guns. It often sharpened existing divisions in countries lacking a culture of civic participation and the rule of law, like Libya. Early elections also risked a return to strife, with the American occupation of Iraq being Exhibit A. One authoritative survey of civil wars since 1945 showed that holding off on elections for five years reduced the chance of open conflict by a third.

In Libya, though, the mood was one of determination. No one in the country believed that elections would by themselves resolve its fissures, and nobody was blind to the growing power of the militias. The great hope, however, was that the new elected authorities would have a stronger mandate and greater legitimacy than the moribund NTC. Libyan leaders also argued that if elections were fair, transparent, and marked by high turnout, they would set an important precedent for national unity. And the United Nations, the Americans, and the Europeans fell squarely in line behind them—if elections were what the Libyans wanted, then that was what the international community should support. After all, as Samantha Power told me, "we weren't running a protectorate."

It was hard not to get swept up by the euphoria: Libyans finally had a say in their affairs. They held elections for municipal councils—an important test run for national voting. They set up free associations, periodicals, and charities, all unfettered by government control. Encouraged by this momentum, the United States and European countries tried to nourish these fledgling institutions, assisting women's rights groups, training journalists, and funding poetry festivals. In Benghazi, I attended an EU-sponsored workshop on citizenship: students, militiamen, teachers, young women, and tribal leaders huddled before a PowerPoint briefing, debating the lessons of Libya's 1951 constitution.

Education seemed a particular focus. The NTC had assured the Americans that it planned to use the country's vast oil revenues for scholarships to send young Libyans abroad. Everything was on the table, from vocational training to firefighting to graduate school—and it would be a windfall of funding for U.S. universities and schools. Chris Stevens lent his support for the effort, going frequently to "shoot the shit with the president of the University of Tripoli," a diplomat involved in the program recalls. But suspicions of the past lingered. "A strata of Libyan bureaucracy was still very hostile to the West," the diplomat said.

Libya's new civil society groups clustered in the marble foyers of hotels, eager for outside funding and attention. I wondered, though, just how far they penetrated into Libya beyond a few key cities. Having left the country decades before to reside abroad, many of the dual-citizen, English-speaking Libyans who ran the volunteer groups had only a dim awareness of the country's new terrain. One American NGO worker supporting Libyan women's organizations discovered that she had actually spent more time in Libya than some of the Libyan leaders she was training.

"These elites are launching campaigns," she emailed home to family, "and claiming to speak on behalf of the millions of Libyan women who never had the opportunity to leave the country."

It was a harsh judgment, but one that captured the sharp divide between Libyans returning from years abroad—many with advanced education and technical skills—and those who'd stayed and suffered under Qadhafi. The latter were often resentful and suspicious. "Double *shafras*," Libyans called the returnees, a mocking reference to the Arabic term for a cell phone's SIM card: the returnees usually had two SIM cards, a Libyan and a foreign one, that they switched out.

As the first year after the revolution unfolded, the full scale of the effort needed to rebuild Libyan institutions started to become apparent.

"We had a profound underestimation of the devastation that Qadhafi had caused," one American diplomat admitted to me. "You had a generation and a half that had never contributed to society."

Meanwhile, public perceptions of Libya's transitional leadership plummeted as Libyans tired of its opacity and timidity. Deferring on difficult decisions to preserve consensus, it doled out appointments based on family ties and militia power in the capital. It often rejected well-meaning UN advice and lacked the requisite staff to handle even routine functions. A vicious cycle ensued.

"The country's new leaders know nothing else but the old ways," a UN official told me, "which in turn fuels the impression that the old ways are back."

The old ways clung especially fast regarding women's roles, in both politics and society. Women's rights had not advanced and actually seemed to be regressing. At best, women received leadership positions in what one activist called "pink ministries," symbolic posts of little consequence, like social or cultural affairs. At worst, they were met with increased harassment, violence, and threats of death.

The disappointment hit Salwa Bugaighis hard. By now, she'd distanced herself from the NTC, bemoaning its lack of women. As an activist, she'd faced pressure not just from Islamists but also from the council's male leaders. "You have your family and your money, what are you doing here?" they chided her.

Then, in October, in Benghazi's main square, the council's chairman, Mustafa Abd al-Jalil, delivered a speech intended to commemorate the liberation of Libya. What he said instead left Salwa and other women activists speechless: Qadhafi-era laws against polygamy were now void.

"We expected this great speech about martyrdom and sacrifice," one of Salwa's cousins told me. "We couldn't stop laughing."

For Salwa, Abd al-Jalil's utterances on polygamy reflected the Islamists' growing power and, more important, Libya's entrenched patriarchy. Both needed tempering, and the way to do that, she figured, was through a constitution that enshrined individual rights, especially those of women. Already, many politicians, Islamists and non-Islamists alike, had argued for *sharia* as a basis for the constitution. So there had to be specific articles in the document guaranteeing women's rights. Here, the upcoming parliamentary elections were vital, given the legislature's role in drafting the constitution. Salwa campaigned for women candidates to appear on the ballots, going frequently on television to do so.

"She realized she had a presence, an effect," her son Wail said.

■

FOR ALL THESE CHALLENGES, it was still possible in early 2012 to remain guardedly optimistic. Oil production had rebounded to nearly prewar levels by March. And despite the specter of militia power and lawlessness, the country was moving steadily toward elections.

"Armageddon predictions [are] a bit overstated," Ambassador Cretz emailed Washington in February. Two months later, he departed Tripoli, a normal end to what had been an eventful and historic tenure. His successor was Chris Stevens.

It was something of a second homecoming for Stevens and a triumphant one at that. He had left Benghazi in November 2011 for a brief interlude in Washington, and now, just after celebrating his fiftieth birthday with family, he was returning. The NTC, the rebel body on whose behalf he'd lobbied the Obama administration for recognition and support, had taken power in the capital. He was not naïve about what lay ahead. Back in Washington he'd followed developments closely, and he knew from his tours under Qadhafi and as an envoy just how devastated and neglected the country had become. But by all accounts he was optimistic—as was much of the administration, especially Secretary of State Hillary Clinton. "He really felt and heard her optimism," his sister Anne recalls. A prosperous and democratic Libya, he'd told senators at his confirmation hearing, "would serve as a powerful example to others in the region who are struggling to achieve their own democratic aspirations."

In Tripoli, he garnered immediate respect, inside and outside the embassy, according to diplomats who served with him. It is of course easy to idealize a fallen colleague—and he was not without his faults. Some diplomats who worked with him questioned the "mythology" of Stevens's high level of Arabic proficiency—a fair enough critique given the difficulty of the language, especially the nuances of the Libyan dialect. Another speculated that, given his modesty, Stevens would probably find the postmortem mythologizing strange and embarrassing. But contemporaneous emails from his colleagues reveal heartfelt admiration for his skill as a leader and diplomat.

"He's incredible to work with," one young diplomat wrote home to family that summer. "Very low-key, great sense of humor, and well-known throughout the country."

He attracted a fierce loyalty, not least from the Libyans with whom he had worked in the first trying months of the revolution.

One of them was a man named Abu Baker Habib, who'd run an English-language school in Benghazi before the uprising. Habib had been a friend of the Americans ever since the reopening of the U.S. embassy in 2006, and during the 2011 revolution, he'd cemented that trust when he helped rescue an American F-15 fighter pilot who'd crashed outside Benghazi. When Stevens arrived as the American liaison to the rebels, Habib became his right-hand man: a combination of fixer, interpreter, and counselor. The bond they formed was unbreakable.

That March, Habib's son was born with a health condition. On top of a frenetic schedule as ambassador, Stevens made near-daily phone calls to arrange for medical care overseas, even calling his sister Anne, a doctor in Seattle, for referrals.

In settling in, Stevens made clear his mandate: Libyans owned their destiny, and it wasn't America's place to dictate how they would go about organizing their newfound politics. "He really bought into the whole light-footprint thing," one diplomat recalled, meaning that the United States would have a minimal presence on Libyan soil. This was of course the imperative set by the Obama administration, and Stevens hewed closely to it.

"He had his marching orders," Colonel Linvill said. When pressed on some matter that might overstep Washington's guidance, he remembers Stevens saying, only half jokingly, "'Now hold on, Brian, I'm just a cautious bureaucrat.'"

As he'd done in Benghazi as the special envoy, he made outreach to Libyans from all walks of life, from all political factions, his priority. One diplomat remembers him staying up until three in the morning with a former Libyan jihadist, a veteran of Afghanistan who'd studied in Berlin during the Cold War, debating, among other things, East German political philosophy. "This was exactly the sort of meetings Chris had," a diplomat told me. "Now there's one more Islamist coming away thinking that, 'Hey, it's okay to talk to the ambassador.'" And he frequently brought junior diplomats to his seemingly interminable meetings, just so they could see firsthand how diplomacy was done. "I learned more about being a diplomat from him than anyone else," was a common refrain from those who accompanied him.

Life at the embassy during that first year after Qadhafi seemed marked by high morale and a sense of purpose. For many in the State Department, Libya offered a welcome contrast to the U.S. presence in Iraq and Afghanistan, where the Department of Defense had held sway. "I didn't want to play second fiddle to another military occupation," a diplomat said.

The ambassador and his fellow diplomats enjoyed late-afternoon tennis matches; Stevens took lessons from the former coach of Libya's Olympic team. He went for runs on a dirt road around the villa compound and led trips to the beach and the Roman ruins outside Tripoli. He lingered with locals over breakfast at Haj Fathi, a popular café. When the embassy's alcohol supply ran short after a militia grabbed a shipment at the port, he started a "prison wine" competition, fermenting anything the diplomats could get their hands on, from fruit juice to "near beer."

"Chris's mix was the worst," a diplomat told me, "but he made everybody drink it."

"That sounds a bit dangerous," I interjected.

"Serving in Libya was dangerous," the diplomat replied.

At a Fourth of July party Stevens had recruited a Libyan cover band that specialized in Western pop; it had stayed largely underground during Qadhafi's rule. Now, in the embassy's garden beside an open bar, the middle-aged musicians belted out Miley Cyrus hits in broken English.

"Chris could hardly keep a straight face," the diplomat said.

■

ACROSS THE COUNTRY preparations for elections picked up. Political parties mushroomed, though the decision to create them was controversial. Qadhafi had criminalized political associations of any sort and had long pushed the line that parties were conduits for meddling foreign powers. During his reign, there were not any organizations that could even serve as the basis for parties, like trade unions.

In early campaigning, the Islamists seemed the best organized, drawing from their long experience as an underground movement. The Brotherhood formed the Justice and Construction Party, courting young people and women. The former jihadists of the LIFG campaigned as well; after convincing the transitional government that his militant days were behind him, Abd al-Hakim Belhaj set up a party called Al-Watan, or the Nation. His old arms supplier, Qatar, pumped in funding, so much so that Al-Watan's election posters bore shades of the maroon and white Qatari flag.

On the other side was the National Forces Alliance (NFA), a broad coalition led by Mahmud Jibril, often described as "secular" or "liberal." But religion was an unhelpful lens through which to view Libyan politics. There were no literal secularists; all of Libya's factions agreed that Islam should play a prominent role in political and social life. Jibril himself had said that Islamic law should be a "frame of reference" for the Libyan constitution. And his NFA was actually a vast collection of outlooks that included forty parties and more than a hundred civil society organizations, including conservative Muslims.

For their part, the Islamists tried to appeal to the center and assuage the concerns of their fellow citizens—and the West. Al-Watan party posters in Benghazi featured an unveiled female engineer running for a seat. I met another of its candidates, a man with a master's in Islamic theology from Saudi Arabia, who spared no effort to portray Al-Watan as tolerant, boasting that half of its candidates were women. America, he assured me, should have no fear of Islamists. "After all," he said, "the United States Constitution is based on Islam."

Nowhere in Libya was the mix of exhilaration and anxiety about elections as palpable as in Benghazi. Since the early days of the 2011 uprising, Benghazinos had prided themselves on being the first stewards of independent politics in Libya in nearly half a century. Yet many in the city now feared a return to the marginalization of the past, especially after the transitional council had rushed to Tripoli in the wake of Qadhafi's fall. In the run-up to the elections, these worries spawned a political movement demanding greater autonomy in the form of a federal system. The more radical of the federalists advocated violence to achieve this.

I saw just how strong eastern grievances had become when I arrived in Benghazi one night in early July 2012, just before the elections. Entering the driveway of the Tibesti Hotel, I heard a loud thud on the roof of my car. Then another. Within seconds angry young men had surrounded me, blotting the light from a nearby streetlamp and banging long wooden poles on the hood and windows. The assault could've ended badly, but my driver escaped the crowd and ushered me into the lobby. "Federalists," he said, shaking his head.

The next day, I went to see the federalists' elderly strategist, a balding professor of management at Benghazi University named Abu Bakr Baira. With a degree from the University of California in Los Angeles and a pedagogical air, Baira was known as the political brains behind the federal movement, though critics accused him of backing more militant tactics, like the mob that had harassed me.

The federalist movement, he explained in a book-lined office, sprang from the conviction by many eastern Libyans that theirs is a distinctive region that had long played a pivotal role in the country's history. Social demography, the federalists believed, set the east apart. While urban centers grew on Libya's coast, most of the inhabitants of Cyrenaica's hinterland remained Bedouin pastoralists, until the second half of the twentieth century, and many tribes of the east traced their lineage back to Egypt and the Arabian Peninsula. Cyrenaican identity was further bound to the Sanusi, the Sufi movement that governed the east until the Italian Fascists came. But most important, Baira said, the east had enjoyed a period of self-governance under King Idris's monarchy, from 1951 to 1969. And that model was what he wanted now. "You have to understand," he told me, "federalism is the only way Libya can survive."

It seemed to me a somewhat idealized take on the monarchy's troubled history. True, the constitution of 1951 empowered regional governments in Cyrenaica, Tripolitania, and Fezzan, but there was constant tension among the three, with King Idris ruling as a sort of tribal arbiter. And in 1963 Idris abandoned the federal system altogether, dividing Libya into ten provinces whose governors he personally appointed. It was meant to help him consolidate his grip, but it came too late to save him from Qadhafi's coup in 1969.

One of the new dictator's first acts was to dismantle the vestiges of Sanusi rule in the east, marginalizing eastern tribes in favor of a three-way alliance among southern and central tribes: his own tribe—the Qadhadhfa—the Warfalla, and the Magarha. Soon after, Qadhafi lavished the west with money while neglecting the east. What made it so galling for easterners was that the majority of Libya's oil reserves— roughly 80 percent—were located in the eastern Sirt Basin. This was the legacy that Baira and his federalists hoped to revert.

Early in 2012, the federalists had softened their earlier demands from a full election boycott to demanding more seats for the east in the new parliament. Baira admitted that an attempt to pressure the transitional council with force had backfired. Just days before, federalist militiamen had set up roadblocks along Libya's main east-west highway at the historical boundary that marks Cyrenaica and the western province of Tripolitania, demanding a greater share of seats for the east in the new parliament. Across Libya, the public rejection of this coercion was unsparing and loud. In Tripoli, I saw protestors marching with signs saying NO EAST, NO WEST, YES TO NATIONAL UNITY and NO TO *FITNA* [CHAOS], NO TO SECESSION, YES TO NATIONAL UNITY. Faced with this backlash, the federalists relented.

"The road is now open," Baira told me. "We realized we were hurting Barqa [Cyrenaica] more than helping it."

But federalist violence continued. Days after I left, federalist militants shut down five oil terminals in the Gulf of Sidra for two days. During the voting, federalists stormed a polling station in Benghazi, set fire to a warehouse of voting material in Ajdabiya, and fired an antiaircraft gun at a government helicopter ferrying voting materials, killing an election official. All of this deepened popular scorn for the federalists. Even easterners who shared their grievances opposed their aggressive tactics. What most of them wanted, along with most Libyans, was not necessarily federalism or a breakup of the state but greater decentralization—for municipalities to have more control over their politics and budgets.

This, I thought, was a step in the right direction. But I was also troubled by the federalists' militancy. The authorities in Tripoli had been powerless to stop it. Bereft of an army and police, they had to count on the shaky goodwill of eastern militias, many of them Islamists, who, luckily, also opposed the federalists' agenda.

Although the federalists stood down, they had set a grim precedent in the new Libya: the first use of armed force against elected institutions.

It would not be the last.

■

AS VOTING DAY approached, Salwa Bugaighis called her son Wail who was in the States, reminding him to vote. "It's historic," she said, "don't miss out."

For most Libyans, the campaign season was at once festive and unfamiliar. Many seemed unsure exactly how to choose candidates. Some looked for impressive-sounding Western degrees, noting the doctorates or MBAs the candidates had listed on their posters and billboards. Others voted for people they knew or knew of, often vaguely, from their town or a tribe close to their family.

After a delay of one month, elections finally occurred on July 7. The results were a relief. To be sure, there was the federalist violence and intimidation in the east. Communal fighting in the western Nafusa Mountains and in towns to the south had disrupted voting. And in the towns of Sirt and Bani Walid turnout was low. But 94 percent of the country's polling stations opened without incident, and the overall turnout, 62 percent, was excellent, especially for a country that had not held national elections for more than half a century. Militias generally steered clear of interfering and in a number of cities they actually guarded the polling stations and transport of materials.

Western countries sent election monitors, who gave the voting high marks. The Carter Center rated 98 percent of the polling stations visited by its observers as "good" or "very good." "This is the least contentious process I've seen," the center's chief of mission, a veteran of democracy promotion in Africa and Latin America, told me at the time.

The results surprised many who had predicted a landslide victory for the Islamists, especially given the Islamists' electoral wins in neighboring Tunisia and Egypt. But of the eighty seats reserved for party-list candidates, Jibril's NFA took the most with thirty-nine; the

Brotherhood-dominated Justice and Construction Party came in a distant second with seventeen. Despite its glossy campaign, Belhaj's Al-Watan party won no seats at all. Many Libyans questioned what exactly the Islamists were offering in a country that was already socially conservative. The Islamists, especially the Brotherhood, admitted they had failed to inspire voters' confidence. Unlike their Egyptian counterpart, they did not have deep social roots in the country.

Yet the common narrative of a liberal sweep was also false. In the remaining 120 seats, which were reserved for independent candidates, the affiliation of the winners was unclear. Moreover, many wondered whether Jibril's fissiparous coalition, which included Islamists, would be able to coax smaller parties and independents into the two-thirds consensus needed to pass legislation. The risk of legislative gridlock was high, especially among politicians for whom democracy was terra incognita. Under its new mandate, the parliament was expected to form a transitional government and govern for the next eighteen months, until the constitution was in place and new elections would be held. It was, some Western observers warned, an unrealistic timeline that seemed doomed to failure.

Overall, however, a mood of triumph pervaded Libya—and Western capitals. President Obama praised the Libyan people for "another milestone on their extraordinary transition to democracy." Senator John McCain, an early supporter of the revolution, arrived in Libya for what seemed a victory lap, mingling with the celebrating crowds in Martyrs' Square after the polls closed. "McCain stood in the middle of traffic and kissed babies, shook hands, and took pictures," a diplomat emailed home. "[Ambassador Stevens] and I stood on the sidewalk watching, shaking our heads at the sight of it."

Among the embassy's diplomatic staff, there was similar elation. So much of the U.S. effort in Libya had been tied to the elections—perhaps too much, in hindsight. "We got distracted by the vote as a success marker," an American diplomat admitted years later.

"There was this sense that, ah, okay, we did this transition in less than a year, smooth sailing. Now on to Syria."

PART II

UNRAVELING

YOUNG MEN WITH GUNS

TRAVELING TO TRIPOLI'S MITIGA INTERNATIONAL AIRPORT is like burrowing through the strata of Libyan history. It was once an Italian airfield, then the Luftwaffe used it during Rommel's march across North Africa. During the Cold War, the Americans leased it from the Libyan monarchy, named it Wheelus Air Base, and built it up as the largest American overseas base in the world. I drove past the remnants of this self-enclosed world: dormitories, a chapel, a bowling alley, and a high school for dependents. "Little America," an ambassador had once called it.

Weeds and wisteria now rioted over the place. Well-armed Islamist militias had taken over too, setting themselves up as a state within a state, with armories, prisons, and motor pools. In all of Tripoli, there seemed no more fitting monument to the militias' power than Mitiga.

You could sense that power at every turn in the capital. While the country was focused on elections, the militias were cleaving Tripoli into sparring fiefdoms. Their skirmishes erupted suddenly, volleys of their heavy weapons booming in the night. They pillaged, tortured, and killed, leaving mangled corpses in their wake. The outgunned police, if they even showed up for work, were powerless to stop them. True, the militias did not challenge the voting, but their power grew quickly, and the changes they wrought on the political landscape would be irrevocable.

The militias' domains in Tripoli stemmed in part from the pell-mell liberation of the capital in August 2011 by Belhaj's Islamists, the Misratans, and the Zintanis. Other armed groups arose from inside the capital itself during the underground resistance that broke into open rebellion in August 2011. An assortment of landmarks demarcated their turf: this or that traffic stop, a fish market, or the zoo. Some admittedly played a stabilizing role, acting as neighborhood self-defense forces in the absence of police, but many were predatory and rapacious. And some had not even fought during the revolution: Qadhafi had released from jail thousands of criminals who now filled the streets and infiltrated the militias, using the cover of "revolutionary" to profit from smuggling and other criminal acts. Anyone with some money, friends, weapons, and vehicles could create a "revolutionary brigade."

In December 2011, the transitional government started doling out payments to the militias using recently unfrozen assets from the Central Bank. It was a fateful error, arguably the most ruinous decision made by Libyans after Qadhafi's fall. Some said it was made under coercion; the government argued it had no choice: it needed to project its authority across the country, and, in the absence of police or an army, it "deputized" the militias. Whatever the reasons, the payments swelled the ranks of the militias far beyond the number that had actually fought in the revolution. Drawn by the promise of a salary, young men joined in droves.

"If the Libyan government said tomorrow it will pay fishermen," a

Libyan friend told me, "everyone would become a fisherman. Same thing with militias."

With oil production rebounding in early 2012, the amounts of money being paid to militias ran into the billions of dollars. When payment didn't appear or was slow or wasn't enough, gunmen set up roadblocks around ministries or barged through office doors waving guns. Unsurprisingly, cronyism grew rampant. Competing officials in different ministries paid only those militias from their own towns, tribes, and regions. Militiamen started double and triple dipping. A young man might be drawing a salary as a police or army officer, then moonlighting in a militia that was also (ostensibly) under government control.

Like the young magician in *The Sorcerer's Apprentice*, the Libyan government was now beholden to an apparition of its own conjuring. Its repeated efforts to disarm and demobilize the militias failed. Its leadership tried to get them to surrender their guns through decrees and appeals—a tactic the transitional council had assured Chris Stevens would work after the revolution. "Look, these are our sons," a council member had said, according to another diplomat, "they will turn in their weapons when we ask." Stevens was not convinced.

After this failed, the government set up a program to try to register revolutionaries and identify their preferences for entry into either the police or the army, or jobs training, or higher education. But this well-meaning endeavor collapsed because of political infighting and because its leadership was tied to the Muslim Brotherhood. What's more, Libya's economy—based for so long on government handouts—could not absorb the young men leaving the militias. The country needed to diversify its economy and build up its private sector: tourism, retail, construction, and tech seemed to be the most promising sectors. Here, Westerners could help, or so it was hoped. A consultant hired by the U.S. Agency for International Development to develop policies for reintegrating Libyan militias recommended building up fast-food outlets. "McDonald's, Kentucky Fried Chicken, and other global companies," he wrote, "come with associated training programs that could be attractive to some militia members."

But it seemed to me it would take more than service jobs or even scholarships to entice the young men away from guns given the salaries they enjoyed. Disarmament after conflict was an inherently political act. It demanded trust among armed actors and their political backers. The absence of that trust created what was known among specialists as a "security dilemma:" no militia wanted to be the first to give up its weapons because that meant ceding power to rivals.

And so a kind of Catch-22 ensued in Libya. The anemic and provisional government insisted that the state could not be built until the revolutionaries (real and self-professed) gave up their guns. And the revolutionaries insisted they would not do so until the state was formed and their interests were secure.

At stake was what the sociologist Max Weber asserted was the very definition of a workable state: the monopolization of force.

■

I'D COME TO Mitiga Airport to see one of Tripoli's powerful militia bosses, a man named Abd al-Rauf Kara. A smooth-skinned thirty-something with a gaze of severe remoteness, Kara was a former metalworker who'd formed a militia after the revolution to ferret out Qadhafi loyalists. Then, since the police had all but disappeared, he tackled drugs: with the collapse of Libyan border control after 2011, a torrent of heroin, cocaine, and hashish flowed into the country. He also seized illegal liquor—a friend of mine cursed him for driving up the price of vodka. His militia, the Special Deterrence Force, enjoyed official top cover from the government, drawing its salary from the Ministry of Interior.

Like many of the Islamists at Mitiga Airport, Kara hailed from the adjoining neighborhood of Suq al-Jumaa, or "Friday Market." For centuries a village of dirt roads and ample irrigation, Suq al-Jumaa's inhabitants had been farmers, fishermen, and artisans who would hawk their wares to city dwellers at a weekly namesake market. It has long been a refuge for dissidents, with a diverse population descending from across western Libya and from points throughout the Mediterranean. Some of its families were also landed merchants from Tripoli who moved there only after losing their wealth during Qadhafi's frenzy of redistribution.

Suq al-Jumaa is also pious and conservative, home to a number of old Sufi orders and Qur'anic schools where boys would go in the summer after helping their fathers in the fields. Over time, other Islamic currents washed ashore, such as the Muslim Brotherhood and Salafism. For the youth of Suq al-Jumaa, these movements offered self-identity and protest. "Growing a beard was how we said fuck the system," one friend from the neighborhood told me. During the revolution, the youths of Suq al-Jumaa worked silently against Qadhafi, even as he kept a tight grip on the capital. Revolting on August 20, they worked with the Islamist fighters backed by Qatar who came down to Tripoli from the Nafusa Mountains. And as the capital fell, they grabbed Mitiga.

Kara received me in a spacious office at the edge of the airfield. In a nearby room, wispy youths in lizard-stripe fatigues and Diadora sneakers lounged on a couch watching a wide-screen TV. A box-fed machine gun rested on a bipod.

Kara is an adherent of Salafism, the conservative, literalist current of Islamism. He sports the thick beard and shaved mustache of a practicing Salafist and speaks in a formal Arabic peppered with Qur'anic allusions. Some observers have accused Salafism of being the doctrinal cognate of al-Qaeda and the Islamic State, but this is an overgeneralization, eliding the currents of Salafist thought and their differing approaches to politics and violence. To be sure, they share similar tenets. But in Kara's case, he adhered to a mode of Salafism that has been described as "quietist," as opposed to the militant jihadism of the Islamic State and al-Qaeda. What defines the quietist school, aside from heavy Saudi influence, is a doctrine of loyalty to a sitting ruler, along with contempt for rival Islamic sects. It is also marked by an aversion to democracy.

"I am not convinced by it personally," Kara told me. "But," he quickly clarified, "this is the best thing for our country now. If everybody wants it I can't go against it."

Critics have detected opportunism and a greed for power in such flexibility, while still others deride Kara as simply another warlord, busily building his fiefdom. Still, he had his supporters, those who applaud his crime-fighting prowess. If Tripoli is Libya's Gotham, they joked, then Kara is its Batman.

■

LATE ONE EVENING I joined one of Kara's Deterrence Force patrols in the capital, young bearded men in their twenties driving tinted-window trucks. They smoked, texted their girlfriends, and stopped for coffee, acting much as any cops on a beat would. One of them riding shotgun scanned the road while cradling a rifle as we headed south: there are Tripoli neighborhoods where Kara's men cannot go, where the bad blood runs deep for this slight or that killing.

By three in the morning, vast swaths of the shuttered city were quiet and cloaked in darkness. A few bony cats pawed through piles of garbage. North of Algeria Square, we passed by one of the city's more astonishing landmarks.

"The Bride of the Sea," as it is known, is an Italian-built fountain with a bronze statue of a bare-breasted maiden carrying a gazelle on her back. It is an icon, beloved by Libyans across the decades. But if you go there today you cannot find her; in 2014, Salafists punctured the woman's belly with a bullet before absconding with her altogether. The desecration was part of a bigger wave of iconoclasm by resurgent Salafists that started first with attacks on Libya's Sufi Islamic sect.

The Salafists had long condemned the Sufis as polytheists for their religious practices: chanting, dancing, the visitation of graves, and the veneration of saints. But after Qadhafi's fall, they went on a rampage. Across Libya, ancient and sacred spaces fell to the Salafists' ire: Sufi mosques, schools, and a library whose centuries-old manuscripts they put to the torch. In Tripoli, they razed the white-domed mausoleum of a Sufi scholar just across from the Radisson Blu hotel.

Back at Mitiga, I asked Kara about the destruction of the Sufi sites. He admitted that his men had participated, but had acted without his permission. "I disagree with the Sufis," he told me, "but we need to use words to talk them out of their deviance, not violence."

For many Libyans, the assaults on the Sufi sites were one excess too many. After all, they said, Sufism was deeply woven into Libya's history; Salafism was a more recent accretion. Its austerity, people felt, was alien to the country. Popular opinion turned against Kara and his men, with some parliamentarians demanding that his militia disband. That didn't seem likely.

I left Mitiga Airport just after dawn. Construction was under way: men clad in overalls hammered at new structures and daubed paint on old ones left by the Americans. The air smelled of sea salt, varnish, and sawdust. One of Kara's associates shook my hand, assuring me not to worry; I was under their protection during my travels.

And then he sighed and said, apologetically, "By God, we will have institutions here."

■

AMONG THE BIGGEST FOES of the Islamists at Mitiga were the militias from the mountain town of Zintan. With Emirati support, the Zintanis had moved into the capital in the last days of revolution and, like the Islamists, had set themselves up as major players by grabbing armories, ministries, and the capital's other, larger airport, Tripoli International. The conflict between the Islamists and Zintan was only slightly ideological: mostly it was about power and the raw spoils of revolution.

The road to Zintan from Tripoli climbs up through the Nafusa Mountains, twisting slowly through limestone gorges brimming with tamarisk. At their highest, these mountains provide enough of a barrier to insulate the capital from the Saharan heat, but they cannot block the *ghibli*, the sandstorms that barrel in over the desert, dumping millions of bloodred granules into the air.

This is an old land. The Nafusa's inhabitants point with pride to the Roman olive presses still in use and ancient granaries and mosques. It is also a heterogeneous one. Like many mountain ranges, the Nafusa was haven to an array of sects, tribes, and ethnic groups. Bedouin Arab tribes lived uneasily next to Imazighen, who followed a minority school of Islam known as Ibadism. Recently settled pastoralists traded with longtime farmers.

When Qadhafi came, he followed a timeworn practice of Libya's previous rulers: pitting these communities against one another by exploiting disputes over land and giving grazing rights to one tribe while denying them to another. Fighting sometimes erupted, but in those days it was limited to knives and hunting rifles. The dictator also quashed expressions of Amazigh identity, including the Amazigh language. For their part, the Imazighen accused him of using Zintan, an Arab town with ties to pro-Qadhafi tribes, to repress them.

During the revolution, the Nafusa towns put aside these differences and fought together. Afterward, the Imazighen enjoyed a cultural renaissance: storefront signs appeared in their language, and their mosques opened once again. The fraternity with their neighbors didn't last, however. The Nafusa fractured, each of its towns setting up its own militia. Old feuds and newer ones grew bloodier as the mountain fighters seized artillery and rockets. Alliances and checkpoints shifted; you had to thread the landscape carefully. Sometimes you were blessed with a visual clue, like the multi-colored flag of the Amazigh militias fluttering above a guard hut fashioned from tin and burlap. More often, though, you were flying blind, hoping that your guide knew the right turnoff, was friends with so-and-so's cousin, spoke the right dialect, or had the right last name.

Zintan, the largest town in the Nafusa, is a windswept tableau of concrete homes, mosques, and water towers perched on the lip of a rocky escarpment. Like the Misratans, the Zintanis nursed a sense of entitlement born of a siege by Qadhafi's forces, and they too celebrated a martial heritage, holding yearly reenactments of their victory over Italian colonial troops. On the outskirts of the town, I walked to the farm of a militia chief, a leader in a coalition of militias called the Zintani Military Council. A garrulous man with a weather-beaten face, he invited me for lunch. But first I had to see his captured armory. We toured the cramped cabins of Russian tanks and self-propelled artillery. Here, he said, his men had found the hog-tied corpses of Qadhafi's soldiers with gunshot wounds to the head—executed by their commanders, he said. I peered into one: the smell of gun oil, tobacco, and urine clung to the air.

We stepped outside for a view of the hills and a forest. The man swept his hand across the vista. "You see here? We cleansed this whole region of Qadhafi supporters." It was true, in a way. After the revolution, Zintan exacted a horrible revenge, firing artillery rounds into a nearby hamlet populated by a tribe that had sided with the dictator. But Zintan had also helped a number of senior regime officials escape across the Tunisian border.

We headed back for lunch. "We also have no extremists here," he assured me. "Here it is all tribes." But this was not the case "down there," he said, pointing toward the capital below—to the Islamists at Mitiga Airport, I deduced—and hinting darkly at conflicts to come.

A few days later I visited one of his allies in the capital, a Zintani militia encamped near Tripoli International Airport. Behind the tall metal gate of its base, a dusty courtyard bustled with men toting belts of ammo and welding steel plates to trucks as improvised armor. Inside an air-conditioned office adorned with brass plaques, certificates, and topographic maps of Libya, the militia's commander, Uthman Mleqta, received me behind a cherrywood desk. With a Kalashnikov and a flak vest propped in one corner, he was trying to look the part of a seasoned general, but in fact he'd run a family catering business for Qadhafi's officials prior to the war and had started a doctorate in business management. The catering work proved useful; it was Mleqta's brother who'd secretly passed NATO the locations of hidden regime facilities in Tripoli on a memory stick. The doctoral work, Mleqta said, gave him organization skills for administering young men under arms.

Mleqta and many of his men were born in Tripoli but had roots in Zintan. When the Zintanis and other Nafusa fighters rushed into Tripoli, he and his fighters acted as the advance team, local guides who could navigate the capital's streets. Then they decided to stay, forming a militia called the Qa'qa Brigade, after the Arabic word meaning the "sound of clashing swords."

"We decided that our goal is to keep the capital safe," Mleqta told me, as an attendant served us tea. "Once everything returns to normal, we will give up our arms."

I wondered what that normalcy would look like. The Qa'qa Brigade had a level of firepower that exceeded that of the army and police. On paper, the brigade and other Zintani militias had subordinated themselves to the Ministry of Defense, which paid the men's salaries. But to whom they really answered was unclear. The Emirates continued to ply the Zintanis with weapons and cash. An influx of former soldiers from Qadhafi's security battalions joined their militias, and Mleqta recruited youths from the poorer sections of southern Tripoli.

For the youths under his charge, militia life was appealing, providing purpose, camaraderie, and an income. Successive appeals to get them to surrender their arms and rejoin society fell flat. What else would they do? Tripoli had few options for work, and their hometown of Zintan, a sleepy village by comparison, offered even grimmer prospects. Then there was the question of whether the militia bosses would let go of the young men under their command. That would mean surrendering power.

As I left his office, Mleqta asked whether I could pass on a message to the American embassy.

"Tell them the United States needs to support me," he said. "With weapons and communications gear."

■

IN A CRUDE SENSE, Misrata is the mirror opposite of Zintan: Zintan is mountainous, insular, and tribal, whereas Misrata is coastal and cosmopolitan, looking outward to the Mediterranean. Zintan is a town of small-time farmers and pastoralists, bereft of a real economy; Misrata is mercantile and entrepreneurial. Zintan had been associated with the ex-regime's security apparatus and welcomed these men back to the fold; Misrata wanted to exclude them from the new order. Key Zintani figures oppose Islamists, whereas Misrata is home to several of them—though the number has often been exaggerated. Of course, these distinctions only partially explained the rivalry between the two towns. Whatever the cause, their enmity would become one of the drivers in Libya's collapse.

Much of the blame, Libyans would complain, rested on the shoulders of Misrata and its unquenched thirst for retribution, born of its epic siege. I had heard that Salim Joha, the city's revolutionary war leader, was grappling with this specter. "Our most important goal is to avoid the evil of our own weapons," he had told a television broadcaster. I wanted to hear how he meant to do this.

East of Tripoli, the highway takes a sharp turn south just beyond the suburb of Tajura. Then, after Leptis Magna, the land turns to date farms and dandelion fields where roadside vendors sell jars of palm juice and African migrants huddle in the shade. Farther on, the Misratan militias had used shipping containers to assemble a checkpoint in the shape of an arch.

On Tripoli Street, the main artery into downtown Misrata, the devastation was shocking—row after row of crumpled concrete and twisted rebar. The walls of the few buildings that remained bore the charred blossoms of exploded rockets and the pocks of gunfire. On the face of one, the European Union had plastered a mural of a white-winged dove breaking off the barrel of an AK-47 with its beak. The Misratans had set up a war museum that held captured weaponry and photoshopped portraits of fallen revolutionaries. It was a visceral memorial, a celebration, I thought, of the city's victimization during its months-long siege.

Ever since the medieval era, Misrata had been a merchant hub, situated at the northern tip of Saharan caravan routes and blessed with a deep-water port. It traded wood, olive oil, and dates with Venice and Genoa; silk came from Persia via Ethiopia. "The inhabitants are rich and pay no tribute at all," wrote the sixteenth-century Andalusian traveler Leo Africanus. The Ottomans used Misrata as a base to project their authority, and then the Italians came, grafting onto the ancient town a grid of villas, schools, and parks. The city's influence waxed and waned after World War II, suffering from Qadhafi's nationalization of its merchants' holdings. And yet, by the new millennium, it was rebounding, its business elites growing wealthy again from the dictator's new investment drive. On the eve of the 2011 revolt, it was Libya's retail and import powerhouse.

Those businesses were now slowly coming back to life. The port, a source of jobs, had started berthing container ships. A dairy factory had doubled its output of yogurt and ice cream. Other, darker commerce was said to be thriving as well, such as drugs and weapons. The city was mercantile to its core. But it had another face.

A prison in the center of town offered the first glimpses. The stucco-walled Al-Huda detention center used to be an internal security building. Now it housed hundreds of prisoners, some of them combatants against the revolution, some just suspected of loyalism. The wardens were committed Salafists and forbade smoking, television, and any reading material aside from the Qur'an and religious tracts. I watched the gown-clad prisoners shuffle en masse into a covered courtyard for compulsory prayer.

Outside investigations uncovered pervasive torture, everything from the dreaded *falaqa*—a pipe beating to the soles of the feet—to flogging with horse whips. In January 2012, Doctors Without Borders halted its operations in Misrata to protest the abuses. In just six months alone, they had treated 115 people for torture-related wounds. "Patients were brought to us in the middle of interrogation for medical care," their director said, "in order to make them fit for further interrogation."

I toured Al-Huda's cramped and darkened quarters. The prisoners slept on thin foam mattresses, ten or more to a room, their laundry stretched across a line. In one dank cell, I encountered a dozen young men from Sudan, members of a rebel group from Darfur, they said, who had fought for Qadhafi during the revolution. The Libyan dictator had long funded and armed the oppositionist Darfurians against the Sudanese government, and during the revolution they returned the favor. Now they languished in limbo. "Please, can you contact the Sudanese consul?" one asked me.

The most brutalized of Misrata's victims, though, were the inhabitants of Tawergha, a bleak dormitory town about twenty-five miles south along the coastal road. Descended from African slaves emancipated in the nineteenth century, the Tawerghans had received public housing and jobs in the army from Qadhafi. They'd long existed in the shadow of wealthier Misrata, with many commuting to work there as trash collectors or dishwashers. During the revolution, unsurprisingly, the Tawerghans stayed loyal, allowing Qadhafi's rocket batteries to use their town to fire on Misrata and accompanying his troops in assaulting the city, raiding the homes of their erstwhile employers.

With support from NATO warplanes, Misrata's fighters turned the tables, attacking Tawergha toward the end of the revolution. It was just the start of their revenge. The Misratans evicted the town's inhabitants, scattering them to squalid camps across Libya, where they remain to this day. "Even the birds fled Tawergha," a refugee told me.

For their part, the Misratans said the Tawerghans were beasts who had sold themselves to the dictator. "They raped my neighbors' daughter in front of her father," one Misratan told me. "It's all on his cell phone." But corroboration of such atrocities often proved elusive. The new government in Tripoli offered little in the way of inquiry or protection, all but surrendering Tawergha to Misrata's furies.

When I saw Salim Joha, the city's moderate and embattled leader, he seemed upset but unsurprised by my mention of these excesses. I met him one afternoon at a seaside resort turned militia base where he sat peeling an orange next to an open window. What struck me first about Joha was his gravelly voice and limpid eyes that caught the light. Sinewy in build, he often favors workers' caps, the black, flat-brimmed type, and untucked denim shirts, which lent him a vaguely industrial or even nautical look. He is known as an intellectual, with an eclectic and well-stocked library. Once when I met him, he was reading Sigmund Freud's *Totem and Taboo: Resemblances Between the Mental Lives of*

Savages and Neurotics. Modern psychologists and anthropologists have rejected Freud's thesis that religion and group cohesion stem from the slaying of father figures by the "primal horde." But perhaps for Joha, it offered some insight into saving Misrata—and Libya—from the excesses of revolution.

In 1981, he graduated from Tripoli's Military College, twenty-one years old and newly married. His father and grandfather had been well-off dealers in animal feed and stock traders. But all that ended after Qadhafi's coup. Deprived of financial means, Joha decided on a military career. The choice connected him to a storied martial lineage.

Joha is the maternal great-grandson of Ramadan al-Suwayhli, who fought the Italians to establish a brief statelet based in Misrata, the first independent republic in the Arab world. A notable from a minor family, al-Suwayhli was famed for his horsemanship and, some said, thievery. His Libyan rivals, competing families in Misrata, said he was an opportunist, pointing to his early cooperation with the Italians. But then he switched sides: in April 1915, at the village of Qasr Abu Hadi, his forces turned on their erstwhile allies. Suffering five hundred casualties, the Italians retreated from Misrata, their influence in Libya now confined to Tripoli and Benghazi.

With the Italians gone, al-Suwayhli consolidated his authority within the city. He courted the Germans and Ottomans—Italy's enemies during World War I—to carve out further influence, with German U-boats docking at Misrata's port during the war. And in 1918, he and other leaders declared Misrata and its environs an autonomous "Republic of Tripolitania," inspired by Woodrow Wilson's Fourteen Points. Until its end in factional feuding four years later, al-Suwayhli's republic printed its own money, ran its own schools and hospitals, and produced its own ammunition. The memory of the experiment lived on through the decades. In 2011, Misratans carried portraits of Ramadan al-Suwayhli into battle.

At the end of the war, Joha found himself the most venerated military leader in Misrata and, arguably, the country. The prospect of great power lay at his feet, yet it seemed a burden to him. He turned down the post of defense minister and chief of staff after the war, chuckling that raising five daughters was enough. What he wanted instead was to work behind the scenes.

First, he tried to unify Misrata's hundreds of armed militias with a regimen of discipline, marked by the registration of weapons and oversight of armories. Joha had also started dispatching militias to quell outbreaks of tribal fighting in Libya's hinterland. By late April 2012, he and other revolutionary leaders sent the NTC a plan to enlist the militias for nationwide service under the control of the chief of staff. The resulting entity became known as the Libya Shield Forces.

Joha lit one of his ubiquitous Rothmans in a black cigarette holder. He leaned across the table and handed me a brochure, meant to sell the Shield program to prospective recruits.

The idea, he explained, was to co-opt and employ the militias until the regular army was trained. The concept proved attractive for young revolutionaries who wanted to play a role in the state but did not want to join the old Qadhafi-era security institutions. For its part, the transitional government welcomed the project as a way to convey its authority and keep order in parts of the country where the feeble army and police could not. But, Joha emphasized several times, the Shields were only temporary, a stopgap measure until the formal army could be trained. Once that happened, he said, they would become the military's reserve force.

Having secured cash payments from the government, the Libya Shield Forces grew into thirteen divisions across Libya, each staffed by regionally based militias. They deployed to put down flare-ups of fighting in the south and guarded borders and oil installations. Their record, however, was mixed. In some tasks, they proved effective, such as securing the Tripoli-to-Tunisia border route and intercepting drug traffickers. But in many instances, they ended up inflaming the local conflicts they were supposed to quell by taking sides with a tribe or a town. Then there was the problem of command and oversight. In theory, they were supposed to report to the chief of staff, but in practice they often acted independently, serving the interests of their militia commanders. And since the chief of staff in Tripoli had roots in Misrata, many of those who joined the Shields were Misratan militias. Meanwhile, Zintani allied themselves with the minister of defense, who came from Zintan.

None of this was how Joha had originally envisioned it.

He lamented that a culture of revolutionary entitlement and revanchism had taken hold, which left little space for compromise with remnants of the old order. His critics in Misrata thought him naïve and too accommodating.

Leaving Misrata at night, I sensed then that I was glimpsing the start of Libya's atomization—here were the fruits of the "statelessness" of the Qadhafi dictatorship, but also a revolution that was starting to turn on itself.

Joha tried as hard as anyone to avert this fate.

■

THESE, THEN, were the three broad militia currents in the capital by 2012: the Tripolitanian militias, the Zintanis, and the Misratans. Each grappled for power, but none advanced a viable, inclusive vision for the country.

What did the internationals in Libya know of this militia firmament, and what could they do? For the first half of 2012, the United Nations Support Mission in Libya (UNSMIL) had no one on its staff with expertise in reforming security institutions. When it finally set up a small section to do this, it was understaffed. Led by an experienced Australian general, the security section tried without success to coordinate the modest security assistance efforts of outside states—the United States, the UK, France, Qatar, and the UAE. These states, one former head of UNSMIL told me, had armed and advised the militias during the revolution but were now either unwilling or unable to transform them into a workable state. At its best, the UN offered limited technical counsel to the Libyans, on the rule of law and on the training of police. But here again, it ran up against what seemed to be an ingrained resistance among Libyans to external advice. All the while, the larger question of growing militia power went unaddressed.

"There were huge tasks for the United Nations," another former UNSMIL chief told me, "but it had no means to accomplish them. If I was to rethink the UN mission, I would've asked for a stabilization force early on." Even a modest-sized peacekeeping force, he argued, could've secured vital facilities such as the airport, ports, and ministries that became the objects of fierce contention by the militias.

Of course, this was beset by obstacles. First, and above all, the Libyans didn't want a foreign military force on their soil: obsessed with not repeating the Iraqi experience of occupation, they ignored precedents for the constructive, limited deployment of peacekeepers in postconflict states such as Bosnia and East Timor. Yet even if they'd acquiesced, the United Nations faced the problem of finding troop-contributing countries, defining the actual responsibilities for the troops, and specifying when force was authorized. Would these troops have enough firepower to deter Libyan militias, or would they become targets themselves? Moreover, the record of UN deployments shows it is exceedingly hard to maintain the perception of total neutrality. A foreign stabilization force in Tripoli would have to coordinate and cooperate with local armed groups to some degree—and that could upset whatever equilibrium existed.

For its part, the United States did not produce any changes in security on the ground. Colonel Brian Linvill, the defense attaché, was little more than an observer to the militia buildup. His budget for assisting the Libyan military was hardly enough to meet the challenge of rebuilding an army from scratch. And it paled in comparison to the amount of money the United States was offering the militaries of neighboring countries. The parsimony was in part due to the U.S. expectation that the Libyans would make a more formal request for assistance and even foot the bill, given their sizable oil wealth. But these were difficult expectations to uphold in the chaos of the time. The result was that the embassy had just a smattering of U.S. personnel to work on military issues in Libya. Of these, a team that tried to locate and disable shoulder-fired surface-to-air missiles achieved some small victories. Canvassing the country, they managed to find and destroy a quarter of the country's twenty thousand such missiles. The vast majority of the remainder, though, was tucked away in the armories of militias.

The Department of Defense also tried to reform Libya's defunct Defense Ministry. The concern within the U.S. military was that you couldn't just sell the Libyans equipment and train their soldiers without the bureaucracy to run an army: personnel, budgeting, logistics, and education. But the visits of the American defense advisors were too sporadic and far between—partly due to logistics and billeting limits at the U.S. embassy. And at any rate Libya needed more sustained and long-term help if it was to remake its military. The advisory effort "was outpatient treatment," Linvill told me, "and the Libyans needed major surgery, not house calls." The British had a bit more success, embedding advisors in ministries and helping the Libyans to write a road map for military reform. It was never implemented.

In the meantime, Linvill renewed his old contacts in the Libyan military, the amicable colonels and generals. Many had sat out the war on the sidelines. Now these men commanded little more than a desk, while militias occupied their bases and armories. The army was simply one militia among many—and the weakest one at that.

"You walk into a government building, you would meet someone who would purport to be a minister," he said. "But the room behind him was empty; there was no depth beyond that one guy and his cell phone. By the time we figured that out it was too late."

∎

LINVILL LEFT LIBYA in the summer of 2012 for a yearlong fellowship at Stanford University sponsored by the U.S. Army War College. His stint in Palo Alto was a time of rest and contemplation. He had been away from his family for more than a year, ever since their evacuation to Malta on that storm-tossed ferry.

He grappled with what he had seen and experienced in Libya, writing a paper entitled "Retaking the Lead from Behind: A New Role for America in Libya." In it, he bemoaned the political and bureaucratic constraints that limited America's actions in Libya. He lamented the failure of the Europeans to play a bigger role, apportioning blame to NATO for its lack of will and capacity, and to Libyans for their unwillingness to engage with NATO. The Europeans, he maintained, had much to offer given their experience with gendarmerie organizations, which was exactly the type of security force the Libyans needed—something in between a conventional army and city police.

Even so, he wrote, all of the efforts to build a police and army would be for naught unless you addressed the young men with guns.

"Libya lacks an alternative to the entrenched power of local militias," he concluded.

"WE DON'T KNOW
WHO'S WHO"

IT WAS BAD ENOUGH THAT TRIPOLI was quaking under the militias' guns. In the east, a strident brand of religious militancy was adding an even more volatile element to the mix. It announced itself one day in June 2012.

It was late afternoon, a time of oppressive heat in Benghazi. Out past the salt lagoons and the container docks, a cloudless sky met the metallic sea. Suddenly sirens bleated and horns honked. A cavalcade of pickups jammed the coastal road, filled with young men manning anti-aircraft guns in cargo beds and brandishing rifles in the air. Sporting balaclava masks or the Afghan *pakol*, they waved black flags and carried signs. Fifteen jihadist militias comprised the procession, from Benghazi and towns across the east and the west of Libya. Their goal was simple: to demand the imposition of Islamic law over the new state. It was the clearest expression yet of a growing radical trend within the Islamists' ranks.

The parade ended in the early evening near an outdoor stage outside the courthouse. Here, a crowd of youths and women had formed, condemning the brazen show of force by these bearded men. "Our situation is fine, go back to Pakistan!" they chanted in rhyming Arabic. "Libya is not Afghanistan!" others shouted. Some acknowledged the Islamists' right to protest but resented the implication that Libyans were in need of greater piety.

"This group comes here and says it wants to practice *sharia* [Islamic law]," said one protestor in a television interview. "But what's their idea? We are Muslims, we pray to God, we are not infidels."

One of the main organizers of the rally was a militia called Ansar al-Sharia, a group that few in Benghazi had heard of until then, led by a husky appliance-store owner named Muhammad al-Zahawi. The details of al-Zahawi's life were sketchy. Some alleged that he had fought in Afghanistan or Iraq or had traveled to Sudan and met bin Laden. What is certain is that he sojourned in Saudi Arabia for many years before Saudi intelligence handed him over to Qadhafi, who imprisoned him in Abu Salim. During the revolution, he fought in Benghazi and then commanded fighters on the Misratan front line. Sometime in early April, after coming back from Misrata to Benghazi, he broke with his erstwhile comrades to start the nucleus of what would become Ansar al-Sharia.

His split with other Islamists was partly over Western intervention in the uprising. "The radicals told us, 'Don't let in the Westerners, they will use you and get rid of you,'" an Islamist militia commander told me. "They were afraid of going back to prison." But more important than this was the group's opposition to the emerging Libyan state after Qadhafi's fall: Ansar al-Sharia condemned democracy as un-Islamic, arguing instead for a government along Islamic lines, with governance through *shura* (consultation). It was a goal that adhered to the Salafist belief that voting for human-made laws meant replacing God's law and constituted polytheism.

Some Islamists who shared bonds of incarceration and combat with al-Zahawi and his followers tried to persuade them to be more accommodating of the new political order. "Ansar al-Sharia said, 'We have to make a state in our system, in *sharia*,'" an Islamist militia leader from Benghazi told me. "I told them, 'Yes, but first we need to join the state in order to change it.'" Another Islamist who ran in the 2012 elections objected to the group's militant theatrics. "Go ahead and protest, but don't bring weapons," he advised them.

But they refused to hand over their weapons, saying that what passed for a state in Libya had been so corrupted it needed to be purified. And nothing was most corrupt than the vestiges of Qadhafi's security apparatus.

"The army protects a corrupt leader," a cleric close to Ansar al-Sharia told me. "And so to avoid corrupting themselves Ansar needs the army to swear allegiance to an Islamic constitution before they surrender their arms and join it." This complaint of corruption was something I'd heard over and over among Islamists who'd been imprisoned by Qadhafi; Ansar al-Sharia was its most extreme expression.

Al-Zahawi's group derived its deeper ideology from a Jordanian jihadist scholar named Muhammad al-Maqdisi. Al-Maqdisi had once mentored the infamous Jordanian-born Iraqi terrorist and progenitor of the Islamic State, Abu Musab al-Zarqawi. But after his former protégé's murderous campaign in Iraq had alienated potential supporters, he cautioned against extreme displays of violence directed at fellow Muslims. And during the 2011 Arab uprisings, he urged his followers not to fight but to take advantage of changing circumstances. Through his online legal forum Minbar al-Tawhid wa'l-Jihad (Platform for Monotheism and Jihad), al-Maqdisi and his allied clerics issued new directives concerning jihad. While preserving armed struggle, they emphasized the peaceful consolidation of power at home through proselytization, education, and organization. At the same time, they roundly rejected democracy—an especially urgent imperative after 2011 when rival

Islamists, namely Muslim Brotherhood groups in Tunisia, Egypt, and Libya, participated in elections, and radical Salafists were eager to expose their error.

In Benghazi, Ansar al-Sharia put al-Maqdisi's teachings into practice with an expansive program of charity and social services. The group's yellow-vested volunteers repaired schools, swept the streets of garbage, and distributed food, heaters, and blankets to the poor. It posted guards at Jala Hospital, winning plaudits from medical staff who'd faced militia threats, and established its own clinics for women and children. It devoted special attention to youth, conducting an antidrug campaign for teenagers and offering camps for soccer, martial arts, and Qur'anic recitation. In Benghazi's rough-hewn Salmani district, it set up "Youth Forum" tents—weekend "retreats" that included roadside work and Salafist instruction.

Emblazoned everywhere was its logo: an open Qur'an, two Kalashnikovs, the black flag, and a raised index finger invoking the oneness of God.

■

DRIVING THROUGH BENGHAZI in the summer of 2012, I sensed the pull of competing claims on the city's future, the ebb and flow between dissolution and what passed for order. Just north of Airport Road was the base of the "Thunderbolt" Special Forces, one of the few functioning Qadhafi-era security bodies. Farther south, in the suburb of Hawari, was the compound of the Islamist Rafallah al-Sahati militia. Out west toward the sea, just opposite the eye hospital, an outdoor arms market named Jinnahayn, or "Two Pounds," did a brisk trade in guns, rockets, and grenades after a recent glut had pushed the prices down. Near Sabri, I saw graffiti sprayed on signposts in medians: NO TO AL-QAEDA.

What was clear was that Ansar al-Sharia was benefiting from the continued weakness of the Libyan state. Alongside its public works, charities, and social morality, it had a darker side, the one that people whispered about.

Starting in mid-2012, Ansar al-Sharia set up training camps to the south of Benghazi for Libyans and foreigners, chiefly Tunisians, wishing to fight abroad. It provided logistics for al-Qaeda's affiliates in the Sahara, the Sinai, and the Arabian Peninsula. It sent convoys of vehicles filled with young fighters from Benghazi, Derna, and other eastern towns to support jihadists fighting French troops in northern Mali. By late 2012, Ansar al-Sharia was helping Libyans travel to fight in Syria; many would later return to form the Libyan branch of the Islamic State.

Who exactly joined the radicals? I asked some Benghazi friends one night at an outdoor café. "Losers and drug addicts," one said. "The jobless and poor," another chimed in. Some members had fought with the group during the revolution, while others came to it later, recruited in mosques or through neighborhood friends. Sometimes families of the youth, I later learned, welcomed the group's efforts at reforming their wayward sons.

"The camps appeal to the parents of these young people," said one cleric I spoke with. He was sympathetic to some aspects of its outreach. But along the way, he explained, they received a heavy dose of militancy. "Movies about holy war," he said, shaking his head.

Yet the narrative of riffraff dominating Ansar's ranks didn't quite square with reality, which was what made its appeal so troubling. The movement included the educated and reasonably well-off; I met one of its members, who was an engineer at the state electrical company. Even youth with promising futures—albeit dimmed by Libya's turmoil—got ensnared by the extremists. Among the sons of Benghazi who trained in its camps and died on battlefields in Syria and Mali were young medical and engineering students. While some of their peers and family lauded their sacrifice, others questioned the loss of life for a cause so far removed from Libya.

Often, membership in Ansar al-Sharia divided families, between those who accepted the new state and those who rejected it. One officer in the Libyan military had two sons in Ansar al-Sharia. An American-educated civil society leader told me how he lost a brother to the group, though he lays the ultimate blame on the regime, for incarcerating him in Abu Salim for the minor crime of posting criticism on social media. Here, he was radicalized.

"Before he went in, he was educated, worldly, and spoke French," he told me. After his release, he was changed. "We tried to save him, to give him a job or a farm," he said. "But we lost him."

The young man died of gunshot wounds in front of a Benghazi police station in 2013.

■

AS SPRING TURNED TO SUMMER, violence in Benghazi surged. In early April 2012, a Libyan contract guard at the American diplomatic outpost threw a *gelatina* bomb over the compound's wall. The same month, unknown assailants rolled a homemade grenade under the armored car of the United Nations' special envoy to Libya. And in the predawn hours of June 6, an improvised explosive device blew a hole in the exterior wall of the American diplomatic facility.

Still, it was possible at this time for people in Benghazi to feel safe and insulated from the violence. "It wasn't against Libyans," an activist had told me, "just foreigners."

But then that changed.

In July alone, more than thirteen ex-regime officials were assassinated in Benghazi. The fruits of careful surveillance of the victims' daily movements, the attacks were well planned. A judge died after being shot in the abdomen on his way to afternoon prayers, and a colonel perished in a car bomb. There were also near misses. On July 29, someone tossed a grenade at the home of General Hiftar; when the general gave chase, the attackers fired back. That same day, a bomb appeared in the basement of the Tibesti Hotel but was successfully disarmed.

Civilians and women started feeling the danger as well. Salwa

Bugaighis had been worried but not panicked. She'd watched the parade of Ansar al-Sharia and other extremists in June with a mix of perplexity and concern.

"Are they trying to send a message to us?" she wondered aloud.

Her friends and family tried to get her to lower her profile.

By this time, her sister Iman had gone back to teaching and all but disappeared from politics and public life. Now she begged her sister to withdraw as well.

"We can't face it," she told her. "Let's keep aside and then if things become better we can be involved."

"Look, if we just move aside," Salwa replied, "we give the opportunity to the others, and then we have only ourselves to blame.

"And," she added, "we can't just start something and leave it."

At the American embassy in Tripoli, Chris Stevens sent a cable back to Washington, "Libya's Fragile Security Deteriorates as Tribal Rivalries, Power Plays and Extremism Intensify," noting with alarm a spike in attacks on diplomats. On June 8, someone stuffed grenades in the chassis of a parked British diplomatic vehicle in the southern city of Sabha, and four days later, assailants attacked the British ambassador's convoy in Benghazi, wounding two security officers. The British pulled out of Benghazi the next day.

An American diplomat working closely with Stevens emailed home to family, complaining about the "dicey security situation." "Rest assured," the message continued, "that we're staying safe and traveling in secure convoys, and if we can't leave Tripoli, then so be it—better safe than sorry."

It wasn't just diplomats who were nervous. A nongovernmental humanitarian organization, the International Committee of the Red Cross (ICRC), seemed to be an increasingly favorite target. In May, its offices in Benghazi had been hit with RPGs; a fringe jihadist group claimed responsibility, accusing the NGO of trying to convert displaced Tawerghans to Christianity. Then at dawn on June 12, a time-delayed IED exploded at the organization's compound in Misrata, wounding one. With its unmistakably Christian emblem, the ICRC knew it would be the first target of the rising extremist trend. So it assigned one of its officers as a sort of emissary to meet with the Salafists, to hear them out and explain the Red Cross's strictly humanitarian aims.

A genial Tunisian, I found the Red Cross representative well versed in Salafist ideology and surprisingly empathetic to their worldview. Like others who studied the movement, he believed the Salafists were not uniform in their views or strategies, dividing them according to whether they focused on social morality, politics, or the use of violence. "But these are not hermetic blocs," he emphasized. "There is interaction between the three currents." It was a crucial insight, one that explained much of Benghazi's murky loyalties.

He believed that the sudden opening of politics in Libya after the fall of Qadhafi had been disorienting for Salafists. Hitherto repressed or co-opted by the Libyan regime, they now found themselves confronted with new opportunities and dilemmas. It was a time of turbulence and debate when acts of violence, such as attacks on Sufi graves, could be used to stake out claims and establish identities—a "recomposition" of the Salafist community, as he put it.

I left that meeting impressed. But the emissary's commendable outreach proved futile. On August 5, the Red Cross in Misrata was hit again, this time with rockets against its residence. None of its staff were hurt, but the organization ceased its operations in Misrata and in Benghazi. Shortly after, Chris Stevens and another diplomat went to see the Red Cross's director in Tripoli, who warned them of a rising pattern of attacks on foreigners. "But Chris and I both thought he was drawing a line between events where there wasn't one, that he was seeing ghosts," the diplomat recalled of the meeting.

Connecting the dots among disparate events is hard enough, but in the bustle of a complex place like Libya, where the United States had not had a presence in decades, it was exceedingly difficult. Still, back in Washington and elsewhere, intelligence analysts tried to do just that. The CIA alone produced fifty-four assessments on the deteriorating security situation in eastern Libya and the growing threat from terrorist groups. Added to this were reports by other intelligence agencies, from

AFRICOM to the Defense Intelligence Agency to the Pentagon's Joint Staff Directorate for Intelligence. Many tried to trace the links between Libyan militants and transnational terrorist groups like al-Qaeda in the Islamic Maghreb.

U.S. diplomats in Tripoli and Benghazi had daily access to this information through "read-books" of the intelligence community's products. Stevens also met frequently with the CIA station chief. One diplomat remembers accompanying him to the CIA's compound in Tripoli, which was physically separate from the "real" embassy. Inside, a CIA officer gave them a briefing. He'd been on the front lines in Benghazi during the revolution, he said, and slept and fought with the militias. And now, he warned, "some of the Libyans who were with us in the revolution are against us," according to the diplomat.

But such warnings were more often focused on transnational terrorist groups than on understanding the homegrown Islamist militias in the east and how their personal networks overlapped with those of the radicals. "There wasn't a lot of reporting on militias," a diplomat said. When the CIA and the intelligence community did focus on militias, it was usually on the well-known groups in Benghazi; the smaller formations often escaped scrutiny. "The Ansar al-Sharia stuff was floating out there," the diplomat told me, "but the CIA was too focused on transnational jihadists and weapons collection." Part of this was simply a matter of resources. "We couldn't do Iraq, Afghanistan, and Libya all at once," one NSC official told me. "Iraq alone was an infinite sink for intelligence."

One place in particular, however, kept cropping up in intelligence products, a town the Americans had encountered centuries before.

■

LOCATED 150 MILES east of Benghazi, the port of Derna sits at the delta of a riverbed on a stunning stretch of coast, flanked by the Green Mountains. It is an ancient town of irrigation canals, orchards, and perennial springs, famous for its night-flowering jasmine and bananas.

Founded by the Greeks as Darnis, Derna always looked outward onto the Mediterranean world, becoming home to Maltese, Armenians, Jews, and Albanians. Refugees from Andalusia built up the city, their influence evident today in the mosques of the old quarter.

Just after the turn of the nineteenth century, Derna's history collided with that of the new American republic. Like most of Libya, Derna then was under the control of the Karamanli dynasty, founded by a former Ottoman cavalry officer. When the Karamanli ruler in Tripoli, Yusuf, started seizing American merchant ships and demanding higher and higher tributes, the American Congress gave the newly elected president, Thomas Jefferson, authorization to use "all necessary force." What followed was but one episode in America's decade-plus war with the so-called Barbary States, the nominally Ottoman principalities based in Tunis, Algiers, and Tripoli. An early American naval blockade ended in failure when the USS *Philadelphia* ran aground in Tripoli's harbor and was seized by Karamanli's forces, who incarcerated her crew of three hundred. That's when an unlikely American adventurer hatched a plan.

William Eaton was not a professional military commander, and his own service as a sergeant in the American Revolution had ended abjectly in a court-martial for insubordination and misuse of funds. But soon after reestablishing himself as America's chief diplomat in Tunis, Eaton found a vital partner: Hamid Karamanli, the older brother of Yusuf. Hamid had fled to Tunis after his brother had violently usurped the throne by killing another brother in front of their mother. With Hamid's help, Eaton plotted to overthrow Yusuf and end America's Tripolitanian war. The project involved recruiting a mercenary force in Cairo and then assaulting Libya from the east, where Yusuf's forces would least expect a land attack because of the difficulty of crossing the desert. American generals scoffed at the plan, but President Jefferson secretly approved it.

On April 25, 1805, after a six-hundred-mile trek through desert, Eaton's marines, and a force of Greeks, Imazighen, and Arabs arrived at Derna. The ensuing battle lasted less than a day and resulted in victory for the Americans. Fearful of an invasion, Yusuf sued for peace—but kept his throne, much to Hamid's outrage. Eaton decried America's "shameful" treatment of an ally.

The victory at Derna, along with the Barbary Wars, was a seminal event in the early history of the United States, solidifying the establishment of the U.S. Navy as a military branch. The campaign also entered the lore of the U.S. Marine Corps through the verses of its hymn and in the ceremonial sword given today to every marine officer, known as a "Mameluke sword," after the jewel-hilted saber that Hamid presented to William Eaton's marine commander. And despite its outcome, Derna's residents celebrate the battle as well, honoring the resistance of their forebears: go to its western beach and you will find a cluster of cabanas called the 1805 Resort, and, farther east, a café called Philadelphia, after the captured U.S. frigate.

The centuries after the battle saw Derna's fortunes rise and fall. Its population grew diverse, with Tripolitanian families from the west mixing with Bedouins and emigrants from around the Mediterranean. It became a center of culture—of education, theater, art, and literature, famed for a nationalist poet named Ibrahim al-Usta Umar. Exposed to the postwar political ideas sweeping the Arab world, Derna's intellectuals agitated for Libyan independence from the British. Its savvy merchants served as local agents for international companies like Rolex and Fiat. Women, too, were empowered, with their own federation and access to education and the arts.

All that changed under Muammar Qadhafi. Derna had a reputation for being too headstrong, too ahead of its time, people said, so the dictator humiliated it. He confiscated land and businesses, making paupers of the town's elite. He shut down the arts, deeming them un-Islamic, and defunded the university. Derna expanded outward, acquiring a shabby sprawl of poured concrete buildings and unpaved roads, enlivened only by the greenery of its hills and gardens. "The 1980s were our cultural drought," one resident told me.

Beset by despair but nourished by a culture of resistance, its young men went to fight the Soviets in Afghanistan. Returning, they sought to topple the dictator himself, joining the LIFG insurgency in the mid-1990s across the Green Mountains. Qadhafi clobbered them, exacting a brutal punishment on Derna that saw the abolishment of social services, subsidies, and youth programs. Unemployment, drugs, and hopelessness soared. But memories lived on, buttressed by deepening piety and a sense of lost glory. On family picnics to the graves of martyrs, fathers and grandfathers evoked the town's storied lineage. They regaled the young with tales of defiance and valor against successive waves of outsiders: the Ottomans, the American marines, the Italian colonial troops.

The rapid spread of satellite dishes in Derna brought home the suffering of faraway Muslims. The vacuum in education created by Qadhafi was filled by hard-line clerics, who'd been trained abroad and now returned to set up small storefront mosques and martial arts classes for young men. And at the turn of the millennium, hundreds of them flocked to fight with jihadist groups against American troops in Iraq and Afghanistan.

In 2008, a political officer at the U.S. embassy in Tripoli, John Godfrey, visited Derna during a rare lapse by his security minders. His cable to Washington, signed by Chris Stevens, describes the town's potent mix of decay, faith, and defiance. "Fighting against U.S. and coalition forces in Iraq," he wrote, was a way for Derna's young "to strike a blow against both Qadhafi and against his perceived American backers." In 2011, these veterans put their years of combat to use in fighting the regime directly. Qadhafi pointed at them specifically when he accused the rebels of trying to form an Islamic emirate during the revolution, and now Western intelligence agencies watched them warily.

After the fall of Qadhafi, a bevy of Islamist militias held sway in Derna, the strongest of which was a group called the Abu Salim Martyrs Brigade formed around two LIFG veterans, Abd al-Hakim al-Hasadi and Salim Darbi. Al-Hasadi was a forty-six-year-old former high school teacher who'd fought with the Taliban before being captured by the

Americans and turned over to Qadhafi; Darbi was another veteran fighter who'd been on the run since the mid-1990s. Their militia quickly consolidated itself in Derna, shutting down beauty parlors and radio stations and demanding gender segregation at the university. The police and security services all but disappeared, cowed by fear.

But as the post-Qadhafi state took shape, the Abu Salim Martyrs Brigade showed its pragmatic face. To be sure, its media outlets still applauded al-Qaeda, and it remained ultraconservative in its values. But its leaders, Darbi and al-Hasadi, believed they had more to gain from supporting the new government than from opposing it. They offered their militia as a bodyguard for the NTC chairman during his visit to the city, and during the July 7 parliamentary elections they sent guards to protect polling stations.

This coziness with the Libyan government did not sit well with more dogmatic jihadists in the brigade's circles, among them an ex-Guantánamo inmate named Sufyan bin Qumu. A onetime tank driver and reputed drug dealer, bin Qumu had gone to Afghanistan to train with bin Laden against the Soviets, then drove a truck for the al-Qaeda leader's company in Sudan, before returning to Afghanistan. Breaking with Darbi and al-Hasadi over their support to the NTC, he founded a militia called Ansar al-Sharia, separate at first from the identically named group in Benghazi. He ensconced his fighters in the hillside forest outside Derna and ran training camps.

The rise of bin Qumu and other radicals also provoked a backlash by liberal-minded citizens of Derna. For them, the Islamists' extremism was anathema to the town's storied heritage and to the 2011 uprising's goals. "They stole our revolution," said one female activist who used the name Maryam to protect her identity. With her red-dyed hair tied in a bun, she had an easy smile and spoke in rapid clipped sentences. I met her in a sleek Cairo café, years after she'd fled Derna fearing for her life. Now she lamented its liberal past.

"Our golden age," she said with a sigh. "Derna of Andalusia, Derna of the night jasmine."

"My father used to direct plays by Hisham Abd al-Hamid," she continued, referring to one of the luminaries of Egypt's cinema scene. Women wore skirts, she wanted me to know, and the town's custom permitted women and men to attend the same wedding. Underpinning it all, she explained, was the moderation of Derna's Sufi orders. She cursed al-Hasadi and Darbi for their insurgency in the 1990s, which brought down Qadhafi's wrath on the town as a whole. Now, she said, when these same Islamists returned in 2011, they killed any hope of an enlightened future.

By late summer another Derna activist pleaded in an email to Chris Stevens for help.

"Please send someone to see the truth for yourselves," the activist wrote.

■

THE NIGHTTIME MEETING in Benghazi began cordially enough.

"We wanted to get to know each other," the Islamist militia leader recalls. "We laughed, we exchanged business cards."

It was September 9, 2012. Seated before him across a conference table was a sandy-haired American diplomat named Dave McFarland, flanked by diplomatic security agents with rifles on their laps. A ten-year veteran of the Foreign Service, with tours in Cairo and Baghdad, McFarland had requested this meeting with Benghazi's most powerful militia leaders.

One of them, a gangly former auto mechanic named Wissam bin Hamid, was by many accounts among the most charismatic and bravest commanders in the revolution. "We called him 'the merciful father,'" a young man who had fought with him told me. "He was always asking about our personal problems, checking on his men." Stories emerged of bin Hamid fighting alone on a hill, with binoculars and a solitary mortar, while his men napped in tents. One UN diplomat even said he was "Christlike" in his asceticism. In meetings, though, he was often passive and simplistic about politics. And his worldview was decidedly conservative.

Joining bin Hamid was another Islamist commander named Muhammad al-Gharabi, a former metallurgy student who commanded a militia called the Rafallah al-Sahati Companies. A third militiaman, a former London cabbie, sat beside them, offering up that he'd spent time in Afghanistan—as a way of saying, "Look, we were enemies once, but now we're friends," an attendee recalls.

McFarland knew that bin Hamid's militia, the Libya Shield, along with Muhammad al-Gharabi's, drew their salaries from the government in Tripoli and were therefore "official" armed groups. But the diplomat wanted to know what that really meant. Whom did they take their orders from? And how did these militias fit into Benghazi's Islamist firmament, especially its radical elements? It was a question of vital importance since the Americans in Benghazi, along with all foreigners, depended on them for their security.

Bin Hamid broke the ice by telling McFarland of his fondness for American cars and his hopes of traveling to America to learn how to repair them. They drank cans of grape juice and ate cream-filled sweets. But then they turned to business.

The American diplomat asked the militia commanders, point-blank, "Is it safe for us in this city?"

By this time, the Americans in Benghazi had concerns about their safety in an increasingly violent city. In person and via cable, they had made repeated requests to State Department headquarters for more security at their diplomatic compound. That compound, the expansive, green-lawned villa complex that Chris Stevens had worked from during the revolution had reverted to a temporary status when Stevens departed Benghazi in November 2011. Bureaucratically, this meant it was hard to acquire funds and staffing—a difficulty that in many ways echoed the neglect that Benghazinos felt after the liberation of Tripoli. The American facility in Benghazi was supposed to have a full contingent of five diplomatic security agents. But it rarely achieved that number. Sometimes, with just two agents at the compound, diplomats were unable to travel for meetings.

"If there is a real mission, fund us and find the staff," one diplomat wrote in a cable. But the response was always the same.

Then, in July, the State Department in D.C. made a request not to extend the use of the U.S. military's site security team (SST)—a team of sixteen special operators based at the embassy in Tripoli—to protect American diplomats. State officials believed that a mixture of U.S. diplomatic security (DS) agents and Libyan guards would suffice in the team's absence. The request occurred at precisely the moment when violence in Benghazi was surging.

On August 15, diplomats in Benghazi convened an emergency action committee meeting, a gathering of representatives from different U.S. agencies that was meant to "evaluate [the diplomatic mission's] tripwires in light of the deteriorating security situation in Benghazi." At the meeting, a State Department officer asserted that the recent violence would become the "new normal." A CIA officer then gave a briefing on the location of ten alleged Islamist militia and al-Qaeda training camps across the city. The embassy's senior diplomatic security agent said he doubted that the post could defend itself against a "coordinated attack due to limited manpower."

The next day, Stevens sent out a cable from Tripoli that spelled out the warning signs. Anyone reading it could not help but be alarmed. The commander of AFRICOM, General Carter Ham, called Chris Stevens after seeing it and offered to keep the military's SST in Libya as a protective force for the diplomats. Stevens declined. The reasons had to do with an unresolved legal dispute over control of the soldiers. AFRICOM had refused to put the SST team under the authority of the ambassador—a point of contention between lawyers from State and the Department of Defense. Added to this were questions about their role: the special operators was supposed to be focused on training Libyans in counterterrorism, but that effort had barely started because of disarray on the Libyan side. And because they did not fall within the ambassador's purview, they were not afforded what is known as "privileges and immunity" or diplomatic protections by the Libyan government. According to one military officer at the embassy, this made Stevens nervous, especially after an attempted carjacking in Tripoli of two SST personnel earlier that summer in which a U.S. soldier shot a Libyan assailant. Stevens whisked the soldier out of the country, to avoid any trouble with the Libyan authorities. But from then on, "he was worried the SST could get thrown into prison."

There were other incidents with the SST that seemed to have frustrated Stevens. Despite being the president's representative in Libya, he had no control of the team—they belonged to AFRICOM. Sometimes the soldiers didn't tell him of their whereabouts—but his diplomats often had to bail them out of trouble. "A brawl at a United Nations party, car accidents," a diplomat said. What's more, back at State Department headquarters, the leadership of the Bureau of Diplomatic Security felt that the team's presence would be a black eye, raising unwanted questions about the department's in-house security capability, according to one diplomat.

In Benghazi, that protective capability remained limited. The temporary mission consisted of four buildings on a compound the length of three soccer fields and one hundred yards wide. Two of the buildings contained residences, offices, and a cantina. Another was the tactical operations center, where security officers worked amid an array of cameras and communication gear, and slept. A fourth, smaller building was where the Libyan guards slept. Some upgrades had been done since Chris Stevens had arrived there in August 2011: increasing the outer wall to a height of nine feet, adding concertina wire and more lighting, and dropping "Jersey barriers"—massive concrete slabs for slowing or stopping vehicles—directly outside and inside the gate. But by the standards for embassies and missions in high-threat posts, it was still lacking. An investigation would later find that the compound "included a weak and very extended perimeter, an incomplete interior fence, no mantraps and unhardened entry gates and doors." It also lacked "weapons, ammunition [nonlethal deterrents], and fire safety." Requests for an upgrade went unheeded, partly because the mission's temporary and uncertain status made the State Department's bureaucracy unwilling to invest in it, especially given the competing demands from other posts.

In contrast, the nearby CIA annex in Benghazi had quickly bolstered its security as far back as June, after the RPG attack on the British ambassador's convoy. Located about a mile away from the temporary mission facility, the annex was a set of villas that housed roughly two dozen personnel known as a CIA base—an adjunct to the larger CIA station in Tripoli. They included analysts, technicians, and case officers who would meet and recruit sources, in addition to well-armed security officers who would escort them when they traveled in the city. As in Tripoli, the CIA was meant to be hidden and discreet, using the public State Department presence as cover. Few Libyans were actually aware that Americans lived and worked in the annex villas.

Meanwhile, the reliability of local forces in Benghazi had grown suspect. The Americans were especially concerned about the Supreme Security Committee (SSC), a coalition of militias under the Ministry of Interior that functioned as a quasi police force. In May and again in June, the ranking diplomat in Benghazi requested that the SSC start a nighttime patrol of the temporary mission's perimeter. But it never did. As the summer wore on, the committee's capacity grew weaker, and by early August, a cable from Stevens warned that it was ill prepared to take on any real policing.

Actual security at the American diplomatic compound was provided by the February 17 Brigade, led by Fawzi Bu Katif, the Islamist oil engineer who'd worked with the Americans and other Western advisors during the revolution. Four armed guards from his brigade provided security inside the perimeter, sleeping in a small building by the gate. Five unarmed (and underpaid) Libyan guards contracted by a Welsh security company, the Blue Mountain Group, patrolled an outer perimeter.

The arrangement had its limits.

To be sure, Bu Katif was a known figure to the Americans, spoke English, and soon became a fixture at the villa. And his militiamen had responded promptly to previous incidents like an IED attack and a gun battle at a medical university that threatened an American diplomat. But there were troubling signs. Sometimes the guards did not show up for work, and they refused to augment their numbers on the compound out of a concern of appearing too pro-American. More worrisome still was their mixed loyalties and the fact that Bu Katif did not have full control over his men. In August, the head diplomatic security agent and later the principal officer in Benghazi expressed these concerns to Stevens, who replied that "we should be in line with the [Libyan government] policy/law on this. What do the local police and SSC leadership recommend?" On September 8, the February 17 militiamen told diplomatic security agents that they would cease accompanying American officials to protest their salaries and hours.

Now, in the meeting on September 9 with Dave McFarland, Benghazi's other militia commanders, Muhammad al-Gharabi and Wissam bin Hamid, added to the worry. McFarland questioned them about security in the city and the militias' ability to preserve it. But al-Gharabi and bin Hamid had questions of their own.

The militiamen told the diplomat that they acted free from oversight by the government in Tripoli, which provided them with salaries and weapons but was ultimately dependent on them. Then they probed him about American support in the upcoming Libyan prime ministerial election, accusing the Americans of backing the National Forces Alliance's Mahmud Jibril, a rival to the Brotherhood candidate they favored.

McFarland pushed back. American policy, he told the commanders, was to not support any one side over another. And he continued to press them on security, trying to understand Benghazi's militia factions and networks.

"What's your role? How do you fit into the security structure?" he asked.

But it was a tangled mess, even to the militiamen.

"We don't know who's who," al-Gharabi admitted.

At the same time, he and bin Hamid tried to assure their guest that they wanted an American presence and especially American investments in the city. McFarland found the mixed signals exasperating.

■

YEARS LATER, I met Muhammad al-Gharabi and asked him about this meeting. Al-Gharabi is a barrel-chested man in his midthirties with the build of a wrestler. Clad in a nylon vest jacket, designer jeans, and black Adidas sneakers, he had spent ten years total in prison, including a stint in Abu Salim. He maintained he was always conservative but never part of any armed or political opposition until the revolution.

That evening by the sea in 2012, he sought help from the Americans to bolster his authority while at the same time warning them of its limits.

"I told them that we need to integrate the revolutionaries into the government, so that we can help the United States," he said.

"What about the rising violence?" I asked.

"With all the assassinations that were happening, I told them, 'I wish you would've helped us from the beginning. Now I am afraid this will happen to you.'"

"Did you ask the Americans to leave Benghazi?"

"No," he replied. "I begged them to leave. I told them, 'We wish you would leave Benghazi because Benghazi isn't safe.'"

THE ATTACK ON THE AMERICANS

"CALL EVERYBODY ON MY CELL phone, call everybody that you know that can help us."

Crouching in the dark, shoeless, the diplomatic security agent Scott Wickland handed his phone to Chris Stevens. He thrust a shotgun into the hands of another diplomat, Sean Smith, a computer specialist, only to take it back after seeing that he was visibly shaken.

The three men had gathered in a room, a gated safe haven inside one of the villas on the sprawling American diplomatic compound. It was September 11, 2012, 9:46 p.m. in Benghazi. Just minutes before, a crowd of armed men had rushed through the compound's outdoor gate.

Two of the attackers now approached the metal grille door to the safe haven and started banging on the locks with their AK-47s. They had grenades.

Hiding in the shadows, Wickland turned to Stevens.

"If they put the grenades on the locks, I'm going to start shooting," he told him. "And when I die, you need to pick up my gun and keep on fighting."

■

JUST OVER A WEEK BEFORE, Chris Stevens had been in Stockholm for a friend's wedding. It was a lavish affair, with the ceremony in a cathedral and a reception in the city's dance museum. "White ties and tails," he wrote in his diary, "boisterous dinner . . . Dancing until 2 a.m." He reconnected with old friends from previous postings and went running in the rain. He met a State Department colleague who'd been in Benghazi that summer and asked her for updates, to refresh his contacts. He was eager to return, friends remember.

Now, on September 10, flying from Tripoli to Benghazi, he had a number of goals. He wanted to meet with the city council, oil and maritime companies, and the February 17 Brigade. And he wanted to open what is known as an American Corner, a cultural hub where young locals can learn about the United States and prepare for study in America by taking the requisite tests. It was exactly the sort of people-to-people initiative Stevens believed was important, and this one was to be housed in the English school owned by his friend Abu Baker Habib. Most important, though, Stevens hoped the visit would position him to obtain funds from the State Department for the temporary mission's upgrade before the U.S. government's fiscal year was over on September 30.

An earlier trip to Benghazi in August had been canceled, "partially for Ramadan, partially for security concerns," Stevens had written in an email. Ramadan was now over but the security concerns remained. In fact, they had worsened. In planning the visit, the head diplomatic security agent in Tripoli warned him of the risks. "I didn't [like] the idea of him going there," he would later testify. But, he said, Stevens "was determined to go."

Stevens knew the dangers and took precautions. There would be no prior announcement of the trip and no media coverage of his meetings. A cadre of five diplomatic security agents would protect him (two traveling from Tripoli and three from the compound in Benghazi). For his meetings outside the compound, highly trained, heavily armed guards from the CIA annex—veterans and ex–special operations soldiers—would accompany him. He also decided to curtail his visit by two days.

Shortly after arriving, Stevens traveled to the CIA annex for an intelligence briefing on threats in the city. He seemed surprised at how rapidly security had deteriorated and asked about the extremist groups that had taken root. They were a veritable rogues' gallery, the briefer told him: al-Qaeda in the Islamic Maghreb, Egyptian Islamic Jihad, al-Qaeda in Pakistan, al-Qaeda in the Arabian Peninsula, and Ansar al-Sharia in Derna. He took copious notes. And when the phone rang to remind him of his next appointment, he ignored it so he could finish the meeting.

Later, at a hotel, he met with twenty Benghazi city council members, who conveyed their frustration at neglect by the Tripoli government. Stevens sensed from them "a sourness about why it has taken so long to get to Benghazi." Yet he of all people didn't need to be reminded of Benghazi's importance.

The next day he held all his meetings on the diplomatic compound for security reasons. He handled routine paperwork, reviewing and signing off on the cable message that Dave McFarland had authored about his meeting with the militias two days earlier. Sometime in the late afternoon, Stevens received a text from the deputy chief of mission in Tripoli: "Hey are you watching TV? Embassy Cairo is under attack."

A crowd of two thousand Egyptian protestors had scaled the U.S.

embassy walls and torn down the American flag. The spark was an amateur film made in the United States that demeaned the Prophet Muhammad as a child molester. It was a shoddy production directed by a Coptic Egyptian, a gas station owner who'd been convicted of bank fraud. But the global effect of its YouTube trailer was seismic, leading to hundreds of protests and more than fifty deaths. Stevens asked his DS agents to monitor its effect in Libya.

After his last meeting, at 7:40 p.m., he strolled past the compound's garden to say goodbye to his final guest for the day, the Turkish consul. Then he returned to his quarters.

"It's so nice to be back in Benghazi," he had written earlier in his diary. "Much stronger emotional connection to this place—the people but also the smaller town feel and the moist air and green and spacious compound."

■

EAST OF BENGHAZI, the country turns even greener and the air cooler and more fragrant. It is a hilly region of cypress and pine where a winding road cuts through canyons of striated limestone. In antiquity, thickets of silphium, an herb famed for its palliative and contraceptive uses, studded the landscape. Greek and Roman colonists harvested the plant to near extinction but not before building the city of Cyrene from its profits. Today, the ruins of Cyrene sit astride the mountain town of Shahat.

The Benghazi militia leader Muhammad al-Gharabi had arrived at Shahat on the night of September 11, en route to a wedding. At around ten o'clock, his cell phone rang. It was Fawzi Bu Katif, the head of the February 17 Brigade, calling from Tripoli, where he was on a visit.

"Come back to Benghazi," he said, "there's an attack on the American consulate."

Over the next few hours, the actions of al-Gharabi and other militiamen in Benghazi would have far-reaching consequences, not just for the Americans, but for Benghazi and Libya itself. Their own lives too would be permanently changed: in the months and years that followed, many would go into exile, some would die, and others would join forces with the Islamic State. That night, some of them struggled to balance the pledges they'd made to protect the city and its guests with their loyalties to one another and their religious convictions, which had been offended by the film and, for some of them, by the Western presence in Benghazi.

Al-Gharabi started making calls. His contacts were abuzz with news that a Libyan protestor outside the "consulate" had been wounded by gunfire from within. Onlookers had rushed home to grab weapons. Then the full outlines of what appeared to be a more coordinated assault became clearer. Eventually, al-Gharabi spoke on the phone with an American in Benghazi named "Paul" and offered to send his men. He received a curt "thank you," he says, but had no further conversations.

"The problem was the embassy didn't trust the revolutionaries to help," al-Gharabi later told me.

But the mistrust went beyond that. Al-Gharabi suspected his own men from the Rafallah al-Sahati militia might be among the crowd of attackers that night. He sent emissaries to negotiate with them, to calm them. "We were afraid people would explode," he told me.

Fawzi Bu Katif had similar doubts about his February 17 Brigade men and their possible involvement in the attack.

"I am in the middle of many waves of things. Things could blow up," he told me. "You see, I had to make a balance between the people in my brigade."

"Between who?" I asked.

"We always had the Islamists, and within Islamists you had, some of them, extremists. But I didn't always have this balance," he admitted.

He maintains, though, that he was unequivocal in telling his men to rescue the Americans that night.

Under a plan that had been rehearsed by DS agents, the four February 17 guards who lived on the State Department compound were supposed to take an "active role" in its defense if something happened. That night, one of them had left for family reasons. And the crowd that now heaved through the compound gates was beyond anything they had imagined—or trained for.

It was a fearsome onslaught; men in Afghan garb, some with non-Libyan accents, armed with all manner of assault rifles and rocket-propelled grenades. Hunkered behind a door in their bungalow, the Libyan guards briefly traded fire with them before fleeing, running the length of the compound to the southern end. One of the guards broke his leg jumping over a wall. The attackers doused the shack in diesel fuel from a generator and set it aflame.

Inside the compound's tactical operations center (TOC), a diplomatic security agent watched the assault unfold on security cameras. He sounded the alarm. "This is not a drill, repeat this is not a drill," he said over the loudspeakers.

Agent Scott Wickland rushed across the lawn to the villa where Chris Stevens resided, stopping first at his bedroom to grab his tactical vest, helmet, and weapons. Banging on the ambassador's door, he shouted: "Sir, get ready." He led Stevens and Smith into the safe haven.

The haven was a fortified area on the first floor of the residential villa, secured by a metal grille gate. "A jail cell door," Wickland called it, with three padlocks. Inside, there was water, food, and supplies, and the windows had been reinforced. When Stevens had first arrived at the compound on the afternoon of September 10, Wickland had given him a short familiarization tour.

Now, in a crisis that neither of them expected, their lives depended on it. Wickland secured the three locks and radioed to the TOC: We are in the safe haven. On the radio he heard gunfire and explosions and "blood-curdling" screams, "like someone had just been shot"—the February 17 guards, he assumed.

The TOC agent phoned the CIA's security detail at the annex compound about a mile away. It was a frantic call: he said he saw about twenty men, armed, and massing on the soccer field just outside the living quarters. Then, minutes later, he made another call to the annex: Could they contact the February 17 Brigade to send relief?

At the annex, the CIA chief, "Bob," started phoning everyone: the Libyan police, the Libyan intelligence service—"they weren't actually very helpful to us"—and local militias. He asked the February 17 Brigade for a gun truck but couldn't get a straight answer. By now the base's security team was arming itself to go and relieve the besieged State compound. When it became clear that there would be no militia support, the team departed into two up-armored vehicles, a Mercedes G-Class SUV and a sedan. It was 10:05 p.m., twenty-three minutes since the first call to the annex came in.

Approaching the compound in the dark, they saw armed men and vehicles.

■

WHEN HE HEARD the intruders at the safe haven gate, Scott Wickland sighted his M4 carbine at the metal grille. The former navy rescue swimmer knew the importance of controlled breathing in moments like this. There were about forty of them, and he figured he could kill ten before dying himself. He glanced to his left: Stevens had closed his eyes.

Then, the banging stopped. The attackers left and the lights dimmed. Wickland thought at first the power was going out, but then he realized it was smoke. The attackers had poured gasoline on the villa's furniture and set it alight, sending black smoke barreling through the grille gate, thick, toxic smoke that smelled of sulfur and shrouded the room in darkness.

The three men dropped to the floor where a precious layer of oxygen still remained. Wickland turned to Stevens and Smith: We are moving to the bathroom. It was just eight meters away, he reckoned. Within seconds, the three men had crawled to the hallway. Cupping his hands to his mouth, Wickland heard the snap and pop of things breaking from heat. He slapped his hands to the ground to signal to the two men behind him in the dark.

Inside the bathroom, he realized he had lost Stevens and Smith somewhere on that eight-meter crawl. He stood up to open the bathroom window, his face "on fire." But all that did was let in more smoke, "like a chimney." He struggled to stay conscious.

He unslung his rifle and shouted again. "Come on guys, I'm moving to my bedroom." He pounded the floor some more as he crawled across the hallway through the smoke. Reaching his room, he was certain he had "seconds left of life." He rushed to a window, cranked it open, and tumbled onto a patio outside where cinder-block fragments peppered his face. He was taking fire.

He returned to the room two or three times. "Come on, guys," he yelled, turning on a bedroom light as a signal. Withdrawing outside, he climbed a ladder to the roof and crawled to a skylight window, banging it with an M4 magazine, hoping to ventilate the room.

Tracer fire whizzed and arced over his head.

■

OUTSIDE, on the dark street leading to the compound, the annex team climbed out of their vehicles to speak with the armed men clad in balaclavas, soccer jerseys, and fatigues. They identified themselves as February 17 Brigade members, and the Americans quickly asked if they could provide covering fire while they entered the besieged diplomatic mission.

One of the Libyan militiamen who joined the Americans that night was a forty-two-year-old father of five I'll call Yusuf. Born in Sabri, the poor, cramped quarter of Benghazi that has been home to many Islamists and jihadists, he had worked as a day laborer before the revolution and had no military experience. That evening he was serving as a member of the Supreme Security Committee, Benghazi's makeshift police force, working out of the February 17 base half a mile away from the diplomatic mission. At around 9:45, he heard startling cries on the radio: a fellow militiaman, a former policeman named Faraj Shaku, was heard screaming on the radio, "Gunfire, gunfire, I am subjected to gunfire!" Minutes later, Yusuf got a call from the prime minister's security office. "You have to get our friends out," the caller said, "they've been surrounded."

He joined five other militiamen in running to the embattled mission. At an intersection they took fire from the northeast, and then Americans from the annex pulled up. Entering the compound together, Yusuf and the militiamen helped secure the grounds and the perimeter.

Meanwhile, the diplomatic security agents moved from the TOC to the villa to assist Scott Wickland on the roof and to look for the missing diplomats. They heard alarming cries from Wickland on the radio—he was barely coherent, vomiting from smoke inhalation. "When is our reaction force coming?" he asked. "When are the February Seventeenth guys?" Searching for Stevens and Smith, the agents donned SCape hoods for visibility, gas masks that protect against a chemical attack but are useless in providing oxygen. The agents took short, shallow breaths, wondering whether their forays into the toxic inferno might only make them victims.

David Ubben, an army veteran of Iraq, was feeling his way in the dark when he came across a motionless body. It was Sean Smith. Dragging him outside, Ubben and other agents checked his pulse and breathing. There was nothing. At 11:01 p.m. they reported him killed in action.

The thirty-four-year-old was a father of two and an air force veteran. He was also an avid and accomplished participant in a sci-fi online game, "Eve," whose four hundred thousand members would later rename galactic outposts in his honor. Logging on to the game earlier that night, he posted a message at 9:40 p.m.: "Fuck. Gunfire."

The diplomatic agents carried his body out and laid it by sandbags near the TOC. Tethering themselves to avoid getting lost, they returned for Stevens, taking turns crawling into the gloom until the CIA team leader from the annex finally stopped them. "You guys have got to get the fuck out of here," he shouted. Overhead drones had spotted armed men massing for a counterattack, and the February 17 men "couldn't hold the perimeter."

As the diplomatic security agents loaded Smith's body into a Land Cruiser, Yusuf's phone rang. It was a Libyan security official from the prime minister's office again. "Where is the ambassador? Is he okay?" Yusuf had just turned to the Americans' Arabic interpreter, when the outdoor lighting went out. He heard a loud explosion to the south.

It was 11:10 p.m. The counterassault that followed, Yusuf recalls, "was like the apocalypse."

From the southern gate, attackers fired assault rifles down the length of the thirteen-acre compound at the Americans and the Libyan militiamen. With only a pistol, Yusuf fired back, diving to the ground and dropping his phone while Faraj Shaku, another militiaman, squeezed off rounds with his AK-47. Spotting an assailant with an RPG, an American annex member on the roof hit him with a ten-round burst of gunfire. That seemed to mark a lull—but for how long was anyone's guess.

The DS agents with Sean Smith's body were the first to exit the gate, at 11:16. With exhausted, smoke-weakened Wickland at the wheel, the DS agents turned right out of the main gate only to encounter gunmen in a fruit grove who fired into the left side of the vehicle. They reversed direction, but then turned around again after someone they believed to be a February 17 militiaman warned them off. Three hundred meters later, another gunman emptied an entire clip at point-blank range into the vehicle, shattering the factory glass but failing to penetrate the ballistic layer.

The annex team at the compound had been covering their egress. One of them turned to the February 17 militiamen to ask for covering fire while they dismantled a satellite dish and its associated equipment. Now they too drove away while Yusuf and the militiamen left by foot.

It was 11:20 p.m.

■

SHORTLY AFTER MIDNIGHT, a surveillance camera covering the compound's tactical operations center went off-line for twenty-eight minutes. But before it did, it captured a remarkable scene: a group of men, armed and unarmed, approached the center and started removing equipment and papers. A robed figure, taller than the rest, moved among them.

It was man named Ahmed Abu Khattala, the leader of one of Benghazi's smaller but more radical Islamist militias. Born in 1971, the six-foot-two Abu Khattala grew up in Benghazi's hardscrabble al-Laythi district. With a ninth-grade education he worked as a mechanic for the ministry of health and then as a construction worker. As a young man, he spent six years in prison for frequenting mosques in al-Laythi that were attended by men who went abroad to jihad. After his release, he lived with his mother and father and six sisters.

Many fellow Islamists took a dim view of him. "He's mentally unfit," a fellow cellmate in Abu Salim prison told me. "A simple person."

Still, he attracted a following: mostly troubled youths, people said, the unemployed and addicts. During the 2011 revolution he formed the Abu Obeida bin Jarrah Brigade with about 140 fighters. Though it had "registered" with the NTC, it still rejected the new Libyan state and sought to impose Islamic law. The February 17 Brigade's Fawzi Bu Katif recalls a meeting of Benghazi's Islamist militias where the assembled leaders agreed to support the civilian government; Abu Khattala, he says, got up and walked out.

In July 2011, the Abu Obeida Brigade disbanded, and its members scattered to other Islamist groups, such as Ansar al-Sharia or the Rafallah al-Sahati militia. Even so, Abu Khattala retained control of his men and could easily rally them, keeping a stash of heavy weapons in his garage and bragging about his skill with mortars.

The Justice Department would later charge Abu Khattala with plotting the entire attack on the U.S. compound. On or before September 11, it alleged in an indictment, he told associates he was "going to do something about the facility," which he believed was a front for intelligence gathering. It was these "associates," hardened men from his childhood in al-Laythi and fellow ex-prisoners who'd joined his brigade, who reportedly first breached the mission compound at around 9:45. They were a motley group: a man named Yahya Sayyid al-Zway with roots in Chad, nicknamed "Jamaica"; a bowlegged man named Ayman Djawi whom Abu Khattala told investigators walked "like a chimpanzee"; a religious authority with Ansar al-Sharia named Khalid Nayhum, along with militants from Derna.

Abu Khattala himself had been spotted on video at the back gate after the first assault, turning away those who tried to help and mingling among the looters. Witnesses described the crowds parting for him, as if out of deference. Footage I viewed by a Libyan journalist shows men outside the south gate with faces covered, some wearing tactical vests and carrying an assortment of light and heavy weapons. A rhyming chant erupted: "Khaybar, Khaybar, oh you Jews, the army of Muhammad will return," in rhyming Arabic—Khaybar refers to an oasis in Arabia and the site of a battle in A.D. 628 when the Prophet Muhammad defeated a community of Jews living there. The journalist said he tried to film Abu Khattala, but his bodyguards brusquely said no.

But most worrisome, Abu Khattala's brigade overlapped with and drew support from the Islamist militias charged with protecting the Americans. Days before the attack, Abu Khattala and his men reportedly arrived at the February 17 Brigade camp not far from the American compound and loaded weapons like mortar shells and machine gun rounds into the back of a truck. During the attack, he warned February 17 guards to stand down, threatening them, "If you kill one of us you will be in trouble," according to a witness, and a cooperative commander obliged.

All of this reminded me of what Fawzi Bu Katif had said: the loyalties of Benghazi militias were blurred together by common belief, kinship, and experiences of incarceration. The murky landscape had a calamitous impact on the Americans that night—and it complicated their later efforts to bring the culprits to justice.

Much of the incriminating testimony against Abu Khattala would come from a witness named Abd al-Salam al-Bargathi, who'd been a commander in a militia outfit called the Preventative Security Apparatus. Relocated to the United States with his family for safety, al-Bargathi testified about Abu Khattala's warning the guards to back off and his earlier trip for weapons at the February 17 camp. Yet eyewitnesses told me that al-Bargathi also shadowed Abu Khattala that night and obstructed the movements of militias who tried to help the Americans. Seizing on these inconsistencies, defense lawyers would later question his motives, citing his demand for $10 million to cooperate with the Americans. They raised the same doubts about another star witness, a forty-year-old Benghazi businessman code-named "Ali" whom the Americans recruited to infiltrate Abu Khattala's circle and who would lure the militia leader to his capture two years later—for $7 million.

These testimonies aside, what is clear is that as the crowds rushed inside the compound after the first attack, Abu Khattala followed them. Here, prosecutors allege he directed and supervised the pillaging, removing documents, maps, equipment, and, crucially, sensitive information about the secret CIA annex less than two miles away. And some time after midnight, they say, he left the compound and went to an Ansar al-Sharia base.

■

IN THE DARKNESS, a Libyan guard emerged on the tarmac at Benghazi's Banina Airport, wearing what appeared to be pajamas. He seemed surprised to see a plane landing at this late hour. The Americans who had just flown in from Tripoli were equally shocked. There were seven of them: four contract security officers from the CIA's Tripoli station, two U.S. military special operations soldiers, and a CIA case officer who spoke Arabic. The CIA station chief in Tripoli had chartered a commercial jet, but when the Americans arrived at 12:53 a.m., it looked as if Banina had closed for the night. "It was completely dead," one member of the team later said. "We were the only plane that had landed in quite some time."

Just after the start of the attack, the American defense attaché in Tripoli had phoned a longtime American contact, General Abd al-Salam al-Hasi, to ask for help. He demurred on sending anyone to the besieged diplomatic mission and also prevaricated when the attaché asked him to send his soldiers to meet the American rescue team at Benghazi's airport. "Okay, I will look into it," al-Hasi replied, according to the attaché.

That was the last anyone heard of him that night. For the rest of the crisis, his phone was switched off, and at the airport, his Special Forces were nowhere to be seen. It was an unsettling absence for one of America's key Libyan allies—but it was hardly surprising. Al-Hasi was increasingly seen as too pro-American and his Special Forces were among the weaker armed groups in Benghazi that night, especially compared to the militias.

Effectively stranded, the Americans at Benghazi's airport were forced to rely on these militias, many with uncertain loyalties. Within an hour, several of them started to arrive on the runway, and sorting out which militia could be trusted proved a daunting task.

Then, shortly after 2:00 a.m., they received the news that an unconscious Westerner had been taken to the hospital.

■

EARLIER THAT EVENING, a young Libyan named Fahad Bakoush was sitting with friends at the Bongiorno Café in Benghazi's Sidi Hussein district when he got news of the attack. Like hundreds of other Libyans that night, he and six friends decided to go check it out. He was twenty-two years old at the time and had never completed his studies, having been thrown out of high school during the Qadhafi years for playing the monarchy's national anthem. His uncle had been killed in the Abu Salim massacre, and he'd long despised the regime.

One of his hobbies was photography and videography. And so when he arrived at the the U.S. diplomatic mission around eleven o'clock, he started filming a crowd with his Sony Xperia. "Bring down the flag," they chanted. He followed the surge of onlookers and opportunistic looters inside the compound, where some of them stormed the villas.

Outside one of them, Bakoush heard shouting.

"I stepped on a body! I stepped on a body!" someone said.

The crowd had dismantled a tall window, gone inside, and discovered a motionless body, next to an iron grille gate. Bakoush clicked on the flash of his camera. What he saw next terrified him: the body of a barefoot Westerner being dragged through the window, the man's face lifeless, with blackened soot encrusting his mouth and nose.

Nobody knew who he was. "We thought at first it was a guard or a chef," he said.

They assumed he was dead, but then somebody took his pulse on his neck.

"He's living! He's living!" they shouted. "God is great! God is great!"

"Put him in my car!" someone said. They carried him to the backseat of a green Daewoo and drove to the hospital. Bakoush would only learn the next day who he was.

Later, a Libyan who had helped pull Stevens from the villa retrieved the ambassador's cell phone (it was actually Scott Wickland's) and started dialing its stored numbers. He said that someone matching the ambassador's description was at the hospital, yet he didn't provide any proof, such as a photo.

The Americans in Tripoli who got the call were suspicious. The call had "a lot of the hallmarks of some type of entrapment," the CIA chief of station later said. "It wasn't straight up."

They had also received information that Ansar al-Sharia was guarding the medical facility. That proved to be false. The chief medical officer at the Benghazi Medical Center that night was an ob-gyn specialist named Laila Bugaighis. Like her well-known cousin Salwa, Laila Bugaighis is educated, articulate, and progressive. During the revolution, she organized medical relief for the front lines. After, she founded and participated in a number of civil society groups related to constitutionalism and women's rights.

On the evening of September 11, she was focused on the following day's scheduled meeting between the Benghazi Medical Center and a delegation from the Massachusetts General Hospital in Boston to open a new emergency medicine division. Chris Stevens was planning to attend.

Late that night, around one in the morning, she got word that a group of Libyans had brought an unresponsive, unconscious American into that hospital. They didn't know who he was and he showed no signs of life. Still, following hospital procedure, the doctor performed CPR for about forty-five minutes, before declaring him deceased and moving him to the morgue.

■

AT BENGHAZI'S AIRPORT, the recently arrived American team had finally settled on a militia leader they could trust. His name was Fathi al-Obeidi.

The fifty-one-year-old al-Obeidi had been a commercial maritime diver before the revolution and then joined Wissam bin Hamid as a lieutenant in his Libya Shield. That night, bin Hamid had gone to the American diplomatic compound and, according to what Abu Khattala told a witness, prevented the assailants from attacking further. Now he was the last hope for the Americans to escape. His deputy al-Obeidi was on duty at the Libya Shield headquarters when a security official from Tripoli called him. "There are Americans at Banina Airport," the caller said. "Send someone to pick them up."

Al-Obeidi arrived at the airport with armored Land Cruisers and

Kia sedans. But so too did a number of other militias, including one that tried to obstruct the Americans' departure. For the stranded Americans, al-Obeidi seemed more reliable than the rest or at least, in the words of one special operator, "less bad."

At 4:15 a.m., just as they were preparing to leave, the Americans received a call that the Westerner at the hospital had been positively identified as the ambassador. A Libyan official had gone to the hospital, taken two cell phone photos of the body, and sent them back to Tripoli—the first positive identification of Stevens. With their hopes for saving him shattered, the American team decided to head straight for the annex, where the survivors of the attack on the temporary mission facility had fled.

Al-Obeidi drove the lead vehicle with one of the Americans seated up front and a Lebanese-accented interpreter in the back. "Left, left, right," the American said, with a map of Benghazi opened up on his laptop. Al-Obeidi had no idea where they were going; nobody in Libya even knew that the Americans had a second location. It was a tense journey, fraught with fears of an ambush. They trusted nobody. At an intersection, somebody stopped them and tried to get them to change routes but they ignored the advice.

When they got to the annex compound just after five o'clock, they found it hunkered down. The base had already been hit by two separate volleys of gunfire earlier that morning, both from a field the security contractors had dubbed "Zombieland." Now the CIA's Mercedes blocked the entrance, and someone had thrown down a glow stick. Al-Obeidi accompanied the team inside—one of the special operators insisted— while his men sat guard in their vehicles outside. He'd expected to evacuate ten to fifteen people but found instead close to forty, including women.

Minutes later, just as al-Obeidi had gone indoors, the car alarms of the parked motorcade started going off. Earsplitting booms: the sound of mortars being fired. A barrage unlike anything they had seen rained down on them: six 81 mm mortar rounds arrived in a minute and thirteen seconds. One of the U.S. special operators on the scene later said that the attackers were more precise and better disciplined than the Libyan army counterterrorism unit he had trained.

Fathi al-Obeidi agreed. These were practiced veterans.

"We were just trying to survive," he told me. It had to be pre-planned, he suspected; the attackers must have been tipped off about the Tripoli team's arrival or at least followed them from the airport.

Inside the compound, the Americans raced for cover, trying to turn off the bright lights that illuminated the compound, making it an easy target. On the roof, two of the CIA's security team and the DS agent Dave Ubben returned fire. Ubben was the first to get hit, with a shrapnel blast to his head and then his leg, which was nearly severed and now dangled "by just skin and some muscle." Reaching to tie a tourniquet, he noticed the round had torn a "grapefruit-size chunk" of flesh from his useless left arm. Shrapnel from another round sprayed a CIA contractor named Mark Geist, hitting his arm as well and stinging him like a "thousand bees." Collapsing, he felt his clothes soaked through and feared he was bleeding out, but it was only water from a nearby tank punctured by the blast. He saw two of his CIA colleagues, Tyrone Woods and Glen Doherty, take hits and die immediately.

With most of its rooftop defenders dead or wounded, the embattled base was at risk of being overrun. The CIA chief decided to evacuate.

Outside the villa, though, al-Obeidi's men appeared to have gone, retreating several hundred meters to a side road as the mortars crashed in. Calling them back, al-Obeidi also phoned Wissam bin Hamid for more cars. Returning at 6:14 a.m., the larger Shield convoy of around fifty gun trucks and pickups loaded the survivors and dead. The Americans scanned the road for danger as they drove to the airport.

Abu Baker Habib, Stevens's close friend and aide, was waiting on the tarmac. Just half a day earlier he had been at his English school, checking the generator and preparing for Stevens's visit to open the

American library. Now he and the remaining Americans received his corpse; Libyan militiamen had retrieved it from the hospital, carrying it in the back of a truck.

And at 9:54 a.m. a Libyan C-130 departed for Tripoli with his remains and those of Smith, Woods, and Doherty.

8

THE REVOLUTION

DEVOURS ITS OWN

IN THE COURSE OF U.S. history, Chris Stevens was the eighth American ambassador to die in the line of duty and the sixth to die in a terrorist act. Assaults on U.S. diplomatic facilities are hardly uncommon and indeed the attack bore an uncanny resemblance to a similar incident in Benghazi in the summer of 1967. Enraged by Egyptian broadcasters' claims that American planes were attacking Cairo during the Six Day War, armed Libyans stormed the American consulate. American diplomats retreated to a second-floor communications vault. "The heat, smoke and tear gas were intense," wrote one of them later. "We only had 5 gas masks for 10 people." The episode ended without any loss of life, miraculously.

Since then, there have been dozens of other sieges and bombings of U.S. diplomatic posts, many in the Middle East. But this one hit the Americans especially hard.

"We didn't just lose our eyes and ears," Samantha Power told me, "we lost the best advocate . . . this person who no matter how bad it got would always say, 'Here are the five things you can do to make it better.'"

The morning after the attack, the American diplomatic staff in Tripoli fled to the better-guarded CIA annex. Fifty-one U.S. Marines arrived from Spain to provide protection. Soon after, embassy personnel deemed "nonessential" were evacuated, and the remaining diplomats went back to the old compound.

The entire character of the embassy would change in those months: the walls became higher and the surveillance cameras more ubiquitous. In addition to the marine platoon, FBI agents came to pursue leads, collect evidence, and interview witnesses. More diplomatic security agents also arrived. The defense attaché office planned to double its presence. All of this meant that the embassy compound was taking on a distinctly militarized air.

This was a change from the early months after the 2011 revolution, when both the administration and State had studiously sought to avoid a military footprint. The fortresslike atmosphere was also a setback for Chris Stevens's commitment to engaging with everyday Libyans. Now the embassy "was like an FOB," one diplomat said, referring to forward operating bases, the fortified outposts of the U.S. military in Afghanistan and Iraq. The number of actual diplomats dwindled, and the sole political officer went for weeks without leaving the compound to meet Libyan contacts, often relying on Twitter and other social media to report on developments. Libyans who wanted to meet Americans at the embassy had to endure an onerous security check that many found humiliating. All of this meant that America's window onto Libya's politics shrank considerably.

The security reaction was in some sense understandable from a bureaucracy that had just suffered the sudden loss of its own. But more important was the response from an administration that was already facing partisan attacks for its conduct on the night of the attack.

"The lesson out of Benghazi just compounded the concern we already had," said Derek Chollet, the former White House advisor. "Because it made it politically radioactive to assume any risk at all in Libya."

The great tragedy in all of this, he added, was that Chris Stevens was "the guy who pushed the envelope."

"And now the attitude was, 'The hell with it.'"

■

THE AMERICAN RETRENCHMENT was happening precisely when the Libya revolution started turning on itself. Political divisions were paralyzing the newly elected government and parliament—the objects of so many American and international aspirations. The militias were becoming stronger and bolder. Activists were cowed by fear, and the space for civic discourse, the kind that Chris Stevens promoted, had shrunk. The fractures that would soon break the country apart were starting to widen with alarming speed. And nothing seemed to hasten the unraveling more than a controversial piece of legislation.

The Political Isolation Law, as it was called, prohibited anyone formally tied to the Qadhafi regime from holding government office for a period of ten years. Polls in Libya suggested popular support for some form of exclusion of high-ranking officials and those with blood on their hands. But this went too far. The law's definition of complicity was so broad that it would ban a vast stratum of technocrats, military officers, and student union leaders, including those who had worked for reform from within and defected early in the 2011 uprising.

Among those targeted was Mahmud Jibril, the head of the National Forces Alliance, whose close association with Saif al-Islam under the Qadhafi regime put him in the crosshairs of the law. Jibril lamented to me that the legislation never distinguished between those who "worked for the state and those who worked for the system," a charge repeated by the law's countless critics, both inside and outside Libya. Where would it end? he wondered. And who exactly would be left to run the country?

The law's proponents saw it differently. They were a coalition that included Salafists, the Brotherhood, ex-members of the LIFG, and leaders of revolutionary towns, chiefly Misrata. Many had spent time in prison, and for them, the ban was necessary justice. They also saw it as a means to push from power their political opponents and to secure access to funds. And starting in late April 2013, they used force to tip the debate: their allied militias laid siege to government buildings, encircling them with armed vehicles and demanding the passage of the law. They warned legislators that a vote against it would be akin to treason.

One of the law's key supporters was a seventy-one-year-old British-trained engineer from Misrata named Abd al-Rahman al-Suwayhli, who'd won a seat in parliament. Though his brother had been Qadhafi's naval chief throughout the revolution and stayed loyal, al-Suwayhli had broken early from the regime and been detained. For him, the Isolation Law was a vital break with the past.

An urbane man with a broad forehead, al-Suwayhli speaks eloquent English. "You see, I grow oranges and lemons," he told me over a lunch of grilled fish. "And to plant new trees, you have to clear the ground of dead roots."

But I discerned another motive behind al-Suwayhli's push for the law. He wanted to ensure Misrata's primacy in Libya's new order and, especially, to clear his own path to leadership of Libya. Here, he seemed to take inspiration from the short-lived independent Tripolitanian Republic based in Misrata from 1918 to 1922.

"This is our destiny," he told me. "The Misratans carried a heavy burden against the Italians."

Like his fellow Misratan Salim Joha, Abd al-Rahman al-Suwayhli is related to the Tripolitanian Republic's founder; he is the grandson of

Ramadan al-Suwayhli's brother, Ahmed. But the affinity with Joha stops there.

"He's obsessed," Salim Joha later told me. "Obsessed with ruling, despite the fact that we share the same family. And anywhere there's fighting, he's involved."

For his part, al-Suwayhli criticizes Joha as being too accommodating of the vestiges of the old regime.

"The problem with Salim is he doesn't mind making peace with the Qadhafi people," he said. "For Salim, the revolution was just a war to stop Qadhafi's forces from attacking Misrata. Then it's back to business as usual."

Al-Suwayhli's push for the Political Isolation Law was not the only expression of an uncompromising streak in Misrata. In the fall of 2012, Misratan militias attacked the town of Bani Walid, a two-hour drive south, after its militias had detained several Misratan youths, one of whom later died from his wounds. A stronghold of the Warfalla tribe, Bani Walid had been one of the last places to fall to anti-Qadhafi forces in 2011. The town's inhabitants had already suffered torture and disappearances since the revolution, but now they endured a monthlong siege, marked by the shelling of its hospital and shortages of water, fuel, and food.

Beneath the Misratans' declared goal of "cleansing" Bani Walid of Qadhafi holdouts lay a historical subtext. In 1920, the Warfalla of Bani Walid, allied with the Italians, ambushed and killed Ramadan al-Suwayhli. Some revanchist Misratans had now grafted that memory onto the present: when Misratan militias finally entered Bani Walid in late October 2012, they affixed a poster of Ramadan al-Suwayhli to a building in the center of the town.

Salim Joha and other moderates had tried to stop the punitive expedition.

"We nearly reached the point where we had an agreement," he told me years later, but extremists in both camps prevented it. Afterward, he paid a huge political price for his moderation. "He lost a lot of his fans in Misrata," a Misratan friend told me.

Joha soon left Libya, taking up a largely symbolic post as the country's military attaché in the United Arab Emirates.

■

THE POLITICAL ISOLATION LAW finally passed on May 5, 2013. It was a watershed in Libya's post-Qadhafi politics, a subversion of its fragile democracy in the name of an elusive "revolutionary purity." Critics compared it to a form of collective suicide. It eroded, perhaps fatally, public confidence in Libya's first elected parliament in decades, the General National Congress (GNC). It worsened militia tensions between towns that backed it, led by Misrata, and those who opposed it, led by Zintan.

For Mahmud Jibril and the National Forces Alliance the law was especially painful. Lambasting the silence of the international community, Jibril called the passage of the law a betrayal by the West of Libya's liberal and secular trend. "We were kicked out by force by Islamists in front of the world," he told me from his office in Cairo, where he lives in exile. Where was the outcry from the United States?

In the coming months, he and his NFA supporters would align themselves even more closely with the Zintani militias while working to undermine the General National Congress.

■

I STRUGGLED AT THE TIME to understand the implications of what was happening and what the rival camps in Libya really represented. The old Qadhafi order, to the extent that there ever was an order, was falling away. That much was certain. But what was replacing it was unclear and often maddeningly complex.

Veterans of other postconflict reconstructions who'd worked in Iraq, Afghanistan, and the Balkans shared my exasperation. Many wondered despairingly whether Libya's problems were so overwhelming and so unique that they defied the received wisdom on rebuilding shattered states. Journalists struggled as well and shied away from Libya—not least because the country was becoming increasingly dangerous. But another reason had to do with the absence of a clear narrative: whereas the 2011 revolution had been a ready-made story, what followed it was trickier to cover and to explain. "Confusion is hard to report," admitted the British television journalist Lindsey Hilsum.

It was too easy to fall for the self-serving explanations of Libya's factions. Jibril and his allies claimed they were all that stood between a liberal, democratic future and a retrograde theocracy run by Islamists. Their opponents led by the Misratans claimed they were fighting a counterrevolution by Qadhafi loyalists. These arguments always struck me as exaggerated, if not patently false. Most everyone in Libya agreed on some role for Islam in political life. True, there were some diehard ideologues—but they remained on the fringes. And few wanted a full return of the old regime's rule, even without its leader.

Instead, the key division seemed to be between those who wanted to preserve or reform the status quo ante and those who wanted its complete dismantling. Even more, the conflict seemed to be a scramble for political supremacy and access to wealth between networks centered most commonly on towns and tribes—and their militias. These were power structures and identities that had emerged during the 2011 revolution, often through foreign support, and had hardened in its aftermath. "Think Renaissance Italy, think city states," a U.S. diplomat later told me.

And yet, I sensed something more was at work in Libya than a squabble among statelets, something that reflected bigger forces buffeting the Arab region and beyond.

The first hints of a revelation appeared to me when I left Libya that summer and traveled to Spain. In a Barcelona bookstore, I picked up a copy of *Homage to Catalonia*, George Orwell's classic memoir of the Spanish Civil War.

Like Spain in the 1930s, Libya was in a revolutionary state, racked by a multitude of factions, some ideological, some regional, some sectarian, all of them artificially grouped into categories by outside observers—into democrats and Fascists, in the case of Spain. Like in Spain, Libya's armed protagonists had splintered into a dizzying array of militias and paramilitaries. (The Spanish pattern was so complex, in fact, that Orwell had to chart it in an appendix.) And Libya, like Spain, was fast becoming an arena for proxy competition between outside powers with clashing visions of politics.

The loss of idealism was another parallel. Orwell, an eager and early partisan in the Iberian conflict, had grown disillusioned with it but had still beseeched his contemporaries to heed the unfolding drama. His warnings were prophetic. I fixated on one of his concluding lines:

"This squalid brawl in a distant city is more important than might appear at first sight."

■

BACK AT THE heavily guarded American embassy, diplomats watched the passage of the Isolation Law with dismay.

"We were horrified," one of them told me. Some would later regret not making a more forceful statement. But what good would such a statement do? Especially after the September 2012 Benghazi attack, when they'd pared down their staff in Tripoli and curtailed their forays outside the villa compound.

The Americans and the United Nations had supported elections in Libya but they could not prevent elected officials from enacting exclusionary legislation, nor could they protect those officials from pressure from the militias. It was a limitation that became most evident in the weeks and months ahead, when militiamen turned their sights on the elected prime minister, a sixty-three-year-old former diplomat and dissident named Ali Zeidan.

I met Zeidan one afternoon in the fall of 2016, in Munich, where he now lives after fleeing Libya's militias. He did his best as prime minister, he says, and did not seem bitter. Escaping to Germany was in some sense a return home: he'd lived there during three decades of exile in the Qadhafi era. He speaks its language haltingly and knows his way around its beer and schnapps. The locals in the neighborhood greet him with deference, the gentlemanly sexagenarian with close-cropped hair and a slight shuffle. He often lifts his thick-framed glasses to focus his eyes or to squint for emphasis.

When he became Libya's prime minister in late 2012, fate handed Ali Zeidan an impossible burden: being the object of intense American expectations. Washington invested in Zeidan its hopes for halting the country's downward slide and, especially, for bringing to justice the perpetrators of the Benghazi attack. Liberal in outlook, conversant in European languages, and a confidant of the late Chris Stevens's, he was a known quantity for the Americans. Now he had the unenviable task of meeting American demands while trying to preserve his dwindling legitimacy at home.

In starting his second term, President Obama wanted a reboot of America's Libya policy after Benghazi. But he needed a Libyan partner to work with, and in Ali Zeidan he finally thought he'd found one.

"The president genuinely felt like America had created a vacuum," said Derek Chollet, who by this time was a senior Pentagon official, "and Zeidan is clearly the guy to put this back together."

The only question was: How long would he last?

His tenure as prime minister was shaky from the start. The General National Congress had elected him by a narrow margin after the first prime minister had failed to form a cabinet. Intended as a compromise between the National Forces Alliance and the Islamist blocs, Zeidan failed to satisfy either camp, despite striving for geographical and ideological diversity in his cabinet.

More important, he faced growing pressure from the well-armed militias who wanted power, each claiming to speak in the name of the revolution. He'd made repeated threats to cut off their salaries but lacked any force of his own to make good on these threats. And as his political survival grew further in doubt, he leaned even more on the Americans and the Europeans for protection, especially in building a new Libyan army.

By this time, Libya's military had all but ceased to function. Save for a few units, it had been hollowed out by years of neglect by Qadhafi, many soldiers failed to show up for work, and the army that now existed was top-heavy, dominated by senescent colonels and generals. Scatter-shot efforts by the United Nations and European countries to build up the Libyan military in the year following the 2011 revolution didn't amount to much, partly because of political divisions and disarray on the Libyan side. The militias now ruled the scene; Zeidan hoped for-eign help would give him much-needed leverage against them.

Visiting the White House in March 2013, Zeidan started off by assuring American officials of Libya's commitment to finding the cul-prits of the 2012 attack—a promise they knew he probably couldn't keep. Then he made an impassioned plea for American help in train-ing an army. President Obama dropped in and spoke with him for about twenty minutes. "All I need is three thousand to six thousand troops," Zeidan told the president and his advisors. Much of it hinged on his ability to deliver two critical things: suitable Libyan recruits and payment to the Americans. Zeidan promised he could do both.

It was a compelling performance, even if the Libyan prime minister gave alternate versions of it to various administration officials. What mattered in the end was that President Obama seized on the idea: the training effort would become a key pillar of his Libya policy—a "quick win," as one State Department official called it.

"The president's attitude was, 'Well, goddammit, if he says he can deliver the recruits and the money, we should be able to do this. This is an achievable thing,'" a senior Pentagon official involved in the project told me.

That summer, British prime minister David Cameron invited Zeidan to attend the Group of Eight at a bucolic golf resort in Lough Erne, Northern Ireland, to push the idea to American allies. In its final conception, the new force would comprise a total of twenty thousand soldiers. The Americans had agreed to train just over a quarter of that number, with the remainder trained by the British, the Italians, and the Turks. It was to be a basic infantry force, in military jargon, a "general purpose force" (GPF) whose goal was to protect Libyan government facilities, personnel, and critical infrastructure from militia pressure.

The project was doomed from the start.

First of all, the arm of the American government charged with executing the project, the U.S. military, was immediately skeptical of it. The defense attaché at the American embassy had argued against it from the begining, believing the scale to be unrealistic. Overruled, AFRICOM was handed the task of planning for the training program just after Zeidan's visit. But its commander "slow-rolled" the initial process, Pentagon and State Department officials told me, convinced that it was unworkable. The American military, after all, knew from experience just how hard it was to construct cohesive militaries in divided and war-torn countries, whether Iraq, Afghanistan, or lesser-known cases on the African continent such as Mali.

Libya was an especially challenging case: as I'd witnessed firsthand, Qadhafi had gutted the regular Libyan army, save for a few now-defunct elite brigades who reported directly to the dictator. To what exactly, AFRICOM asked, would the Libyan recruits return once their training was complete? Libya lacked the bureaucracy to support a new army, especially vital functions such as payroll and housing, to say nothing of the armories and bases, which the militias controlled.

Then there was the issue of recruits. Could the Americans and their allies find an adequate number of competent and healthy conscripts, with sufficient geographical and tribal diversity from across the country? From past experience, they expected at least a 75 percent attrition rate during the training. And given the decrepit or nonexistent state of Libyan records, how would they be vetted for past criminal activity and human rights violations, as an American law—the Leahy Amendment—required? Finally, AFRICOM pointed out that the plan would take longer to execute than some of its proponents realized: training the entire force was expected to take five to eight years, yet the life span of Zeidan's government could be counted in months, if that.

Still, AFRICOM had no choice but to salute smartly and proceed.

President Obama wanted the general purpose force to happen. And so too did the new American ambassador.

On the very same day that President Obama had received Ali Zeidan at the White House, he announced his appointment of a successor to Chris Stevens, a veteran diplomat and Arabist named Deborah Jones. A New Mexico native descended from Mormon pioneers, Jones had served in the United Arab Emirates and as ambassador to Kuwait. To Libya, a country dominated by men and weapons, she brought a determined authority; shortly after arriving, she outshot General Abd al-Salam al-Hasi, the Americans' favored Special Forces officer, on a shooting range. She'd grown up hunting with her father, after all, and was a "better shot than all my brothers," she told me. Her pet dog, an excitable terrier named Dusty, greeted visitors to her office.

Her assumption of the post in June 2013 ended months of caretaker leadership in the American embassy and was meant to signal to Libyans a redoubling of America's efforts in the failing country. She embraced Obama's commitment to Zeidan while also meeting with a range of Libyan officials, including Islamists opposed to Zeidan—a normal enough diplomatic function. Unfortunately, these meetings led Zeidan and his allies to perceive an American naïveté about Islamists or, worse, an active preference for them. Zeidan in particular would accuse the ambassador of infatuation with Misrata, and even "subcontracting" American policy to the powerful coastal city.

"She went to Misrata, saw that it's clean and well organized, and asked, 'Why is the rest of Libya not like this?'" Zeidan told me.

In fact, Jones stuck by Zeidan to the very end and pushed hard for his signature program, the general purpose force. But the obstacles to the program continued to mount.

For both political and security reasons, the Americans and their allies had decided to conduct the training outside Libya. Early Libyan recruits to the program signed up expecting to go to the States for training but were mortified to learn that they would be spending six months at a military base in Bulgaria, where the Americans had decided to conduct their training. Bulgaria occupies a uniquely painful place in Libyan memory: in 1998, five Bulgarian nurses were arrested and sentenced to death for allegedly conspiring to infect four hundred Libyan children with the HIV virus. A standoff ensued, with international health experts attributing the outbreak to bad sanitation at the hospital in Benghazi and human rights experts decrying Libya's imprisonment and torture of the nurses. The nurses were released only after European Union mediation.

The training location was not the worst of the problems. AFRICOM wanted to send hundreds of personnel to Libya to vet and process recruits before they went to Bulgaria, but the State Department refused both for practical reasons (the lack of billeting space, mainly) and out of deference to Libyan concerns about a foreign military presence. When the recruitment finally started with a fraction of that footprint, the American screeners had trouble identifying enough Libyan recruits who met the basic requirements.

These faults were bad enough, but even more serious was Zeidan's inability to deliver payment for the training, which the Americans had demanded before starting. The price was exorbitant to begin with, $600 million for the total package, yet Zeidan could not even deliver the first installment, despite repeated promises. Officials in his own government opposed the training, and militias, especially from the Islamists, saw the new force as a threat to their power—and to the revenue they continued to draw from the government. Their political supporters controlled the parliament after the Isolation Law, and parliamentary approval was required to release the funds.

While the Americans waited and chased Zeidan for payment, their NATO partners proceeded with their part of the training. The results were mediocre at best and tragic at worst. The Turks rushed through their vetting of recruits, eager to win follow-on contracts for the equipping of the Libyan army. Ill-prepared trainees suffered what one AFRICOM officer called "astronomical" attrition rates, due to medical or discipline issues. Zeidan himself admitted this, accusing those who trained in Turkey of "smoking hash, being drunk, and going with girls." The Italians fared slightly better in their training.

Then in late October 2014, disaster befell the U.K.'s program. A group of the three hundred Libyan recruits who'd gone to train near the staid village of Bassingbourn snuck out of their barracks late one night and pedaled on stolen bicycles to nearby Cambridge. Mayhem ensued. The Libyan trainees roamed intoxicated through the town's cobblestone streets, groping and assaulting women, and exposing themselves. Two of the cadets were later convicted and sentenced for gang-raping a young man walking home from a wedding. The British sent the remaining recruits home and canceled the program altogether.

American officials watching the fiasco took note. By this time, the growing security crisis in Libya was making the American program increasingly moot. But it was the British experience that sealed the fate of the general purpose force for good. "It died when the United Kingdom canceled their training," a State Department official told me.

It was not the only U.S. military assistance effort to end in failure.

In the summer of 2012, the Americans had opened another front, a program to train an eight-hundred-strong battalion of Libyan special operations forces in counterterrorism. They'd decided to hold the training sessions at a Libyan military base known as Camp 27 that lies some sixteen miles west of Tripoli along the coastal road to Tunisia. Fenced by junipers and imposing walls, it was a rarity in postrevolution Libya: a military facility that was largely intact and secured by a pro-American faction, the Libyan Special Forces under the command of General Abd al-Salam al-Hasi.

The only problem was its location. The camp sat squarely on a disputed boundary between two tribes, strategic real estate in a long-standing tussle over control to the western approaches to Tripoli—important especially for smuggling. But at the time, the Americans were unaware of this significance—and General al-Hasi never informed them of it.

There was another pitfall. I learned from the Libyan commander of the counterterrorism battalion that it recruited nearly all of its soldiers from the western region of Libya and especially from one town, Zintan, to the exclusion of other areas. It was an imbalance that was bound to stoke suspicion among Zintan's rivals, especially Misratans and the Tripoli Islamists, who would likely view the unit as simply a Zintani militia. And what was to guarantee that the Zintanis wouldn't use their new-found military capability against these rivals, whom they had branded "terrorists"? The project risked splintering an already fractured country, and America's association with the force could taint its image as a neutral party.

The training started slowly. At first, the Americans focused only on physical training and first aid, because the Libyan soldiers lacked weapons. By 2013, though, the Americans had built up Camp 27, provisioning it with mock-up buildings for urban combat training, a firing range, armories, and weapons such as pistols and assault rifles. At the end of the daily training, the American soldiers returned to gated villas just down the coast to sleep, leaving Libyans to guard the expensive facility at night.

One morning in August 2013, while the Americans were still at their villas, the guards at the camp opened the gates to armed raiders, who set about pilfering. The Libyan commander at the site told his men to stand down in order to avoid bloodshed and sparking a broader conflict between tribes. In the weeks that followed, equipment and weapons started appearing on Facebook for sale. The Americans got some of the guns and night-vision goggles back, but most of the matériel was never accounted for. A livid ambassador Jones ordered the closure of the project and sent the U.S. special operators home. Soon after, Islamist militias moved in and occupied the camp. It was yet another failure of American assistance efforts and an object lesson in the pitfalls of Libya's tribal politics.

Zeidan held a press conference days later, lambasting the looting of the camp and chiding the Libyan public for what he saw as an unruly contempt for government property. And in the coming weeks and months his fortunes would further decline, with the United States and its allies powerless to help him.

"I am inside a *ghibli*," he pleaded with them, referring to the fierce desert wind.

■

SHORTLY AFTER THE RAID, Zeidan's government suffered a string of crises. In late August, an eastern militia commander seized three oil terminals in the Sirt Basin and declared them the possessions of the eastern region of Cyrenaica, or Barqa. The controversial eastern federalist movement had lost steam after the 2012 elections but never went away. Now it controlled half of Libya's oil exports.

The movement found a military champion in the form of a brash thirty-two-year-old from the eastern town of Ajdabiya named Ibrahim Jadhran. An ex-prisoner in Abu Salim, Jadhran had become, after the fall of Qadhafi, the central regional commander in Libya's Petroleum Facilities Guard. In seizing the oil ports he was supposed to guard, Jadhran claimed the right to sell the oil to outside parties, citing corruption in Tripoli and Zeidan's bias against the east.

There had been sporadic shutdowns of oil facilities in the past, by guards demanding salaries, for instance. But Jadhran's blockade was of a wholly different magnitude: he'd grabbed six hundred thousand barrels of oil in export capacity, or about half of Libya's total. It marked a dangerous new turn: an attempt to ransom the country's economic lifeline. Critics called him a thug and an opportunist, and even easterners who'd complained of Tripoli's neglect blanched at such barefaced extortion.

As oil production plummeted, the embattled prime minister scrambled for options, threatening to break the blockade by force or even bribe Jadhran's militiamen. Lacking an army of his own, he also tried to enlist the Misratan and Zintani militias, which risked plunging the country into internecine war. When he asked the Americans to intervene and bomb Jadhran's forces, they refused, urging him to talk.

The stalemate exposed yet again his government's feebleness—and the fictive sovereignty of the Libyan state. And as the standoff stretched into fall, Ali Zeidan faced more challenges.

On October 5, 2013, U.S. Delta Force commandos, FBI agents,

and CIA officers snatched a wanted Libyan al-Qaeda figure on the streets of Tripoli. Abu Anas al-Libi, the nom de guerre for Nazih Abdul-Hamed Nabih al-Ruqai, had just returned home from dawn prayers when two white minivans blocked his car and gunmen leapt out. The abduction was over in thirty seconds. The forty-nine-year-old al-Libi had long been wanted by the United States for his alleged involvement in the deadly 1998 al-Qaeda attacks on the American embassies in Kenya and Tanzania. The Obama administration hailed the bloodless operation as proof of the long arm of American justice. But in Libya, the incident only added to Zeidan's woes.

Zeidan's opponents quickly seized on al-Libi's abduction as a violation of the country's sovereignty, even if most Libyans I met shrugged it off or even applauded it. Zeidan tried to deflect the criticism. He met with al-Libi's grieving family and assured the press that he had demanded an explanation from the Americans. Zeidan told me the Americans had not informed him of the abduction; a U.S. diplomat told me that indeed they had, though they hadn't specified the exact time and the place—and that the prime minister did not object.

Then, five days later, on October 10, Zeidan was abducted himself. In the predawn hours, gunmen stormed the Corinthia Hotel, where he'd made his residence, and roused the prime minister from bed. Whisking him to a secret location, they demanded money, though in public they claimed to be acting on the authority of the public prosecutor, who denied he'd issued any such order. The militiamen who grabbed him were hard-line Islamists and revolutionaries, some of whom had pushed for the Political Isolation Law. This time, though, they'd miscalculated: the public backlash to their seizure of Zeidan was swift, temporarily lifting his popularity. Released through an intermediary, the prime minister railed at what he saw as a coup.

As Zeidan's situation worsened, the White House tried to redouble its efforts to train the fledgling Libyan military. But the political obstacles in Libya were growing worse, and hopes for the general purpose force soon dimmed, especially after the debacle of recruits in Britain. The Americans' seizure of al-Libi had only intensified domestic opposition to the foreign training program, particularly from the Islamists. Fearing that the Islamists threatened his security, Zeidan moved his living quarters into a building controlled by Zintani armed groups. This only confirmed the growing perception among Islamists and Misratans that Zeidan was siding with the Zintanis and their political allies, the National Forces Alliance.

As Zeidan grew increasingly powerless, Libyans themselves mobilized to curtail the militias' power. On Friday, November 15, two thousand protestors organized by Tripoli's city council gathered in front of a villa complex occupied by Misratan militias in a neighborhood called Gharghur. These militias had long been despised for their mafioso-like abuses, which were said to include secret prisons. What followed was a massacre, leaving forty-eight dead. Misrata militiamen fired first in the air and then at the protestors, spattering blood on white prayer gowns and killing dozens. Some of the survivors went home, changed out of their prayer dress, and returned with weapons.

I was in Tripoli at the time, watching a ribbon of black smoke unfurl against the skyline of a winter's dusk. As the awful thump-thump of antiaircraft guns echoed across the city, I got in a taxi and tried to make my way to the sound of the shooting. A few blocks from the fusillade I encountered a roadblock manned by soldiers and police, who did nothing to stop the violence. I heard the afterburners from a few old MiGs tearing overhead—the government's futile show of force.

For Ali Zeidan, the killings at Gharghur were yet another humiliation. His American patrons couldn't help him; in fact they were hunkered down during the clashes. He appeared on television after the massacre, offering his condolences and admitting that his security forces had not intervened because they were too weak.

But it was in Benghazi, city of the revolution's birth, that Zeidan faced his starkest challenge, the one that would tear the country apart.

∎

THE 2012 ATTACK on the Americans had left Benghazi reeling, and after the exodus of Westerners, it seemed all but forgotten by the world. Yet the tragedy was also the spark for a remarkable protest movement. The following Friday, thousands of Benghazinos marched in the streets demanding the eviction of the militias and the return of the army and police as the guarantors of security. The "Friday of Saving Benghazi," as it was known, was a stunning expression of people power. The death of the Americans, especially Chris Stevens, had been the spark, but its real roots were deeper: the marginalization of the eastern city after the revolution and its growing lawlessness.

Salwa was there along with her son Wail, carrying Libyan flags. "It was so beautiful," Wail remembers. Another cousin marched as well with a sign that read THE PEOPLE DEMAND ACCOUNTABILITY FOR THE KILLERS OF BENGHAZI'S MARTYRS. So too did Iman and Laila. "We were demanding a civil state, not a state of militias," Laila told me.

Tragically, the protest ended in bloodshed when some marchers stormed militia compounds, which was never part of the organizers' plan. Even worse, government officials appeared the next day defending the city's Islamist militias: they were on the government's payroll, they said, and would remain in Benghazi as de facto police. The organizers were crestfallen.

"We couldn't believe our ears," one of them told me after hearing this speech. "How could these militias be legitimate," he asked, "given their behavior?"

For their part, the Islamist militias wondered why they'd been targeted by the demonstrators: after all, they'd protected polling stations during the 2012 elections and had even tried to help the Americans the night of the attack.

Regardless, in the summer that followed the attack, violence rattled the city. Unseen assailants sprayed checkpoints and passersby with automatic weapons or slapped sticky C4 on the bottom of cars. People stopped going out at night. By the winter, scores had died, mostly ex–security men, officers, activists, and judges. Crime and vendettas probably accounted for some of the deaths, but radical Islamists such as Ansar al-Sharia were widely believed to be conducting a systematic campaign. It was hard to say for sure because the weak police never followed up and the culprits went undiscovered and unpunished.

Charged with restoring security in Benghazi, Zeidan had few options. Islamist legislators in the General National Congress favored a strategy of dialogue with the militants, to try to coax them into abandoning violence in favor of politics, arguing that even within groups like Ansar al-Sharia there were hard-liners and moderates. I'd met an Islamist parliamentarian from Benghazi, a former Abu Salim inmate who'd tried to do just this. "Let's try to convince them to be flexible," he told me. But as the killings continued unabated, many in Benghazi scoffed at this approach, seeing it as naïve if not willfully complicit in the violence.

Lacking options, Zeidan tried to work with the seemingly more pragmatic Benghazi militia leaders who drew their salaries from his government and were supposed to follow his orders. But he found them at best unreliable and at worst two-faced in their loyalties. Wissam bin Hamid, the commander of the Libya Shield One, in particular seemed to frustrate him. Previously, his militiamen had cooperated with the Libyan government and with foreigners, lending their support to the American diplomats on the night of the 2012 attack and after to the FBI investigation. But now he seemed to be turning more hard-line, possibly due to the growing influence of his more radical comrades-in-arms.

"He's very naïve," Zeidan told me. "Anybody can program him. We decided on a lot of things and then when time came to do it, he changed his mind."

I'd met bin Hamid one warm night on the patio of Benghazi's Juliana Hotel, its resort-like feel seemed strangely incongruous with the bursts of gunfire that punctured the night. Surrounded by his coterie, he was evasive and often dismissive about cooperating with Zeidan. And in the coming months, many local activists, along with the United Nations, would accuse him of tacitly supporting and even orchestrating the violence that plagued Benghazi.

As the summer unfolded, opposition to him grew. On June 8, 2013, an angry crowd had gathered in front of bin Hamid's Libya Shield base in Benghazi, demanding that his men depart. Many of the demonstrators, some of them armed, belonged to a powerful eastern tribe that laid claim to the land bin Hamid's men occupied and resented what they saw as his overweening presence. Gunfire erupted; when it was all over, thirty-one people had died and dozens were wounded.

In Tripoli, the chief of staff, who'd advocated the Libya Shield program, resigned, and the parliament once again passed a law directing Zeidan to dismantle Benghazi's unlawful militias. But like other decrees, this one would fail as well.

■

THE VIOLENCE CONTINUED. Many in Benghazi had all but given up on Zeidan, holding out instead for a new deliverer. And that summer, events in neighboring Egypt, the most populous Arab state and a bellwether for the region, gave those hopes a boost.

On July 3, the Egyptian army's commanding general, Abd al-Fattah al-Sisi, removed from office Egypt's first democratically elected president, the Muslim Brotherhood leader Muhammad Morsi. The coup drew support from a popular movement that included liberal activists who'd criticized Morsi's autocratic rule—and now approved his removal through a most undemocratic means. A little over a month later, the Egyptian army and security forces killed between eight hundred and one thousand Brotherhood members and supporters who'd staged a sit-in over Morsi's removal. Many Egyptians, including liberals, responded with blithe ambivalence or even approval. It was the worst massacre in Egypt's modern history, and it cast a long shadow over the Arab world, signaling, in retrospect, the end of the Arab Spring.

Its effect in Libya was deeply polarizing. I started hearing Islamists and the revolutionary camp speak darkly of Libya's "deep state"—a term they had not used before. The Egyptian coup would also push some Libyan Islamists to become more reluctant to cede or even share power:

What guarantees did they have that they would not be thrown in jail—or worse? "We thought a door from hell had opened," an Islamist parliamentarian from Benghazi told me.

But for other Libyans, al-Sisi's coup was a boon and a blessing. Libyans who opposed the Islamists suddenly had an exemplar just across the border, a potential ally who could tilt the balance of power in their favor. Many hoped that a similar uniformed savior would come to Libya. "We need a Sisi here," a tribal shaykh had told me that summer. "If it worked in Egypt it will work here."

It was a sentiment I heard from many people in Benghazi who were tired of the ceaseless chaos, who looked to Egypt's military rule as a solution. But it was a flawed parallel. Whereas the Egyptian general had a powerful national army behind him, embedded in Egypt's politics, economy, and society, Libya was a hollow state, bereft of a real army. Still, the hope persisted. And the Egypt-like fractures, between Islamists and their opponents, only widened as security in Benghazi deteriorated.

On Friday, July 26, gunmen in a car fired a bullet into the heart of a well-known activist and lawyer named Abd al-Salam al-Mismari as he walked home from a mosque. Salwa Bugaighis was devastated at the loss of a longtime friend; he'd joined her in the early protests at Benghazi's courthouse in 2011. Like her, he had been a critic of the Islamists—though even more vociferous—and his killing triggered a wave of vigilante attacks on the homes and businesses of suspected Islamists and Brotherhood members. In a vicious cycle, the murder of civilian activists picked up.

"By the second half of 2013 we started worrying," Laila Bugaighis told me. "It wasn't a joke anymore."

The Bugaighis women in Benghazi seemed to be particular targets. Laila and her cousin Salwa started getting ominous phone calls and text messages. "When you ring back the number, it's usually blocked," Laila told me. Threats on Facebook pages accused them of being secularists.

By this time Salwa was the deputy chair of the National Dialogue

Preparatory Commission, a reconciliation body that engaged citizens on politics, development, justice, and security. She was enthusiastic about the work and traveled to dozens of towns across Libya. By many accounts, she was wildly successful and popular, especially among youths. To be sure, security weighed on her, and she avoided certain towns because of the dangers. But she refused to abandon Benghazi, her home.

That winter, her son Wail sat with her in the living room of their house. Salwa had gone on television again and pointed her finger at Ansar al-Sharia after a courthouse bombing. Now her family knew she would be a target.

Wail implored her to leave. "You are just another dead body to them," he told her.

But he already knew her reply.

■

THAT NOVEMBER, I'd flown back straight from Benghazi to Washington, testifying before the Senate Foreign Relations Committee the next day. What I'd seen in the eastern city and in Tripoli weighed on me, as did the pleas of Libyans I'd met. "Public patience with the militias has reached a tipping point," I told the senators assembled before me.

The congressional inquiry into Benghazi was picking up and would reach its full force in the coming year, when Republicans in the House of Representatives would establish the Select Committee, chaired by Congressman Trey Gowdy from South Carolina. In 2014, I testified before a precursor to that committee, the House Committee on Oversight and Government Reform, chaired by Congressmen Darrell Issa, who would later join forces with Gowdy. The hearing was entitled "Benghazi, Instability, and a New Government: Successes and Failures of U.S. Intervention in Libya." I'd hoped to steer the discussion away from partisan politics and back to what to do about Libya's precipitous decline. Yet any mention of Benghazi on the Hill invariably fell back to the night of September 11, 2012, and the administration's response.

It was only the beginning. Over the next two and a half years the Select Committee would spend hundreds of hours, thousands of pages, and millions of dollars investigating the Benghazi attack. This would add to seven other inquiries by Republicans in Congress over the course of four years. None would uncover a "smoking gun" or any evidence of wrongdoing by Secretary of State Hilary Clinton. Toward the broader failings in U.S. policy and preparedness that night, none would add much beyond what the State Department's own internal review had concluded.

What they did accomplish was politicizing a beleaguered country that was in desperate need of assistance.

"The only face of Libya that presented outward was a violent one," Samantha Power recalls. "And the complexity of what was going on behind the scenes, or even who the good guys were that one could turn to, a lot of that knowledge was lost."

Back in Tripoli, American diplomats watched the carnage in Benghazi with dismay and horror. The daily violence was thinning the ranks of their Libyan interlocutors; the FBI director had testified that summer that nearly fifteen Libyans who'd been assisting the Americans in the investigation of the 2012 attack had been killed in the east. Something had to be done.

"We needed to show presence in Benghazi," Ambassador Jones told me, a view shared by the military. "Our [special operations] guys were champing at the bit," she added.

And so in early 2014, she hatched a plan to discreetly ship ammunition to the embattled Libyan Special Forces in Benghazi, commanded by a man named Colonel Wanis Bu Khamada. The Special Forces were among the first military units in Benghazi to defect from Qadhafi's regime in the early days of the 2011 uprising. Now they seemed to be all that stood against the rising chaos, and many Benghazinos looked to Colonel Bu Khamada as their last best hope. "He was the only one fighting extremism," Jones said.

I'd seen Bu Khamada that winter at his base in the farmlands outside Benghazi. By this time, the number of killings had surged, in front of mosques, outside homes, in the streets. Driving there one night, I passed shuttered shops and sandbagged checkpoints manned by his soldiers, rail-thin and jacketed against the chill, warming their hands on charcoal fires. Inside the base, bearded supplicants loitered outside his door: a confusion of camouflaged fatigues and clouds of cigarette smoke.

The fifty-something Bu Khamada has a face etched by years of smoking and a furrowed brow that suggests concentration or preoccupation. He has little interest in politics and is known as more of a negotiator than a commander, getting things done through charisma and tribal clout. He'd used these skills to work with Benghazi's Islamists, cooperating even with radicals such as Ansar al-Sharia on policing the city. It had worked at first, but by the late summer of 2013 it was failing.

Within Ansar al-Sharia and other Islamist militias, uncompromising extremists got the upper hand, while moderate Islamist commanders such as Fawzi Bu Katif and Muhammad al-Gharabi, who supported the government, fled the scene. Increasing acts of vigilantism, often by eastern tribes, drew the Special Forces into conflict with the Islamists. By the fall of 2013, Benghazi had fallen into open street battles between Ansar al-Sharia and the Special Forces.

Terrified residents threw their support behind Bu Khamada even more, but the colonel and his men were outgunned, lacking armored vehicles and running short on ammunition and funds. He pleaded with Zeidan's government for help and railed against parliamentarians in Tripoli, whom he accused of funding the Islamists while ignoring the army.

Enter Ambassador Jones. She thought she'd found help for Colonel Bu Khamada's Special Forces through a third party, what she calls a "sympathetic Gulf country" with which she had excellent relations from a previous diplomatic posting. This country's government agreed to supply Bu Khamada with ammunition, but only if its involvement was undisclosed, to which Jones agreed, offering up an American plane to fly the matériel into Benghazi's Banina Airport. But the Pentagon's lawyers killed the proposal because under the terms of the UN arms embargo, the sources of any arms shipments into Libya had to be declared.

It was yet another failure to avert the city's descent, though at least one Pentagon official I met was skeptical that Jones's plan would have had any impact in curtailing the violence.

"Does Benghazi really need more 7.62 ammunition?" He shrugged. But if the Americans couldn't save Benghazi, who would?

9

"THIS IS DIGNITY"

GENERAL KHALIFA HIFTAR SEEMED CONFIDENT when I went to see him one day in June 2014.

Three years after his failed bid to lead the Libyan revolution, he was back on the scene. Demonstrators throughout the country cheered him as a hero, and his visage appeared on newspaper pages and television screens across the region and the globe. Foreign patrons would soon ply him with weapons. It was by any measure a remarkable turnaround for the septuagenarian officer whom many in Libya had only months before written off as an also-ran.

But he had good reasons to be paranoid. Weeks earlier, a car laden with explosives had crashed into a villa outside Benghazi where he was holding a meeting, killing three of his soldiers. It was hardly the first attempt on his life. So when I went to see him, I expected tight security.

Hiftar had set up the field command for his self-styled Libyan National Army in the farm country east of Benghazi, where the terra rosa soil nourishes tracts of barley and almond trees. Entering an old army base, I passed a derelict helicopter leaning oddly to one side. Inside, bodyguards with bull-pup assault rifles escorted me through a scanner and an invasive pat-down. They asked me to leave my belt and my shoes behind while I conducted the interview. "That's total Qadhafi-style," a Libyan friend later joked when I told him of the security gauntlet. He meant it in more ways than one, I would learn.

Then, just before they ushered me in to see the general, they decided to take away my pen and notepad, handing me instead a few sheets of paper and a pencil.

■

I'D NOT HEARD anything from General Hiftar since late 2011 and early 2012 when he'd suffered a string of embarrassing setbacks. He'd tried to have himself appointed as the chief of staff and later minister of defense but been rejected. His men had raided a Tripoli hotel used by the NTC, searching for millions of dinars supposedly stashed away by Qadhafi. They fought gun battles with Zintani militias near the airport, and his oldest son, Saddam, had been wounded in the leg during a bank melee. When it was all over, Hiftar was run out of town and all but disappeared from view.

Then, on February 14, 2014, he surfaced. Dressed in his army uniform, he appeared on television announcing the suspension of the elected parliament, the General National Congress. He called on Libyans to come out and support him, but they didn't, shrugging off his stunt as an "electronic coup" or the "coup that wasn't." How could you mount a coup, they wondered, when you didn't have an army? It seemed yet another failed bid by the aging general.

But Hiftar wasn't finished.

Far from exiting the stage, Hiftar started quietly building support, tapping into multiple grievances, the most potent of which were anti-Islamist sentiment, eastern feelings of exclusion, and the desire for security in chaotic Benghazi. In early 2014, he started recruiting fellow army officers, and then he went to the eastern tribes, especially the poorer tribes that ringed Benghazi, whose sons had staffed Qadhafi's security services. One evening, in a floodlit tent near the sea, he stood before an assembly of their shaykhs, telling them he wanted to liberate Cyrenaica from terrorism.

"I want you to join me because the army and police are being killed," he proclaimed, according to an attendee. The shaykhs assented and gave him money, arms, and vehicles.

On May 16, 2014, he moved again into the spotlight, but this time he would not be shunted aside. With little more than two hundred fighters, backed by a few old jets, Hiftar attacked the bases of Benghazi's militias—not just the radicals like Ansar al-Sharia, but pro-state militias like the Libya Shield and the February 17 Brigade. "Operation Dignity," he called it the next day on television. He spoke in mumbled, solemn tones about his duty to the nation, about cleansing Benghazi of terrorism. The fighting that ensued was the fiercest the city had witnessed since the 2011 revolution.

Back in Tripoli, military officials decried the operation as illegal and unsanctioned. No matter; Hiftar believed he had a mandate from the people and accused the government in Tripoli of being part of the problem. The GNC, or parliament, was a particular target of his ire: it was supporting the Islamist militias, he said, and had overstayed its term. His Operation Dignity, then, was intended to force its dissolution and hasten the convening of a new legislature, one where the Islamists would be marginalized.

In this goal, Hiftar enjoyed the support of a popular protest movement against the GNC's extension of its mandate. Dubbed "No Extension," it was backed by the National Forces Alliance, many of whose members now supported Hiftar. Added to this, Hiftar's allies in the capital used military force against the parliament. Two days after the start of Operation Dignity, Zintani militias who'd put aside their differences with Hiftar shelled the convention center where the Congress held its sessions.

In the coming weeks and months, eastern military units would join Hiftar's Libyan National Army in waging Operation Dignity, the most important of which was Colonel Wanis Bu Khamada's "Thunderbolt" Special Forces. Like Hiftar, officers in these units resented the power of the militias, who enjoyed privileges denied to what they saw as the "legitimate" military. The federalists backed him too, hoping that his campaign might presage greater autonomy for the east. In the west, the Zintani militias, longtime foes of the Islamists, joined, along with a western tribe that had enjoyed Qadhafi's favors. From abroad, a wealthy tycoon with links to the former regime pumped in money and beamed in flattering coverage of Hiftar on his satellite media channel.

Then there were Libyan politicians, namely those who had been shunted aside after the Political Isolation Law, like Mahmud Jibril. Some came to his side uneasily and after first opposing him, most notably, the prime minister, Ali Zeidan.

Zeidan had publicly denounced Hiftar's February coup attempt as "ridiculous," but later hoped that the rising general would save him from his opponents. But Dignity arrived too late. On March 10, 2014, the oil blockader Ibrahim Jadhran finally made good on his threat to sell oil to outside parties. That day, a North Korean–flagged tanker, *Morning Glory*, departed the port of Sidra with more than 230,000 barrels of crude. A team of U.S. Navy Seals swooped in on the vessel off the coast of Cyprus, handing it over to Libyan sailors who steered it back to shore. It proved a fatal blow to the beleaguered Zeidan. The next day, he fled Libya for Germany after the GNC had threatened him with an investigation into "financial irregularities."

In the end, the line that divided those who supported Operation Dignity and those who didn't wasn't really about ideology, though anti-Islamist sentiment certainly contributed to the movement. Instead, it was about how much of the old order to preserve and how much to discard. In this sense, it reflected fissures that had been present in the Libyan revolution from the very start, going back to the killing of Abd al-Fattah Younis. It also signified the failure of consensual politics. Sadly, this wasn't surprising for a place that had known only repression and one-man rule.

"Now we've got thousands of Qadhafis," a Libyan friend lamented, "rather than only one."

■

SIX DAYS AFTER Dignity started that May, a friend in Benghazi emailed me.

"I'm fine but I'm not sure until when," he wrote. "Killing, kidnapping, random shooting and slaughtering every day! But we as Benghazi residents support our national army . . . and Major General Khalifa Hiftar and his Operation Dignity."

Some of Hiftar's earliest supporters were Libyans in Benghazi who were sick of the grinding violence. Throughout the first half of 2014, the number of killings had risen—and not just security men and military officers, but civic activists and journalists, many of whom now backed the general, albeit uneasily. They wrestled with the implications of supporting a man who promised to restore security but who'd also threatened elected institutions.

One of them was Salwa Bugaighis.

The worsening violence in Benghazi vexed her, and her outspokenness had resulted in several death threats. In January 2014, these threats finally forced her to leave the city of her birth, moving to Tripoli. But the family who remained was still at risk. That summer, her eldest son, Wail, had narrowly survived an ambush by gunmen near their house. Fleeing to a police station for help, he was met with a disheartening response. "Look, we can't even protect ourselves," the officers told him.

Fearing for his life and that of her other two sons, Salwa took them that month to live in Jordan. While sitting in an Amman hotel room, she got a phone call and burst into tears. Yet another activist had been assassinated, a newspaper editor named Miftah Bu Zaid, who'd been one of her closest friends and who'd protested with her at Benghazi's courthouse on February 17. Would any of them from those heady days still remain? she wondered.

She came back to Libya from Jordan in late June to gather her belongings from her house in Benghazi before moving permanently to Amman. More important, though, she returned to vote on June 25, for the follow-on legislature to the GNC, known as the House of Representatives (HOR). Friends begged her not to; couldn't she vote from Jordan? they asked. She returned anyway, stopping first in Tripoli, where I met her two days before the elections.

I sat waiting for her in the lobby of the Radisson Blu hotel with one of her colleagues and friends, a California-educated entrepreneur named Tamim Baïou, who worked with her on the Libyan National Dialogue. When Salwa entered, she strode through the security scanner unveiled, wearing a tailored coat, an open-collar lavender blouse, and heels. The Radisson then was under the control of Islamist militias who brought their morality with them: a sign at the entrance forbade unmarried male and female guests to share a room. The bearded guards with rifles eyed her warily.

"If these Islamists say they want to protect the state," she told me over coffee, "they need to protect state institutions." And especially, she added, they should protect civil society. She lamented the shrinking role for activists and for secularists. Why, she asked, was America inflating the role of Islamists like the Tripoli militia leader Abd al-Hakim Belhaj?

"If he didn't have Mitiga [Airport] and Qatar, he would be nobody," she exclaimed.

We came to the topic of Khalifa Hiftar.

For all of his faults, she said, Hiftar had "shattered the taboo of calling out the extremists by name.

"He's allowed a venue for secular and democratic voices to come out," she continued. And since we can't stop him, she argued, we should try to bring him into the fold, to give him legitimacy. She asked that the United States help his Libyan National Army with intelligence.

"The U.S. needs to align with the right actors," she said.

Hiftar's war divided Salwa and her relatives—as it divided many families. Iman, the orthodontist who'd retired from the limelight, was suspicious of his aims from the beginning, while a cousin backed him with enthusiasm. Salwa seemed torn, at least initially.

"She knew him very well. She knew his motives," Iman told me. "But she was very scared about the domination of the extremists in Benghazi. So we had this debate: Okay, who is more dangerous?"

Tamim, Salwa's colleague, agreed.

"She was frustrated," he told me. "We all were. And sometimes you have to pick the lesser of two evils, whatever that may be."

■

THE DAY OF THE ELECTIONS, I flew east into Bayda, where Hiftar's men met me on the runway and escorted me to my hotel. Around midnight I awoke to a telephone ring.

It was Tamim, asking whether I was okay. He paused.

"Salwa's been murdered," he said.

"She's been killed in her home," he continued. "In Benghazi."

Tamim now was worried for me. I mumbled some appreciation and assured him I'd take care.

I was sleepless for much of that night. Salwa had seemed such an immutable fixture of Libya when she'd walked through the lobby that day, defiant and different from many Libyans I'd met. Though I'd hardly known her I could sense the inspiration she must've provided. And now she was gone.

In the days before the voting, Tamim and others had tried again to dissuade her from going to Benghazi. Her son Wail did as well, and she'd agreed, not wanting to worry him. "But I'd forgotten about the elections," he later told me. At Tamim's urging, she agreed to use her brother's bodyguard during her time in Benghazi, to keep a low profile and avoid media.

She phoned Tamim from Benghazi the day of the elections. "Don't worry, everything's fine," she said. He could hear the nearby voices of her security escort.

Later that day, she posted a photo on Facebook of herself after voting. She called Wail in Jordan; he remembers seeing her father's number, a Benghazi number, and being furious with her. Go vote, she told him. Before sunset, she climbed to the balcony of her house and posted another photo of smoke rising from clashes. In a phone interview with a television station she beseeched her fellow citizens: the polls are closing soon, don't be deterred by the fighting.

Salwa was on the phone with her sister, Iman, when she heard the voices of men outside. Her husband went downstairs to speak with them. "I'll call you back," she told Iman.

Later that night across town, Salwa's cousin Laila Bugaighis—the doctor who'd been on call the night of Chris Stevens's death—had finished work at the Benghazi Medical Center. It had been a busy day of treating casualties from the fighting, which had flared despite a ceasefire. As she was leaving around nine forty-five, her cell phone rang.

"Have you left yet?" the doctor on the other end said. "Come to the ER."

There were nearly twenty gunshots in total on Salwa's body and a massive bludgeon wound to her head: this was no ordinary break-in but an act of brutal malice. The gunmen also kidnapped her husband, who would never be heard from again. Her son Wail heard about his mother's death that night and tried dialing his father's cell number, only to get ringing and then silence. "I thought the battery had just died," he said.

There would be no investigation or justice for the culprits. I read the police report: it was a jumble of contradictory and inconclusive testimonies, much of it reportedly coerced. The Egyptian guard who was working at Salwa's house was shot in the leg. The only witness, he would later die in police custody after confessing his complicity. The other attackers would never be brought to justice.

Salwa's death was an earthquake, rippling across a city and a country already exhausted by violence. No one felt safe after that, especially women: Salwa's sister, Iman, got threats and left the city, while Laila stopped traveling to the hospital and worked from home.

Seven months later, though, she too would leave, just before dawn, after being told she was "on a list."

"I didn't even pack," she said.

■

SALWA'S MURDER was also a boon to Hiftar and his iron-fisted approach toward the Islamists in Benghazi, putting an end to calls for dialogue. The general redoubled his pledge to wipe out the militants, but more important to bring order to people's lives. This was what he believed they really craved.

The morning after Salwa's death, a security man collected me from my hotel. We drove down a narrow road toward Hiftar's military base, cutting through coppery fields hemmed by thistle. My escort looked down at my seat belt and urged me to fasten it—the first time this had happened in all my travels in Libya.

"This," he said, pointing to the seat belt, "is Dignity. After Dignity we will have a *system.*"

■

KHALIFA HIFTAR is a tall, mustachioed man with fleshy jowls and a dimpled chin. Receding white hair sweeps back and to the side; the hooded eyes are not unalert but suggest weariness. Taken as a whole, it is a rumpled face. He wore a crisp beige tunic, untucked and festooned with gold-trimmed epaulets. We sat on a couch in his office.

He began by thanking me for my visit. I was the first American he'd received since he started his operation, he said, and he pressed me for American support. "Apaches, drones, C-130s," he said. He asserted that he was fighting America's foes, so America should help him.

But America's stance on Hiftar at the time seemed ambivalent, and in the coming months American policy makers would wrestle with how to respond to his rise. By 2014, the White House was still hoping to stabilize Libya and especially to remove the legacy of Benghazi as an issue in the 2016 presidential campaign. Here was a man who perhaps could do that.

"What about General Hiftar?" I later asked the White House senior director for counterterrorism at the time, a Yale-trained lawyer named Joshua Geltzer.

"Well, it's one of those grudging things," he said, after he'd left government. "You look at him and you say, 'Well, he is keeping some bad guys at bay,' though at times with what seemed to be great brutality. But I am not sure we ever fully figured out a long-term answer to that question."

Hiftar divided U.S. government agencies. Those charged with defeating terrorists, the Central Intelligence Agency and the Defense Department, especially the special operations community, saw utility in his campaign against extremists. A retired member of Delta Force, the military's elite and secretive counterterrorism branch, told me that his former colleagues had expressed "relief" at the start of Dignity.

On the other hand, the State Department, which focused on the political task of building the Libyan state and reconciling its opposing factions, took a dimmer view. This was, after all, an unsanctioned operation that further divided the already shattered country. Even so, there were early hints that diplomats welcomed the chance to strike at extremists who'd killed their colleagues.

"I am not going to come out and condemn blanketly what he did," Ambassador Deborah Jones told a think-tank conference in D.C. in May 2014. After all, she said, the general was "going after very specific groups . . . on our list of terrorists."

One of those terrorists, in fact, was America's principal suspect in the 2012 Benghazi attack, Ahmed Abu Khattala. The towering militant had continued to move across the city after the attack with the support of sympathizers and Islamist militias. "He walked freely between his house and his mosque and nobody could touch him," a friend from his neighborhood told me. But that didn't last. After the Americans snatched al-Libi, he started getting nervous, a witness would testify, and would later join forces with Wissam bin Hamid in fighting Hiftar.

Then, just after midnight on June 15, American special operators landed by helicopter on the southwest edge of Benghazi and seized Abu Khattala. Code-naming him Greenbrier River, the abduction was in many respects a textbook raid: one of his confidants, who was secretly working for the Americans and had spent months ingratiating himself with the militant, had lured him to the coastal villa on the pretext of finding a haven from General Hiftar's forces. The waiting Americans overpowered Abu Khattala after a brief struggle, leaving him with gashes and bruises, and ferried him to a U.S. naval ship off the coast. On the trip home, the Americans would interrogate him for thirteen days without access to lawyers—a detention criticized by his defense lawyers and human rights groups.

Three years later, the jury in a Washington, D.C., district court would find him guilty of providing material support to terrorism and three other charges, while declaring him not guilty for the remaining fourteen, including the murder of the four Americans. The outcome was a disappointment for many, but it reflected the jurors' doubts about the motivation of the prosecution's three Libyan witnesses. One of those witnesses was a commander allied with General Hiftar's Dignity campaign, whom U.S. prosecutors had deposed in Cairo. A tribal militia leader named Salah Bu Lighib, he had earned notoriety for his social media posts endorsing battlefield brutality against Islamists, which undermined his credibility in the trial.

When I'd sat with him that day in June, Hiftar was adamant that he was fighting the murderers of Americans. But the lines were hardly clear-cut: several of the Benghazi militiamen who'd helped the Americans on the night of the attack, men from the February 17 Brigade and the

Libya Shield, were among those targeted by his Dignity operation. I wondered if he distinguished between these groups and the truly extremist jihadists.

"Do you see any hope for reconciling with the Islamist militias in Benghazi?" I asked. "Are there some, less radical ones that might be brought in?"

He shook his head.

"There are three options for them," he said. "In prison, under the ground, or out of the country."

Already, he continued, they had violated a cease-fire he had declared to observe the elections, and Salwa's murder the night before was further proof of their perfidy.

His contempt extended beyond armed groups to Islamists of all stripes.

"We don't need *sharia* here," he said, tracing with his fingers the outline of a beard. "It's in our hearts already."

All of this—the messianic vision, the visceral dislike of Islamists, and the reverence for the uniform—had a precedence in Libya's neighbor to the east. Indeed, Hiftar's speeches bore a strong similarity to those of Egypt's strongman, General Abd al-Fattah al-Sisi, who had recently been elected president. I asked him whether the Egyptians were supporting him militarily, and he replied he'd not yet asked them. In the coming weeks and months he would receive Egyptian arms, matériel, and advisors.

An attendant walked in with a platter of sandwiches—tuna, chicken, and cheese. Hiftar beckoned me to eat, pinching one of them carefully to avoid soiling the sleeve of his uniform.

"How long will this last?" I asked.

"That depends," he said, "on how much help we get. The Russians and Chinese have offered to help us, but we are waiting for America."

It was classic bargaining, lifted straight from the Cold War. In the coming months, Russia would in fact repair his aging fleet and supply him with newer aircraft. And that was just the start.

"After we control Benghazi, we'll move our military forces to Tripoli. There's al-Qaeda in Tripoli, after all," he said.

He certainly did not lack for military allies there. Among the most important were the Zintani armed groups inside the capital, the most powerful of which was led by the caterer turned militia chief Uthman Mleqta, whom I'd met years before. Mleqta and the Zintani militias had threatened the General National Congress before and shared the general's dim view of the political Islamists—especially those from their rival, the city of Misrata.

Moreover, they controlled Tripoli International Airport, the most strategic asset in the city and a gateway for Hiftar's forces to invade western Libya. During the spring and early summer, the weapons flowed through the airport into Zintani hands, much of it from the United Arab Emirates. In parades, the Zintanis showed off fighting vehicles, assault rifles, and even new uniforms. The balance of power in the capital was clearly tipping in their favor. And now Hiftar himself was threatening to invade.

But then the Misratans acted first.

PART III

COLLAPSE

CIVIL WAR

ON THE MORNING OF JULY 13, 2014, a small force of Misratan fighters, along with militiamen from Tripoli and other western towns, launched a surprise attack on Zintani positions at Tripoli International Airport. The salvos sent passengers in the waiting hall scrambling for safety and crippled Libya's passenger fleet parked on the tarmac. Pressing their attack on nearby Zintani armories and bases, the attacking coalition termed the operation "Libya Dawn," a direct counterpoint to Hiftar's Operation Dignity. The conflict in Benghazi had reached the capital; Libya was now in a state of civil war.

The man leading the assault was a Misratan militia leader and parliamentarian named Salah Badi. A fifty-eight-year-old former air force fighter pilot, he had resigned in protest over Qadhafi's war in Chad and

spent time in prison. During the revolution, he won plaudits for brav-
ery as a commander, and after he never stopped fighting. As a parliamentarian, he spearheaded Misrata's punitive attack on Bani Walid
and had pushed for the Political Isolation Law. Libyans have a word
for such a person: *thawriji*, a diehard, someone who loves revolution
for revolution's sake, while others took more lighthearted jabs. "We
called him the frying pan," said a fellow Misratan, "because he's facing
fire on many sides."

A balding, thickly built man with a heavy brow and broad lips,
Badi looks the part of the stubborn pugilist. Justifying his attack, he
complained to me about the Zintanis' accumulation of power in Tripoli
through their control of the airport and other key sites. The airport, in
particular, was a concern, especially now that the Zintanis had allied
themselves with Hiftar: he claimed to have intelligence on the specific
date when Hiftar and the Zintanis planned to attack Tripoli.

"They are bringing in everything they need through the airport,"
Badi explained. "Weapons, people, drugs. And now war." His move on
the airport, he explained, was aimed at forestalling what he said was an
impending coup.

There were other reasons as well. Losses on the political front
added to the Misratans' and Islamists' alarm over the Zintanis' military
buildup. Across the country, in the June 25 elections for the House of
Representatives, Misratan, Islamist, and revolutionary factions suffered
losses to figures affiliated with the National Forces Alliance. Many of
the Islamists now worried that the new parliament would undercut
their influence, reverse the Political Isolation Law, and divert funds
away from their militias. Some even feared for their lives. The Islamists
wanted guarantees and assurances that they would not meet the same
fate as the Muslim Brotherhood in Egypt—imprisonment or worse.

"Right now," one of them told me, "the only realistic guarantee is
a gun."

American, British, and United Nations diplomats had tried to
avert a showdown, proposing to Zintanis and Misratans a plan for a
face-saving compromise that would include the Islamists. But the mili-

tias and their political backers on both sides seemed set on conflict. During one UN-brokered meeting, Zintani militia commanders stormed out theatrically, announcing their intention to die as martyrs. In Misrata, moderate figures tried in vain to rein in Salah Badi: Salim Joha traveled back to Misrata from the United Arab Emirates and pleaded with the militia chiefs to compromise, but they would have none of it. For too long, they said, they'd watched Zintanis get stronger in the capital, noting with alarm provocations like the shelling of the GNC. Now, with Hiftar's threat to invade Tripoli, they sensed a window closing. Misrata was ready for war.

"You had two choices back then," Joha told me. "To fight or to be called a traitor. And from that day I was a traitor."

Failing to talk down the hard-liners, he fled Misrata in the middle of the night, an undignified exit for a man who'd once been hailed a wartime hero and who'd pushed for magnanimity after the revolution. Soon after, someone broke into his house and scrawled on his door, "Salim Joha the Traitor."

They even destroyed his library.

■

AS THE FIGHTING in Tripoli continued, the Americans hunkered down. The embassy villa complex sat in the middle of Zintani-held territory, right in the cross fire. Rounds arced over the compound; airbursts rained down shrapnel, clinking on the roof. Grad rockets were the worst: inaccurate missiles made even more unpredictable by improper storage and unskilled gunners. The marines and Libyan security guards rushed indoors for shelter.

"It's not worth losing even a finger over this bullshit," Ambassador Jones thought to herself.

The United Nations had pulled out its staff as soon as the clashes started. Now, in mid-July, she decided it was time to leave as well. But the options were few and far between: Tripoli International Airport lay in ruins, and there were no operational seaports. The Pentagon had proposed using Ospreys for evacuation, tilt-rotor transport aircraft that can take off and land vertically, but Jones was leery of their record of mishaps. Moreover, their limited passenger capacity would require a large number of planes to ferry out the Americans, increasing the vulnerability to ground fire.

The remaining option was a 250-mile land route to the Tunisian border. But that meant navigating a patchwork of militias, some with questionable, if not outright hostile, views toward America. The United Nations had already made the dangerous trek in two separate convoys just after the fighting erupted. At a checkpoint near the western town of Sabratha, known for its jihadist sympathies, masked men walked methodically down the line of UN vehicles, asking the drivers, "Are there any Americans here?"

The preparations started. Diplomats and marines took sledgehammers to classified computer drives and burned documents in the empty swimming pool: "the bonfire of the vanities," Jones called it. She directed the diplomats to pack only one piece of luggage, though they noted wryly that Jones did not follow the rule herself.

Finally, early on the morning of July 26, at around three forty-five, the embassy team and the CIA annex departed in thirty-nine vehicles. It was the holy month of Ramadan, and across the capital the militias had just woken up, lighting their butane stoves to cook the Suhoor meal before starting their fast at sunrise. The fighting all but ceased in those predawn hours, giving the Americans a vital interval of safety.

As they threaded their way across Tripoli, through the Nafusa Mountains, and onward to Tunisia, F-16 fighter jets and drones loitered overhead. Planeloads of armed marines in Ospreys followed the convoy as well, ready to touch down if the Americans encountered trouble. Crossing the border at noon, they departed Tunisia in a C-17 the next day, and when they landed in Italy, Jones poured the diplomats glasses of Veuve Clicquot champagne from bottles she'd stuffed in her extra luggage.

In the coming months, the remaining Western embassies would

depart. With its airports destroyed or inoperative and foreigners gone, the country's isolation was now complete. Libyans were incredulous.

"Even Mogadishu has an airport," a friend told me. "It's easier to get there than Tripoli."

■

AS THE FIGHTING RAGED, the country split into two.

On August 4, the newly elected House of Representatives relocated to the far eastern city of Tobruk, installing its own cabinet and prime minister in the town of Bayda. It branded Libya Dawn an outlawed terrorist group, and in the months that followed, it would ally itself with Hiftar and his Libyan National Army, eventually appointing him general commander. Its prime minister would order Hiftar to "liberate" Tripoli. But in the meantime in Tripoli, Libya Dawn had set up its own government.

Since its attack on the capital's airport, Libya Dawn had expanded into an amalgam of militias from the city of Misrata, which provided the bulk of the firepower, western towns such as Zawiya and Gharyan, Imazighen communities, certain Tripoli neighborhoods, the Muslim Brotherhood, and former Libyan Islamic Fighting Group figures. Not all were Islamists, contrary to common media depictions. What held them together was their opposition to Hiftar's Dignity operation and sympathy with the Benghazi militias he was fighting. More broadly, though, they claimed to be more "revolutionary" in outlook, meaning they sought the complete remaking of Libya's political order and security institutions. These were the same revolutionary impulses that drove the 2013 passage of the Political Isolation Law; the fissures from that episode had never closed and had now burst open.

In Tripoli, Libya Dawn reconvened the General National Congress and installed its own political authority, the National Salvation Government, opposed to Hiftar and the Tobruk House of Representatives. This meant Libya now had two rival governments, two parliaments, and two constellations of loosely loyal militias. Even Libyan embassies abroad were split. Foreign journalists had to get two different visas and two separate media passes. Traveling between Tripoli and the east was akin to crossing the borders of two countries at war. It was not uncommon to be interrogated as a spy for the other side upon arrival.

Making matters worse, Middle Eastern states intervened.

On August 18, shortly after midnight, airstrikes hit the positions of Dawn fighters in Tripoli, followed five days later by another, this time before sunrise. The strikes were far more precise than anyone had seen in the battle for the capital, killing more than twenty fighters, mostly from Misrata. General Hiftar quickly claimed responsibility, but many were suspicious: the bombing was too accurate for the old Russian jets in his fleet, and they lacked the ability to fly at night.

And then, the mystery was solved.

From the craters of their camp, Dawn fighters recovered fragments of an advanced, laser-guided weapon—a fin-kit with American factory markings. The Americans denied involvement, pointing instead to an Arab ally: the United Arab Emirates.

The Emiratis had meddled militarily in Libya during and after the revolution, but not like this. This was, above all, an impressive feat of airmanship and logistics. They'd flown their jets, Mirage 2000s, from a base in western Egypt, fueling somewhere along the 770-mile route to Tripoli, most likely over the Mediterranean from a French-made Airbus tanker. The Pentagon had long trained and equipped the Emirati air force to become more autonomous, but this wasn't what it had in mind. This was brazen interference that worsened a civil war. The Americans had detected the Emiratis' preparations for the strike, officials said, and tried without success to warn them off.

Libya was now a theater in a bigger proxy war between two competing poles in the Middle East.

On one side, backing Hiftar's forces, were the Emiratis and the Egyptians, with some Saudi and Jordanian support. The Emirates and Saudi Arabia in particular had supported General al-Sisi's toppling of the Egyptian Muslim Brotherhood back in the summer of 2013 and had since sustained his rule as president through massive subsidies. Now they saw a burgeoning Islamist threat in Libya, on Egypt's western doorstep. Hiftar was a natural partner for them.

In addition, Egypt had a number of real security concerns regarding Libya. The shared border between the two countries had always been porous, even under Qadhafi, and since the Libyan revolution it had grown more so. Illicit goods and weapons flowed across as well as Islamist militants. Al-Sisi believed that Egypt's own Islamist militants in the Sinai were using Libya for training and logistics, and while there is evidence to support the idea, it is likely that the Egyptian ruler was exaggerating the extent of that support.

Al-Sisi started a pipeline of military aid to Hiftar: Mi-8 helicopters with the Egyptian flag clumsily painted over, MiG-21 fighters, small-arms ammunition, and light weapons. Hiftar's sons supervised the transfers from Egypt and from other foreign suppliers. Then Egypt itself intervened: Egyptian warplanes flew reconnaissance and strike missions, and Egyptian troops joined an Emirati commando team in destroying an Islamist militant camp outside Derna.

On the other side, backing the Dawn forces with money and weapons, was Qatar, which worked through Turkey and Sudan for logistics. Qatar channeled funds to Misrata and Sudanese aircraft flew arms into Tripoli's Mitiga Airport or smuggled them through the southern desert, following old caravan routes. Yet the extent of Qatar's involvement was not a great as the Emirates' and Egypt's.

All of this meddling infuriated international diplomats who were trying to resolve the conflict. "The Emirates and Qatar were really awful," a UN official told me. "They didn't give a damn about Libya, they were always worried that the other would come out on top."

The arms shipments from all sides breached the UN arms embargo on Libya and the airstrikes violated the still-in-effect no-fly zone. Noting the offenses, the UN sent letters and teams of investigators to demand an explanation but in nearly every case received nonresponses, denials, or evasions. "I think we should be slightly careful in replying to the [UN] Libya Panel," read one leaked email between Emirati Foreign Ministry officials in August 2015. "The fact of the matter is that the UAE violated the UN Security Council resolution on Libya and continues to do so."

The regional proxy war in Libya was the clearest evidence yet of the failure of Western and international plans for postrevolution Libya. The country had collapsed, and regional states had stepped in, each trying to bend its destiny to its will. It was part of a broader trend among the Gulf Arab states, of an increasingly muscular foreign policy, not just in Libya but also toward Egypt and Iran and in Syria and Yemen. Their aggressive stance, critics said, was the result of America's hands-off policy toward the failing states of the post–Arab Spring and its dismissive attitude toward the security concerns of its Gulf Arab allies.

But it also stemmed from differing prescriptions for the region's ills. The Obama administration believed that inclusivity and political openness would diminish the dark forces of sectarian strife and radicalism. No, the authoritarians of the Emirates and Saudi Arabia, along with Egypt, responded. What was needed was a tighter ruling grip and a healthy dose of Islamic orthodoxy for the wayward youth who'd been led astray by terrorists—and by the Brotherhood, which they considered one and the same. This is not to say that their opponents Qatar and Turkey were pushing liberal democracy across the region: they had their own self-interested motives as well, ones that were better served by promoting the inclusion of Islamists.

Whatever the case, Gulf intervention ruined the lives of even innocent Libyans. And not just in Libya.

Shortly after the airstrikes in Tripoli, Emirati security forces rounded up ten Libyans who'd been living and working in the UAE, some for as long as ten years and some with dual Libyan and Canadian or American citizenship. There was never a court warrant and the Emiratis publicly denied holding many of them, admitting to detaining only four. Two Libyan Americans, a father and a son, were formally charged with supporting the Brotherhood, which by late 2014 the Emirates had listed as a terrorist organization. They would remain in prison for a total of twenty-one months, enduring bouts of torture before they were finally acquitted.

■

IN EARLY 2015, I returned to Tripoli. By this time, the Zintanis had withdrawn from the airport back to the mountains. But whatever victory the Dawn forces could claim was a Pyrrhic one.

The fighting in the capital had been indiscriminate and costly, waged with rockets, mortars, and even air-launched missiles that hit homes and hospitals. The UN reported that the clashes had displaced more than a hundred thousand. Retribution, disappearances, and vigilantism were rampant; anyone affiliated with Dignity or sympathetic to its factions was at risk. Dawn militias looted the Tripoli homes of eighty families of Zintani origin and vandalized the studios of a television station favorable to Dignity, briefly kidnapping its chairman. They attacked a camp of displaced Tawerghans, longtime objects of Misratan enmity. Car bombs hit the Emirati and Egyptian embassies.

Driving through Tripoli in those days, I spotted a new fashion that had taken hold: masked gunmen manning a checkpoint. Abd al-Rauf Kara's militia had started the balaclava trend, and now, friends said, it was chic. The city and its approaches were dotted with gunmen, and passing through the sieve was fraught with risk. In the Libyan vernacular, they were called somewhat sarcastically *ashaws*, translated loosely as "tough guys," though many thought them little more than posers.

The neighborhoods they guarded went for hours without electricity. I saw people waiting in long lines for gas and scavenging for wood as fuel. Schools had emptied, and hospitals faced dire shortages of medicine.

Still, in parts of the city people carried on, gathering at cafés for a morning brioche and latte, marrying, and, if they were wealthy, shopping at the Mango outlet on Gargaresh Road. One night, I watched a tracksuited man jog around a weedy field while Ferris wheel lights spun in the distance.

Some Libyans I met feared that an invasion of Tripoli by Hiftar was only a matter of time, while others secretly welcomed it. Yet as time wore on, even those in the capital who opposed Hiftar and his Dignity campaign started to tire of having the Misratan militias back in the city, especially after the chaos they'd sown with their attack on the airport—not to mention the Gharghur massacre the year before.

The old epithets reappeared. *Shiraksa*, they called the Misratans, meaning Circassians, non-Arabs—a label that referred to some of the town's inhabitants' Ottoman-era roots in the Caucuses. Others jabbed at them as *Mazarit*, "those who ruin things," a grammatical play on the Arabic plural form of Misratan. Some people stopped shopping at Misratan-owned stores.

The Misratans and their militia allies didn't stop fighting even after the Zintanis left the airport. They fired onto the homes of a pro-Dignity tribe to the west and south of Tripoli, forcing thousands to evacuate. In late September, they pushed farther south, besieging an air base controlled by the Zintanis. And then, they went for the oil.

That December, Misrata-led forces under Libya Dawn attacked the oil terminals at Ras Lanuf and Sidra, intending to wrest them from the militia commander Ibrahim Jadhran, who'd by now allied himself with Hiftar. The facilities accounted for over half of Libya's oil production, and the Misratans and their allies in Tripoli wanted control. They worried that the east was trying to set up its own versions of the National Oil Corporation and the Central Bank of Libya to sell the oil and disperse its revenue.

In the weeks that followed, the fighting slowed to a steady exchange of artillery. Neither side advanced. On December 25, the oil tanks caught fire, igniting an inferno that burned for nine days. Heroic firefighting finally extinguished the blaze, but not before it had destroyed 1.8 million barrels of crude. Each side blamed the other for the rocket attack that had started it.

The following February, I traveled to the Dawn-held front.

■

THE FIRST ARTILLERY ROUNDS landed just as the setting sun threw shadows on the empty stretch of coast. Dark puffs of smoke blossomed from the pale sand. Atop an earthen berm, a young fighter in an oversize flak vest peered through a periscope, while below, men in ski caps huddled near antiaircraft guns. An offshore breeze carried whiffs of rocket propellant and sweat. The prize was six miles away: white storage tanks filled with oil.

Over the walkie-talkie came a hurried voice: "Saadun, Saadun, the bird is here! The bird is here!" Saadun was the code name for a portly commander in the Libya Dawn militia and my escort on the front line. His men had teased him earlier for struggling to haul his hefty frame up the berm.

The "bird" was a MiG-23 fighter-bomber belonging to the rival Dignity forces. The overhead roar of an afterburner gave way to crackling flashes across a cloudless sky—flak from Misratan antiaircraft guns. We ran behind a concrete wall. The MiG dropped its bomb half a mile away, shaking the ground beneath us. Saadun seemed unperturbed. "The day and time you will die was written before you were born," he told me.

I went to the Misratans' base at Bin Jawad, a drab little town inhabited by Bedouins who'd long since departed. Hiftar had bombed it repeatedly. The Misratan fighters showed me a demolished auto repair shop and a school. Inside a bank with a smashed ceiling, I saw remnants of a Russian-origin cluster bomb, an insidious weapon that kills long after it lands by dispersing submunitions. An international convention bans its use, and what I saw was evidence of its first employment in Libya since 2011.

In a field hospital decorated with a mural of an eagle and the American and Libyan flags, a few saline bags dangled over box-spring beds. A German-trained doctor complained about the lack of blood coagulants. A week earlier, he said, the other doctor had died when a bomb landed next to him while he was talking on the cell phone with his father. The shrapnel had ripped through his upper chest and his neck. They couldn't stop him from bleeding to death.

It seemed to me a vicious little war, one that had escaped the head-lines amid the far bloodier fighting in Syria. And yet stubborn narratives of righteousness sustained each side—as well as cash from the oil flow they sought to monopolize.

"We believe in defending Libyan rights," Saadun told me. "This oil is not for Hiftar or Jadhran but all of Libya."

There had been a brief cease-fire the day I arrived. Then, at around two in the afternoon, an artillery strike killed a nineteen-year-old Mis-ratan fighter. Saadun radioed back to his commander for permission to respond, receiving it at once. At a staging area in the rear, fighters hoisted long Grad rockets into a launcher mounted on a truck. Rinsing it down with water, an ablution of sorts, they uttered cries of "God is great." Minutes later, the barrage began; there was pounding in the distance and lightning flashed across a darkened skyline.

That night, I joined the fighters gathered in makeshift barracks. Some were only teenagers. They watched *Braveheart* on Tunisian televi-sion and drank *bokha*, the local moonshine. They slept four or five to a room on thin mattresses and awoke to a breakfast of mashed dates and olive oil. In the morning, I sat in a vacant courtyard with a fighter, a for-mer day laborer from Misrata, watching a few goats wander in and out of the shadows. A short man in his early thirties, he fought in revolu-tionary militias to topple Qadhafi. He thought it was over then, but it wasn't.

"Three years after the revolution and look at this." He shook his head. He had two kids back in the city, and he had a father undergoing treatment for a heart condition.

He wanted to go home. But Misrata was fighting too many wars.

■

NOWHERE WAS LIBYA'S CIVIL WAR more pitched than in Benghazi. For many in the Dawn coalition and especially in Misrata, defeating

Hiftar's forces in the eastern city remained the ultimate goal. It was the seat of the revolution and the soul of the country, they believed, and the outcome of the fighting there would be decisive. "Whoever controls Benghazi controls Libya," a Misratan commander had told me.

Shortly after Hiftar had launched Dignity in May of 2014, his campaign in Benghazi stalled. By targeting all the city's Islamist militias, by branding them all as radicals, Hiftar had forced them into a unified front. Before, there were disagreements between the Islamist commanders, especially about whether to affiliate with the state; some supported the elections and others did not. But when Hiftar attacked, they put aside these differences, and on June 20, the most powerful of these groups, Wissam bin Hamid's Shield, Ansar al-Sharia, the February 17 Brigade, and the Rafallah al-Sahati Companies formed the Benghazi Revolutionaries' Shura Council. It was a fateful move that allowed disparate militias to coordinate their forces and maximize their firepower.

One Libyan who fought in the Shura Council was Tariq, the Islamist lawyer who'd protested at the courthouse on February 17 with Salwa and others. I'd met him years later, after his wounding on the battlefield and his harrowing maritime escape to Misrata, where he was then sent to Turkey for medical care. Tariq looks a bit older than he is, with circle-lined eyes, and he is heavyset, a result, partially, of long stretches of immobilization. There is a titanium rod screwed into his left femur, and he walks with a cane. The bone marrow has stopped growing, which means more rounds of surgery.

He wanted me to know that the Shura Council was not all radicals and wayward youths. Yes, he said, those existed. But many of the fighters, like him, were lawyers, doctors, and engineers. They wore black balaclavas to protect their identities; some still had families in Benghazi, vulnerable to retribution by Hiftar's forces. Tariq believed that he was fighting not just against Hiftar and a return of the old regime but for his family's right to live in Benghazi.

Thousands of families had been displaced by pro-Dignity militias, he explained, simply because their male relatives were fighting Hiftar.

Still others had been targeted because their families' origins, like his, were not in the east but from the west. "It's ethnic cleansing," Tariq told me.

A new nativism had taken hold in Benghazi, he said, among some of the eastern tribes backing Hiftar. A tribal racism, he called it. Those families they deemed not indigenous to the east they branded as *ghuraba*, or "westerners," especially the Misratans. No matter whether your family had been here for centuries, like Tariq's, you did not belong now. Worse, some easterners questioned the very Arab identity of the Misratans, deriding them as Turkish and Circassian implants—a reference to the city's distant Ottoman ties.

I wondered how and when this exclusionary trend had come about. Benghazi had always been cosmopolitan and Mediterranean in its outlook, a tapestry of all of Libya's tribes, with intermingling and intermarriage. And the Misratans had been an inseparable part of it, arriving in the sixteenth century and flourishing as builders and businessmen. "The Misratans founded in Benghazi . . . the first urbanized society in largely Bedouin Cyrenaica," a noted Libyan scholar wrote in his history of Libyan tribes. Soon they dominated Benghazi's trade and real estate, "to the point of monopoly," overtaking the Jewish community. Some of the city's older streets and quarters by the sea still bear the names of Misratan families. Now they were incredulous at being told to go home.

But conflicts between tribes, and between east and west, could not fully explain the violence. Libyan tribal identity always seemed elusive and sometimes constructed to suit the circumstances. It was sometimes more of a social identity than a political one. What made the conflict in Benghazi so complex was that the battle lines, and the radicalization of youth, cut across tribes and families. The Islamists in Benghazi included not just families with origins in Misrata and western towns but members of tribes from the east. Sometimes the fighting was within these tribes themselves. What lay at the core, it seemed to me, was Libya's utter absence of institutions, worsened by the economic and political disparity between east and west. Malignant tribalism had arisen as a by-product.

For their part, supporters of Dignity accused the Misratans of exaggerating their victimization. The real battle in Benghazi, they maintained, was against Islamists and terrorists, full stop. And since the city of Misrata—and behind it, Turkey—had backed these militants, Benghazi's rage against Misratan-owned homes and shops was understandable, they argued, if not justified. Still, I couldn't just discount the chilling tales I'd heard, from families in Misrata who'd fled from Hiftar's forces in the east.

At the end of Ramadan in 2014, the Shura Council launched a ferocious attack on Hiftar's largest military base in Benghazi, the Special Forces compound, overrunning it. It dealt a humiliating blow to Hiftar, who'd failed to evict any of the Islamist militias as he'd promised. Now most of his troops had retreated outside the city, hunkering down at Banina Airport, which the Shura Council struck with artillery. By the end of summer, the Islamists claimed control of nearly 80 percent of Benghazi.

Days of terror followed. The Islamists fanned out, setting up checkpoints. From the Special Forces base, they'd seized the rosters of the military and police; anyone on the lists they killed on the spot. Others they dispatched with car bombs or in drive-by shootings. Sometimes they tossed the corpses near an animal feed plant south of the city, where families went to look for the missing.

It wasn't just security men or those aligned with Dignity who died. One Friday in mid-September, gunmen killed a popular eighteen-year-old activist and blogger named Tawfiq Ben Saud and a friend of his named Sami al-Kuwayfi as they were driving. The killings shook a city already reeling from the murder of Salwa Bugaighis and others just months before. The exodus of activists quickened.

As the fighting surged in Benghazi, the Misratans and the Dawn government in Tripoli kept the funds and weapons flowing. As ever, it was hard to distinguish Misrata's two faces—the merchant city eager for trade and profit and the revolutionary hotbed. Often the two overlapped. When I asked some civilian leaders about the arms shipments, they claimed not to know. Others tried to justify it. The politician

Abd al-Rahman al-Suwayhli had insisted to me that they were only giving arms to "revolutionaries" led by Wissam bin Hamid and not to hard-core jihadists such as Ansar al-Sharia. But the line between the two had largely collapsed ever since the forming of the Shura Council: once the weapons arrived at Benghazi's port, who knew where they went? The radicals could be dealt with later, some Misratans replied; all that mattered now was beating Hiftar.

"If Hiftar grabs Benghazi," al-Suwayhli told me, "he will divide the country."

■

IN SEPTEMBER 2015, I traveled back to Benghazi. I wanted to see what had happened to the city since the launch of Operation Dignity and why the fighting had been so protracted.

I came in through a northern suburb called Kuwayfia, the only route open. Filled with date palms and murmuring springs, Kuwayfia was said to be the source for the mythical Garden of the Hesperides. Now it was barnacled with urban growth: breeze-block homes, mosques, and a prison where torture was rampant. At the edge of a lake, the serpentine chutes of a disused water park stood coated in grime while black smoke rose from the shelling. I passed a bleached-out election poster for Ali al-Tarhuni, a liberal, American-trained economist, his grinning visage at once otherworldly and quaint in the stricken landscape.

To the south, the war had all but obliterated the Old City. The colonnaded fish market where families once gathered on Ramadan nights among the date vendors and children's games was now a shambles of concrete. Artillery had scarred the Italianate facades of Tree Square, once beloved for its cedar, and destroyed the covered bazaar of Suq al-Jarid, once filled with tailors, jewelers, and leather smiths. In other parts of the city, the war was never far. At the end of this or that street, behind a darkened berm or a tank, lay the front, and the sound of the heavy guns. I went to a field hospital where Filipino nurses tried to revive a wounded soldier. Two holes in his stomach spurted rivulets of blood. "The snipers are the worst," the man's commander told me. They wheeled him into surgery.

Displaced families now crowded into schools turned shelters, their classrooms doubling as bedrooms and kitchens, separated by diaphanous sheets hanging from clotheslines. In one of them, I met an old woman and her granddaughter who'd lived by the sea in Benghazi all their lives before leaving as the clashes had started. The girl, eight years old, got up to make coffee for us. Her father had died a year before, she said matter-of-factly, when someone drove by his shop and sprayed it with gunfire. "We never knew that these sorts of people were among us," her grandmother said.

In the central neighborhood of Majuri, I met a young man in his twenties I'll call Issam. A former university student, he sported skinny jeans, a stitched denim jacket, and a G-Shock watch. A Beretta in his waistband belied his new calling: leading men, or rather boys, in battle.

Issam was the head of one of Benghazi's many neighborhood and tribal militias who fought alongside Hiftar. Known as "support forces" or "youths of the neighborhood," these paramilitaries comprised upwards of 60 to 80 percent of the Dignity forces. Their opponents, the Islamists, labeled all of them *sahawat*, or "awakenings," a derogatory reference to the U.S.-backed tribal councils in Iraq that had revolted against al-Qaeda.

The support forces, Issam explained, had started out as small-time vigilantes, guarding checkpoints and intersections during the months of assassinations that rocked Benghazi in 2013 and early 2014. They were young men mostly, college students like Issam or day laborers, bound together by neighborhood or kinship. Hiftar started funneling weapons to them in the summer of 2014, building them up as a fifth column inside the city, and on the eve of his counterattack that fall his media outlets called on them to rise up. As Hiftar's forces rolled through Benghazi, the support forces erected barricades to block the

Islamists' movements and fought side by side with the army. Many attacked the families of suspected militants, demolishing their homes and businesses. Thousands of families, like Tariq's, fled Benghazi from these attacks. A Dignity commander justified the destruction in the interest of saving "Libyan social fabric," but of course, just the opposite occurred.

Issam and I walked together to the front, where a dreadlocked fighter manned a recoilless rifle. Issam pointed to a poster of his brother, killed in recent clashes, and to an armored truck with a sign affixed to its fender: WHEN THE WAR IS FINISHED AND THE MARTYRS GO TO HEAVEN THE COWARDS GO TO THE STREET AND TALK OF HEROISM. I met his militia's resident poet, a former teacher now feted as the "Bard of Dignity," who wrote elegiac verse for fallen fighters—and sometimes picked up a gun himself.

It was intimate combat, a battle of snipers' nests, tunnels, and artillery duels, where both sides blew up buildings to clear fields of fire. Children as young as fourteen or fifteen years old fought in the Majuri militia; one of them, Issam said, had a particular talent with the 14.5 gun. They often turned over captured militants to Hiftar's uniformed troops, though sometimes they did not: one day, after disabling an Ansar al-Sharia vehicle with a rocket, they took two prisoners, a Sudanese and a Tunisian, and summarily shot them.

One night in October 2014, Issam and dozens of his militia fighters attacked the four-story home of a wealthy businessman of Misratan origins in Majuri who allegedly supported Ansar al-Sharia. The family owned several factories and stores for building materials, including an aluminum workshop where Issam had once apprenticed. During the twelve-hour battle with RPGs and heavy machine guns, the man was killed and his brothers surrendered. Issam turned them over to the Special Forces and then looted and burned the home. I learned from the family's survivors that the Special Forces shot two of the brothers in captivity while another had to have his eye surgically removed due to injuries sustained in the battle and torture.

Across Benghazi, I saw signs of similar vigilantism everywhere:

the blackened ruins of burned-out houses and the skeletons of cars, oxidized to a tawny red.

■

AN ARAB FRIEND, an exile from Yemen's unending catastrophe, once told me, "Short wars change regimes, long wars change societies."

By the time I left Benghazi in the fall of 2015, the war for the city was entering its sixteenth month, longer than the war that toppled Qadhafi. It would continue. Hiftar had promised repeatedly to finish it in a week. Instead, the fighting had killed thousands and forced half the city to flee. It had caused devastation in Libya worse than that of World War II.

The general had said he was leading an army to vanquish terrorists and Islamists. That much was evident. But along the way, his war was unraveling the threads that had held Benghazi together. And the effects were spreading across the country, given the connections of different tribes, families, and factions to the city. "Benghazi is all of Libya," Libyans like to say.

I once asked Laila Bugaighis whether she hoped to return. She paused.

"Benghazi without the sea is not Benghazi," she said. "And you can't see the sea."

EUROPE'S
AFRICAN SHORES

THE YOUNG TUAREG DRIVER I'll call Faraj shifted into high gear to clear a dune. He paused, waiting to see that the path was open. We'd driven off the asphalt road to avoid an ambush, but Faraj was cautious: his Land Cruiser bore the stippled scars of a mortar round in recent fighting. He'd been sleeping inside at the time and emerged unscathed.

It was just past dawn and behind a layer of clouds the sun cast a blue-gray light on the sands. Faraj navigated the desert as he had countless times before, using no map, no GPS, only the stars and, during daytime, landmarks such as power lines or an odd-shaped rock. He didn't have much education. Still, he had skills as a smuggler, so in the chaos of war he survived—and even prospered.

By 2014, the civil war that engulfed the north had come to his home in the arid south, rupturing bonds between neighbors just as it did in Benghazi. The warring factions, Dignity and Dawn, started sending weapons and cash to feuding southern groups. As the hardships mounted, the fighting ensnared and corrupted the region's youths, and the elders of Faraj's people, the Tuareg, lamented their despair.

■

NO OTHER PEOPLE in Libya, or North Africa for that matter, have cast such a spell on the Western imagination as the Tuareg. For centuries, they were a nomadic culture stretching across the Sahara and the Sahel in southern Libya and parts of Algeria, Mali, Niger, and Burkina Faso. In the West, the Tuareg are famed as the "Blue Men of the Desert" for the indigo head covering worn by men that leaves only the eyes exposed.

It's easy to see why they've been idealized and romanticized. They were warriors and camel riders. A matriarchal society, historically, it was the men who were veiled, not the women. The origins of their language, a dialect of Amazigh, are still unclear. In conquering the Sahara, French colonialists were both terrified and enchanted by the Tuareg, seeing them as living embodiments of the noble savage: gallant, free, and uncorrupted by modernity.

It is a trope that persists in the present. In 1999, *National Geographic* visited the Sahara's Tuareg regions seeking the "rhythms of life unbroken since the time of Muhammad, 1,300 years ago." When Qadhafi opened Libya to tourists, the romance of this image drew Western visitors to the south. The Tuareg suddenly found a new income, one that allowed them to escape from menial labor. European tourists demanded that their guides into the dunes be Tuareg, so they could re-create the fantasy.

None of it bore much resemblance to reality. Modernity had changed the Tuareg, bringing poverty and social erosion. Breaking with the pastoral ways and hierarchy of their elders, younger Tuareg entered a remittance economy of migrant labor. The new itinerant culture of these Tuareg had a name: *ishumar*, from the French word for unemployed, *chomeur*.

For the *ishumar* from drought-afflicted Niger and Mali, oil-rich Libya was paradise. Qadhafi encouraged them to come north for work. Once they arrived, however, he recruited many into a pan-Saharan military force called the Islamic Legion, meant to project his power in Africa and the Middle East. Alongside Mauritanians, Eritreans, Sudanese, and Bangladeshis, the Tuareg fought in Chad and Lebanon during the 1980s. "We were cheap soldiers," one of them told me. Some had joined expecting that the Libyan ruler would help empower them back home in Mali and Niger, and he certainly encouraged this belief. In 1980 he set up a camp to train Tuareg militants fighting for an independent "Central Sahara" republic. Yet when Tuareg veterans of the Islamic Legion went back to Mali and Niger to lead rebellions in the early 1990s, Qadhafi abandoned them.

Under Qadhafi, the Tuaregs' lands, and all of southern Libya, remained places of desperation and poverty, despite the discovery of abundant oil, aquifers, and gold. The dictator extracted these riches from the land in the south, but southerners themselves saw none of the benefits. Bereft of a local economy, they became smugglers or joined the regime's security services.

As he'd done elsewhere, Qadhafi warped the social tapestry of the south by playing tribes against one another.

■

FARAJ STEERED US along the edge of the Ubari Sand Sea. A long ridge of dunes rippled northward to a dust-cloaked horizon: half-crescent barchan dunes, star dunes with radiating arms, linear dunes in slantwise corridors. To the north lay the depression of Wadi al-Shati; farther beyond, the basaltic plateau of the Haruj volcano. The parched nothingness was not always so. It used to be a lush, watery land, covered by a paleo lake. South of the Sand Sea the rocks are blackened with a varnish of iron and manganese oxides from the once-high humidity. Carved on their surfaces, there is climatic evidence of a different sort: petroglyphs of crocodiles, hippopotami, giraffes, and oxen. In one, two cats face each other on their hind legs, their forearms stretched in playful sparring.

This was the art of hunters and herders, who eked out a pastoral existence on the drying savannas. In the second century B.C. came the Garamantians, an urban culture of farmers, warriors, and traders. They built underground irrigation tunnels and pyramidal tombs, and wrote in a proto-Amazigh script. The Garamantians were also slavers, raiding "Ethiopian cave dwellers with four-horse chariots," according to the Greek historian Herodotus. They shipped this human chattel northward to the Roman markets at Leptis Magna.

The Arab invasions of the seventh century ended the Garamantians' rule. As the centuries passed, other invaders would come and go: the Ottomans, the Italians, and then the French, who tried to attach the southwest region of Fezzan to Chad shortly before Libyan independence. These outsiders tried to govern the tribes, to levy taxes on them, to enlist them in their wars, but they never could, not completely.

In his fabulist novel, *The Bleeding of the Stone*, the Libyan Tuareg writer Ibrahim al-Koni describes how an Italian army officer named Captain Bordello kidnaps a young Tuareg shepherd from a southern oasis. He wants to dragoon him into fighting in the Italians' conquest of Abyssinia, but the youth escapes his shackles by changing into a *waddan*, a rare type of horned ram of spiritual importance to the tribes. Later in the book, an American marine named John Parker comes to the south from Wheelus Air Base in Tripoli. He brings machine guns and flies in a helicopter, helping a pair of Libyan hunters scour the desert for gazelles. The men demand that the shepherd show them the hiding place of the elusive *waddan* inside a warren of mountains. He refuses. They crucify and behead him, but not before he transmogrifies again into a *waddan*:

"His body was thrust into the hollow of the rock, merging with the body of the *waddan* painted there. The *waddan's* horns were coiled around his own neck like a snake."

Then the heavens darken and it starts to rain. The man-animal's spilled blood on stone has fulfilled an ancient prophecy of an earth-cleansing deluge.

■

FARAJ AND I passed by a *mashru'*, or project—a giant, circular field of grain, watered from wells dug into aquifers. The whole of southern Libya contained such underground reservoirs, which were meant to supply Qadhafi's "Great Man-Made River," a scheme of pipes to transport water to the north. It was costly, vain, and never realized, and for the Tuareg it was another extraction of resources whose wealth they never saw.

Faraj had turned on the CD player. Floating above the flapping wind from his open window was an electric guitar set to antiphonal drumming, clapping, and a male and female chorus. Faraj said it was the famous Malian Tuareg band Tinariwen.

Ibrahim al-Koni might have won literary prizes abroad, but the hearts of Tuareg youth across the Sahara belonged to Tinariwen. Fusing Tuareg rhythms with Western rock and blues, they drew inspiration from the solos of Jimi Hendrix and the chords of Dire Straits. It was an incomparable sound that eventually won them European recording contracts and a global audience. But for years, young Tuareg exchanged their cassettes in secret, fearful of arrest. The music is seditious and revolutionary. We were listening to the anthem-like "Voice of the Beasts." The singer exhorts the Tuareg of Niger, Algeria, and Libya to rise up, chiding them for being "ignorant" and "basking in the shade."

The Tuareg in Qadhafi's Libya remained on the margins. They

faced the dictator's Arabization policies, even if he treated them as honorary Arabs and went so far as to claim some Tuareg lineage for himself. Their towns in the south were sorely undeveloped, despite the discovery of oil nearby. Lacking education, young Tuareg joined the security forces, like the 32nd Reinforced Brigade or the Revolutionary Committees.

When the 2011 revolution started, some Tuareg broke with the regime, but many others stayed loyal. After the war, Tuareg soldiers of Sahelian origin looted Libyan armories and went to Mali, where they led an insurgency and helped establish a short-lived semistate in the north of Mali known as Azawadh.

Still other Libyan Tuareg struggled with the taint of having sided with Qadhafi.

■

IN THE WAKE of Qadhafi's dictatorship, the Tuareg cooperated with another non-Arab minority in pressing for their rights. The Tabu are a dark-skinned African people who dwell in the Tibesti Mountains of northern Chad, southeastern Libya, and parts of Niger and Sudan. Historically a clan-based society of camel herders, the Tabu speak a language of Nilo-Saharan origin. In Libya, they have always been a people apart. They suffered under the monarchy; new citizenship laws required written family records, but the Tabu were an oral culture then, seminomadic and mostly illiterate.

Their status under Qadhafi got worse. Using them as pawns in his dispute with Chad over the uranium-rich Aouzou Strip, which includes the Tabu-populated Tibesti Mountains, he offered citizenship to thousands of Tabu, while enlisting others in his army. When the International Court of Justice awarded the Aouzou Strip to Chad in 1994, he abandoned them, revoking their citizenship and denying them access to jobs, education, and medical care.

Unsurprisingly, the Tabu joined the uprising in 2011. Qadhafi dispatched emissaries to woo them with cash, weapons, and, again, offers of citizenship, yet it was too little, too late. At the war's end, they controlled southern border crossings, oil fields, and armories. They grew rich. But more important, for the first time they had hope.

"Everything was like a paradise then," a Tabu fighter turned activist told me. But, he added, "I knew we would face problems. Everybody was talking about Tabu power."

The afterglow didn't last. In towns across the south, in remote Kufra and in the provincial capital of Sabha, clashes broke out between the Tabu and Arab tribes who felt threatened by the Tabus' newfound economic power and usurpation of smuggling routes. In Tripoli, meanwhile, the transitional government proved unwilling to address Tabu grievances, especially on citizenship. "The government doesn't want to open that door," the Tabu activist told me. Behind the inertia, he said, was a not-so-latent racism evident among even the most liberal and educated Arabs. The most pernicious slander was that the Tabu were African, not Libyan.

A fellow minority in an Arab-dominated state, the Tabu found a natural partner in the Tuareg. Both had been denied citizenship and both suffered from underdevelopment. Their activists joined together in staging sit-ins at government ministries in Tripoli, demanding employment and identification cards. They issued a joint statement threatening autonomy for the south.

Much of the cooperation between the Tabu and the Tuareg stemmed from a remarkable treaty the two peoples had signed in 1894 called the *midi-midi* (roughly, "friendship," from the French *amitié*). For years they'd fought, mostly over control of caravan routes and pastures, but the *midi-midi* accord put an end to that by defining a boundary between them in Libya and in the desert to the south. For over a hundred years, the *midi-midi* kept the peace, through drought, displacement, and dictatorship.

The sun climbed higher in the sky, warming us in the truck. Faraj pointed to a flat-topped bluff towering in the distance. The Tuareg call it Tende Mountain; *tende* means "drum" in their language. It is a strategic high ground, and from its summit mortar and heavy machine-gun crews have a panoramic view of the town below.

It was here, in September 2014, where the *midi-midi* finally collapsed.

■

FARAJ AND I entered the town of Ubari, passing windbreaks of juniper and oleander followed by chicken coops and thatched huts for livestock. At a cinder-block market, dusty mufflers hung next to goat cadavers. Someone had painted a mural of Che Guevara next to a cigarette kiosk selling Manchesters, a bootleg favorite.

Like other conflict-ridden towns in Libya, Ubari is a mix of tribes and ethnicities. Most of the population is Arabized Africans of sub-Saharan origin, the so-called *ahali*. The Tuareg are the next-largest group, and the Tabu are a minority. The Tuareg say that Ubari is firmly in the Tuareg zone defined by the *midi-midi*, but the Tabu say they have just as much a right to be there, and in the first years after the 2011 revolution they started asserting it. Flush with cash from smuggling profits, they started buying property in Ubari. And then they grabbed the oil.

About forty-five miles west of Ubari is Libya's second-largest-producing oil field, Sharara, accounting for 20 percent of Libya's output. The militia that controls it can get security contracts and, even more important, leverage with the Tripoli government.

I'd spent a night in Sharara's compound, a lunar-like complex of villas, a pool, and a cafeteria surrounded by a featureless desert plain. In its heyday I suppose it was a tolerable if cloistered existence for the expatriates who lived and worked there. Those foreigners had now disappeared save for a few technicians, hardy Serbs and Ukrainians in stained overalls, who did maintenance. The water in the swimming pool had turned a dirty brown.

After the revolution, militias from Zintan who controlled Sharara started recruiting Tabu as guards, a move that alarmed the Tuareg who believed the field lay squarely on their turf. Tensions mounted in nearby Ubari.

One afternoon in September 2014, a Tuareg security force tried to arrest some Tabu men who were selling illegal gasoline in the town center. The Tuareg insist that the Tabu weren't just selling fuel: inside their canisters were hidden narcotics. The situation escalated, with a Tuareg shooting a Tabu and then vice versa. A committee of elders arrived and managed to establish a truce, but that night a convoy of sixty or so Tabu fighters arrived and attacked Ubari at dawn.

A Tuareg commander I'll call Anwar was manning the base that bore the brunt of the assault. A beefy, melancholic man with a russet-colored head wrap, he had a chrome Colt .45 tucked in his baggy pants. As a boy growing up in Ubari, he enjoyed playing soccer on dirt fields and listening to music. Lacking opportunities, he joined Qadhafi's security apparatus like many other Tuareg, becoming a lieutenant in the 32nd Brigade. He defected early in the revolution, he says, and in the years that followed, he became an ardent Tuareg nationalist. "We are the lords of the Sahara," he told me.

Anwar was in charge of a militia on the city's eastern edge, which the Tabu hit with heavy machine-gun fire. In the week that followed Tabu militias pushed through Ubari, burning Tuareg homes as they went. Anwar's men and other Tuareg militias raced to the top of Tende Mountain and started firing on the Tabu neighborhoods below, with antiaircraft guns and artillery. The firing spread beyond Ubari. In November 2014, the Tuareg, aided by the Misratans, seized the Sharara oil field from the Tabu, prompting Zintani militias in the north to close down a section of the pipeline that connected Sharara to a port on the Mediterranean. Immediately, 340,000 barrels of oil per day went off-line. Such were the rules in Libya's zero-sum game.

By mid-2015 the battle in Ubari had turned to daily exchanges of mortars and snipers, forcing 80 percent of its inhabitants to flee and killing hundreds.

I went to one of the poorer Tuareg neighborhoods damaged in the fighting. Tangles of electrical wire crisscrossed mud-brick homes, and sewage coursed through the dirt streets. I met a few nurses who'd done their best to tend to the wounded. We sat in a courtyard under a mango tree; their henna-dyed hands and batik jewelry belied their ordeal months before. In a school turned clinic, they'd used plaster tape bandages and strips of clothing to stanch horrific wounds. They pleaded now for medical supplies and psychologists for traumatized children.

As fighting between Dawn and Dignity escalated in the north, it reverberated in the south. The Misratans backed the Tuareg, while the Tabu got support from General Hiftar's Operation Dignity and the Tobruk-based government. Southern elders lamented that their young men had become, in effect, hired guns for the north. Each side pushed a number of toxic narratives about the other.

"The Tabu brought mercenaries, guys with dreadlocks, African guys who couldn't speak Arabic," a Tuareg commander said. "This was the Chadian army we were facing." To be sure, the Tabu did recruit Chadian Tabu and even some Darfurian fighters. But the scale of this outside help was vastly exaggerated.

For their part, the Tabu and their Dignity backers said they were fighting Islamist militants and especially al-Qaeda, who enjoyed safe haven in the Tuareg areas. Some of their suspicions sprang from a militia run by a Tuareg Islamist named Ahmed Umar Ansari, whom the United Nations accused of funneling weapons to Mali via Niger. Hailing from an elite Tuareg clan, he was the first cousin of a Tuareg militant leader in Mali with ties to al-Qaeda, and he enjoyed at least some backing in Ubari. His militia operated in plain sight; I once passed by its headquarters just north of Tende Mountain.

But the Tuareg I met in Ubari downplayed radicalism in their community, dismissing the accusations as Tabu and Dignity propaganda. Their culture, they insisted, with its Sufi influences, matriarchy, and openness, was an antibody against the severe Islam of the militants.

Many Libyan Tuareg had in fact returned to Libya from Mali, disillusioned after Islamist radicals gained the upper hand in the northern semistate they'd tried to create.

Still, the extremists had a presence, they admitted, especially in the uncontrolled mountains to the west, near the Tuareg town of Ghat on the Algerian border.

■

IT IS HARD TO IMAGINE a more remote town in Libya than Ghat, a six-hour drive from Ubari. It seemed cut off from the world, but this was hardly the case for much of its history. For over a millennium, Ghat had been a center of Saharan trade—salt, dates, gems, and slaves—and a stopping point for pilgrims from as far away as Timbuktu. It was also the seat of the Tuareg sultanate, where the Tuareg and Tabu had signed the *midi-midi* agreement, before declining when Italian-built roads replaced the camel routes. In the 1990s, the town enjoyed a renaissance when tourists arrived for the annual festival of Tuareg music. "The dancing city," Libyans called Ghat.

I walked one afternoon through the sun-bleached arches and crumbling parapets of its old quarter, dating to the Garamantian era. The modern town of Ghat lay to the south and beyond it the Algerian border and the ink-blue peaks of the Tassili n'Ajjer. To the east lay the Acacus Mountains, their steeples of volcanic rock inspiring the legend of the Cave of Genies. Here, the Tuareg believed, apparitions dwelled, emerging to battle one another with fire. It was through these valleys that jihadist militants were ferrying arms and men between Algeria and Libya.

Border guard commanders I met in Ghat acknowledged the movement of al-Qaeda in the Islamic Maghreb and other groups. Yet whatever freedom the militants had, the commanders insisted, was due to Ghat's poor control of the border rather than to any active collusion or sympathy. The guards needed vehicles and guns, along with radios and walkie-talkies, and especially salaries. Deprived of a livelihood, the young men who encamped at lonely outposts adopted a moral calculus in patrolling the frontier: they tried to stop arms, illegal narcotics, and militants, but allowed cigarettes, migrants, and subsidized food to cross—for a price.

Sometimes, of course, the jihadists paid to get through as well.

■

I LEFT SOUTHERN LIBYA in a windstorm. It was late winter, the season when the easterly *sharqi* winds collide with the *gharbi*, or western, wind. The "battling of the winds," Libyans called it, and my Tuareg guide was quick to see it as a metaphor for the south's afflictions.

Communal fighting would continue to flare in this vast neglected region. The opposing northern factions, Dawn and Dignity, would continue to meddle in the south's affairs: in the coming months, Hiftar's forces and the Misratans would wage a seesaw battle for access to southern airfields. But perhaps most important, the south remained mired in economic despair. Faced with such hopelessness, young men joined the ranks of smugglers, militiamen, and criminals in increasing numbers.

The south of Libya, it seemed to me, could no longer exist on the periphery of international concerns. The post-Qadhafi chaos, with its collapse of borders and economic decline, had erased the distinctions between the Sahara and the coast. Africa's misery was spilling across Libya into the Mediterranean, and Fezzan was the new southern shore of Europe.

The desert around me was the proof. The caravan routes that once ferried slaves to the north now carried a new but equally grim traffic.

■

THERE ARE TODAY an estimated seven hundred thousand to one million migrants residing in Libya. Just over 50 percent are believed to have Libya as their final destination, seeking menial jobs that are still available in the war-torn country, and the rest intend to make the sea crossing to Italian territory, the most perilous stretch of human travel in the world. In 2016 alone, nearly five thousand died on this journey, an average of about fourteen deaths a day. The vast majority of them come from sub-Saharan Africa.

Linked by culture and trade to Africa, Libya has long existed as a portal of sorts between the Mediterranean and the Continent—a role that Qadhafi played up, even though his relations with his southern neighbors were often stormy. In the last decade of his rule, having been spurned by Arab regimes, the dictator reinvented himself as an African leader. He'd first backed African liberation movements and then the despots who came to power, all the while sending arms to various insurgents from Liberia to Sudan. In 1999 he called for a "United States of Africa," which led to the creation of the African Union, whose presidency he assumed in 2009. That tenure was marked by frequent clashes with African rulers, though his largesse paid off in the 2011 revolution when a number of African states, especially South Africa, supported him.

African migrant flows to the north were a useful tool for Qadhafi, who portrayed himself to Europe as a gatekeeper who could turn the taps on or off at will. Yet the dictator's commitment to stopping these flows was always illusory; European countries were in fact cooperating with a government that was itself embedded in trafficking. In the chaos that followed his death, migrants flooded Libya, abetted by smugglers and militias who'd replaced the regime. The civil war between Dignity and Dawn with its attendant economic decline only worsened the crisis as the circle of complicity in smuggling widened, especially in Libya's south.

Most migrants just want work and pay a lifetime's savings for the journey to Libya. Many have wrenching stories, traveling by camel across the Chadian desert or dodging marauding Janjawid militias in Darfur. The Eritreans seek asylum, fleeing their country's open-ended conscription that amounts to a prison camp. Nigerians constitute the majority. One of them is a young man I'll call Ibrahim.

When Ibrahim was six years old, his parents sold him into servitude to a wealthy villa owner near the city of Kano, in the north of Nigeria. It is a common enough practice in a region where child trafficking has reached epidemic proportions, stretching across borders and netting millions of dollars. Ibrahim was lucky; he washed clothes and did domestic work. Other children his age were forced to work in quarries, fields, or fisheries, or were sold into prostitution and pornography.

One day a sympathetic guard at the villa opened the gate for him. He slept in a park for weeks, begged for money, and made his way north to Agadez, Niger. A windblown outpost of adobe buildings, Agadez was once the seat of an ancient Sahelian sultanate. Today it is a way station on the journey north, with an estimated 170,000 migrants passing through it in 2016 alone. Some never make it beyond the gates of the town. "I saw death in Agadez," Ibrahim said.

In Agadez, the worst of the odyssey lies ahead of them, across the Sahara into Libya. They pack into the beds of Hilux trucks, clinging to whatever they can. Ibrahim could not recall the route through Libya they took; most could not. He stopped at any number of southern towns where migrants are robbed, beaten, and raped. I'd met groups of them on the street in the southern provincial capital of Sabha, rife with violence and crime: they said smugglers force them to work in fields, brothels, and casinos, or cleaning toilets at militia bases in order to pass to the next leg. The militias that passed for police, I learned, are just as brutal as the smugglers. When they discover a truckload or carload of migrants at a checkpoint, they haul the migrants over the border to Niger and dump them in the desert.

The journey north could take weeks or months. The smugglers left behind those who fell off the truck "for the animals," Ibrahim told me, and beat him with long wooden sticks. An asthmatic boy in his group died from thirst, and Tuareg bandits shot another in the leg. Arriving in Tripoli, the migrants faced more perils waiting for a boat. The smugglers herded them into safe houses, dozens or more to a room.

I met a smuggler who ran such houses, a man I'll call Karim. Like Ibrahim, Karim was a Nigerian but had been in Tripoli for decades, where he'd been imprisoned for smoking hashish. After the revolution, working as a human trafficker was an easy choice. He ran two safe houses, including one reserved for children. Karim would lock their rooms from the outside, forcing the migrants to pay about a thousand dinars to leave, to proceed to beachheads east or west of the capital.

And if they don't have the money? I asked.

"We help them," he replied.

Forced labor was what he meant. The smugglers press-ganged many into slavery or prostitution, calling their families back home to demand a ransom.

A child from Ghana who'd escaped this servitude had ratted out Karim to Tripoli's counter-smuggling police.

"He's a big fish," one of these policemen now told me. We were sitting in his Tripoli office, where he'd brought Karim from his cell.

"And what's next for you now?" I asked Karim. He glanced at the plainclothes officer. It was clear he'd endured weeks of interrogation—and he wasn't leaving soon.

"I'll tell you what's next for him," the officer interrupted. "It's a surprise."

He smiled at the prisoner and jeered, "Maybe we will kill you, eh, Karim?"

■

THOSE MIGRANTS who'd made it to the shores of the Mediterranean stood on a threshold, at the continental terminus of an epic journey. Some had not planned to make the sea crossing but did so only to escape abuses they'd suffered at the hands of smugglers and militiamen. Regardless of motive, what remained before them was the perilous final leg, a distance equivalent to a road trip from Abuja to Kano. Many had never seen the sea before, and most could not swim.

They crowded onto vessels of proven unreliability. In the past, the smugglers had favored wooden fishing boats: some could pack several hundred souls on their deck or in airless holds, with predictably fatal results. Later, with the increase in patrols by European navies and humanitarian ships run by private NGOs, the smugglers shifted to even less seaworthy craft, huge inflatable Zodiacs with outboard motors. Bought from Chinese suppliers on the Internet, these craft could never make the entire voyage to Italy. But they didn't need to: all they had to do was to reach the twelve-mile limits of Libya's international waters, where the rescue boats awaited. To cut costs further, the smugglers would skimp on fuel or, worse, send someone out to retrieve the motor, letting the migrants drift.

It was a moonless night when Ibrahim set off from a beach east of Tripoli. He straddled the side of the dinghy, one leg dragging in the sea. The shores of Italy, his goal, lay some 290 miles away. Two hours out from Libya, not quite in international waters, the boat started to leak.

This can happen for any number of reasons. The sealant on the seams of the dinghy can break or the hull can get punctured. Most often, the water-soaked plywood floor snaps from a large wave or starts dissolving into soggy splinters. The women, who usually sit on the floor out of a misplaced sense of security, are the first to feel the seeping seawater.

"The ladies stood up," Ibrahim told me, "and that made it worse."

A sinking boat is subjected to a new set of rules. In the panicked struggle, a harsh Darwinism sets in. The bodies of rescued and drowned migrants bear the marks of scratches, bites, and abrasions. Women have drowned in just a few inches of water on the floor as the occupants trample their heads.

That night, Ibrahim watched a Nigerian friend topple into the sea and vanish into the darkness. He was sitting in another part of the boat, and he couldn't reach him amid the heaving and flailing passengers.

"Nobody helped him because they didn't want to fall in themselves," he said.

■

IN THE SUMMER OF 2016, I traveled by small skiff from Tripoli to Zawiya, a onetime hub of sponge fishing and Sufi orders that was now home to an oil refinery—and smugglers. On a dirt road west of the port, past a checkered lighthouse, sat an abandoned tire factory that was now a detention center for migrants. This was where I met Ibrahim. He and others who'd been rescued at sea sat in the shade of an acacia tree near a gaggle of geese and wild turkey.

The migrants' future here was uncertain, and many languished in limbo; their home countries had long since closed their embassies in Libya. The Libyan wardens acknowledged they could not send the Eritreans home, under international law, because the repressive government there would persecute them as defectors. The International Organization for Migration worked to repatriate other nationalities. The other route was bribery, or the Libyan guards would force the migrants to work to pay for their return. Sometimes the smugglers themselves would free them with a bribe, only to extort them for another crossing.

An NGO called the Nasr Organization had run the center in Zawiya since July 2015, and it had finally come under Libyan government control in 2016. It was one of roughly twenty centers under the nominal authority of the minister of interior's Department of Combatting Illegal Migration; many others are off the books, under militia control. Yet even in the "official" centers, the militias hold sway, and the conditions are abominable.

I'd seen quite a few of them. At one center in Tripoli's Abu Salim neighborhood, the warden was a soft-spoken Salafist who readily admitted mistreatment by his guards.

"I can't deny they hit the migrants," he said. "They get fed up."

The first thing I noticed in the cells was an overpowering smell, of dried urine and sweat. Then the sight: a mass of bodies, hundreds of them, lying or sitting on the floor. Laundry hung by the windows. The men stirred and stood up, eager to talk. A Gambian lifted his shirt to show me two welts on his shoulder.

"They beat us with horse pipe," he said. "We can't speak their language, and this is how they punish us." The bruises added to the speckles of scabies on his abdomen. He washed from a single faucet, he said, and shared two toilets with hundreds of detainees. He'd been there for months and rarely saw the sun.

"We can't let them go outside," the center's supervisor admitted. "It's too dangerous."

At another center, in Misrata, Nigerian women told me of rape. Militias had rounded them up in a safe house, accusing them of being prostitutes. They shared a giant bin of greasy rice and a tub of watery tea. "We are Humans, not Animals," they'd scrawled on the wall of their cell.

In Zawiya's center, the director led me through a catacombed hall lit by a single bulb. Attempts at escape were not uncommon, he explained. One night in April 2016, a detainee had grabbed an AK-47 from a guard serving dinner and started firing, killing four fellow migrants and injuring twenty-five. Outside sources including the United Nations and NGOs offered a different version: the militiamen who guarded the facility shot the escaping migrants in what was a mass breakout. Hearing the gunfire and thinking that the entire center was revolting, the Libyan locals in Zawiya started shooting any Africans on sight.

The director tried to show me how things in the center were getting better. He'd given the migrants kits of toiletries provided by European aid agencies and even checkerboards. The center had struggled as well to improve its medical treatment for the rescued migrants: hepatitis, HIV, and tuberculosis were rampant. Then there were the injuries sustained at sea, the most appalling of which were gasoline burns.

When gasoline and salt water come into contact with exposed skin, they cause a searing chemical burn. This happens most often to migrants, usually women, who are sitting on the floor of a waterlogged boat next to a leaking canister. The pain is immediate and excruciating. A "vegetable peeler applied to someone's buttocks," is how a volunteer doctor on a rescue ship described it; people have drowned after leaping off the boats to relieve the burning. The detention center treated the burns with what they had in the way of salves and ointments, but serious cases required more advanced care to avoid death.

Still, the injured were the lucky ones.

I met a young Libyan who dealt with the countless who perished at sea, a lawyer named Riyad who volunteered with the Red Crescent. A typical day would begin with a call in the morning from someone who'd spotted corpses washed up on the shore. He and his team would arrive an hour or so later in white protective smocks.

The dead they gathered were nameless. Libyans did not want them buried in their cemeteries, and the Red Crescent lacked a morgue of their own. The bodies were swollen and bloated, Riyad said, and some of them had been eaten by fish.

"Nobody eats the fish here anymore," he told me. "Nobody swims either. They're afraid of the bodies."

■

I WENT TO SEE the coast guard commander who had picked up Ibrahim and the other migrants at sea, a twenty-eight-year-old lieutenant named Abd al-Rahman Milad al-Bija.

At his office in Zawiya's port, he explained the sheer magnitude of his responsibility; he had to cover a 125-mile stretch of coast, from Zawiya west to the Tunisian border. All he had were rigid inflatable boats—I'd seen two of them on the quay—and a larger trawler with an inoperable radar. These were meager resources to fight a sophisticated and growing epidemic. He chuckled at the terms "black market" and "underground." The migrant traffickers were in fact a multinational corporation, he said, with electronic money transfers to suppliers and brokers in Malta, Rome, Frankfurt, and Dubai. He pleaded for outside help.

In the fall of 2016, it finally came: the European Union, and especially Italy, started training and equipping the Libyan coast guard. Having cut off the migrant traffic from Greece and Turkey, the Europeans turned their attention to closing down the central Mediterranean route, which by the end of 2016 had seen an unprecedented number of crossings. That meant enlisting Libyans themselves to stop the flow and working with men like al-Bija.

Al-Bija shrugged his shoulders. He doubted the assistance would work.

"This, the sea, is the last point if they want to rescue people," he said. "They need to stop the smuggling sooner." He meant on land, in the south of Libya, and he was right. The Europeans had a plan for that as well: led by the Italians, they provided money and training to towns in the south to curb smuggling and set up holding centers.

Then Italy began paying the traffickers themselves, via the Tripoli government, to compel them to stop carrying migrants across the desert and the sea and to crack down on those who continued to do so. It seemed a shortsighted practice that only bolstered the power of Libyan militia bosses. Libya's interior minister called it a "reconversion" of smugglers that dramatically reduced the migrant flow, but in fact many armed groups simply shifted to other illegal and highly profitable activity, like the smuggling of subsidized fuel. And in some coastal towns, Italian funding sparked conflict: fighting broke out between militias who enjoyed Italian payments and those who didn't.

Al-Bija lit a cigarette. He had an equine face and gelled hair swept back to the nape of his neck. Something I noticed upon meeting him was a hand with missing fingers: the result of an injury during the 2011 revolution, where he'd lost a brother. The wound, however, did not prevent him from flipping open the lid of his Marlboros pack, nor from participating in coast guard operations at sea.

A video surfaced of one such rescue in September 2016.

Al-Bija's boat pulls alongside a listing dinghy packed with migrants. Clad in fatigues and a beret, al-Bija kneels on the side of the boat and whips a migrant with a rubber pipe. The frightened man shields his face with his forearms. "Easy, Bija," one of the coast guard crew says off camera. "Easy, Abd al-Rahman." This wasn't anything like the videos al-Bija had shown me in his office, of his men clashing with armed fuel smugglers or draping grateful migrants in blankets.

After the fall of Qadhafi, al-Bija's tribe captured Zawiya's port and a nearby refinery and set themselves up as the area's notional coast guard. But the migrant detention center run by the Nasr Organization was in fact complicit in the trafficking trade, the United Nations alleged, a front for militias who forced migrants to work and released them for a ransom—or not at all.

All of it made a mockery of European hopes of identifying and training Libyan partners to combat smuggling.

■

I TRAVELED BACK from Zawiya to Tripoli on an Italian-made speedboat, the type favored by smugglers. The island of Lampedusa, the tip of Europe, lay just to our north, visible if you strained your eyes. Along the Libyan coast to the south, we passed the frames of half-finished buildings, spindly cranes, and funnels of smoke. At sunset, we pulled into port, where young boys net-fished and dove off a jetty. I thought of something Riyad, the Red Crescent corpse collector, had told me.

One summer morning he'd gone out to a beach and found that the dead migrants who had washed up that night were all women. One or two were pregnant, he said. Then, something offshore caught his eye.

It was the body of a small boy, wedged between clusters of rocks amid the pounding breakers.

"We couldn't get to him," Riyad said, "because of the waves."

Eventually, the tide freed the boy and carried him out to sea.

12

THE ISLAMIC STATE'S
AFRICAN HOME

AS LIBYA'S CIVIL WAR BETWEEN Dawn and Dignity ravaged
the country, a new menace arrived, burrowing deep into the vacuum wrought by the fighting. Hiftar and the Misratans were so busy
fighting each other that they failed to notice the growth of the Islamic
State on Libyan soil.

Born in Iraq and Syria, the Islamic State first arrived in Libya in
the spring of 2014, drawing from a younger generation of Libyans
who'd come of age during and after the revolution. It peeled away
adherents from weakened al-Qaeda affiliates like Ansar al-Sharia,
co-opting them, instead of attacking them as it had in Syria. It called
foreigners to come to its new North African affiliate. And by the
fall of 2015, the Islamic State's leadership declared Libya its best

opportunity for expansion, oil-rich and ideally located between Africa and Europe.

None of this would've happened without the return of Libyan volunteers from the Syrian jihad. In the months that followed Qadhafi's death, thousands of Libyans left to fight in Syria. A mix of motives propelled them: belief, adventure-lust, friendship, and desperation. The first of them felt a revolutionary fraternity with the anti-Assad rebels, fighting with relatively moderate groups such as the Free Syrian Army. As time wore on, more and more zealots went, fired by jihadist ideology. The young Libyan I'll call Ahmed was one of these early volunteers.

Ahmed had grown up comfortably as the son of a grocer in Janzur, on the western edge of Tripoli. For decades, Janzur had been a seaside settlement famed for its watermelons and home to a tuna cannery. With the oil boom and a rush of migrants, the capital swallowed it up with housing tracts, gated "tourist villages," and an American school favored by diplomats.

In 2013, Ahmed entered the University of Tripoli to study engineering. He was not observant back then; he did not go beyond the usual instruction in Sufi schools. He smoked cigarettes and drank home-brewed alcohol, the potent *bokha*, as his friends did. It was his first term of study, a time of dislocation and questioning, wrought by upheaval in Libya and in the world.

In 2011, he'd been too young to fight against Qadhafi, but then another Arab uprising, in Syria, gripped him. "We'd suffered, and we knew the Syrians were suffering too," he said.

He watched the Syrian war from afar, on the Internet and on Saudi satellite stations, where two Saudi clerics, Muhammad al-Arife and Ayidh al-Qarni, beseeched their audiences to support the revolution. It was a religious obligation, the preachers said, incumbent upon all believers. But these exhortations alone did not recruit Ahmed.

In the predawn hours of August 21, 2013, a Syrian Republican Guard artillery crew in Damascus launched a volley of rockets into the eastern neighborhood of Ghouta. The largest of the shells carried fifty to sixty liters of sarin, an odorless, colorless liquid, twenty times more lethal than cyanide, which vaporized on impact. U.S. government estimates put the death toll of civilians at over 1,400. Thousands more were hospitalized.

"After Ghouta, I really decided," Ahmed told me.

It was not hard to get to Syria. A Syrian man in Tripoli gave him a contact in Turkey. "Call this guy," he said, "he will tell you where to go."

In Aleppo, he joined a small militia called Muthanna, named for the nom de guerre of its leader, another Libyan. There were twenty of them, from Derna, Benghazi, Misrata, and parts of Tripoli. These were places of faith, with long pedigrees of resistance, whether at home, against the Italian colonists and Qadhafi, or abroad, in Afghanistan and Iraq. For the young men, this history mattered; they walked in their forebears' footsteps.

The Libyans joined an alliance of Syrian Salafist fighters, some more radical than others; some, like the Nusra Front, linked to al-Qaeda. They encamped in the farmlands near Aleppo, where Ahmed trained on a 14.5 mm gun. Winters were colder and cloudier than in Janzur, but less wet and without the salty gusts from the sea. He liked the easy camaraderie of jihad, the communal cooking, the muted pageantry of flags and emblems, even the hours of waiting.

In October 2013, the Syrian army launched an armored blitz aimed at choking off Aleppo and cutting the rebels' supply lines to Turkey. The Libyans fought in the battle of Brigade 80, an army base near the international airport, then retreated north to a hamlet of beehive homes and olive groves called Tiyara. Here, Ahmed manned the defenses of an old plastics factory just east of a hill where Hizballah snipers and Syrian soldiers had the commanding heights and an easy defilade. When a Libyan fighter next to him fell to the ground, shot in the head, it wasn't just any death. He was a childhood friend from Janzur, two years his senior; they'd joined the war together. And so, in December 2013, Ahmed decided to leave the front.

Leaving Syria was harder than entering. The next month, the rebels fell into factional fighting. The Free Syrian Army attacked the Libyans, killing their leader, Muthanna, as part of a burgeoning feud with jihadist groups. Ahmed barely escaped with his life, traveling west of Aleppo until he reached the Turkish border.

February saw him back in Tripoli, safe and exhausted. But he wasn't finished with war. When the capital fell into fighting in the summer of 2014, he joined a neighborhood militia on the side of Dawn. One day in October, a group of seven Libyan veterans of the Syria war arrived at the abandoned TV station where he was based with his friends. He remembered one of them from the Aleppo front. It was another Libyan, though, a brawny thirty-five-year-old from Bani Walid named Malik al-Khazmi, who pitched them to join the Islamic State.

"The *tanthim* [organization] is coming to Libya," al-Khazmi told them, using the common moniker for the Islamic State.

"Don't you want to be the first to join? The nucleus?"

■

THE FIRST PLACE in Libya where the Islamic State secured a foothold was in Derna. This wasn't surprising. Hundreds of Derna's youths had gone to Syria, where many had joined a jihadist militia called the al-Battar Brigade, which enjoyed financial support from Derna's charities and businessmen. It wasn't long before al-Battar pledged allegiance to the Islamic State and acquired an outsized reputation for fearsomeness and brutality on the Syrian battlefield. It attracted non-Libyans, especially French, Belgians, Moroccans, and Tunisians—among them, the future mastermind of the Islamic State attack on the Bataclan theater in Paris, Abdelhamid Abaaoud. Its fighters returned to Libya in waves. And by the fall of 2014, al-Battar veterans, along with local jihadists in Derna, had declared the Libyan city part of the Islamic State's province in Barqa or Cyrenaica.

The liberal activist Maryam remembers signs appearing over Derna's buildings announcing departments in the Islamic State's new government and calling residents to join. STRETCH FORTH THE HANDS TO PLEDGE ALLEGIANCE TO BAGHDADI, they read. At a nighttime meeting convened by the Islamic State for local citizens, a respected professor and federalist stood up, demanding angrily to know from the bearded Saudi speaker why his group appropriated the hallowed historical term "Barqa" for their dark project. He died the next morning in a hail of bullets on a tree-lined street near Derna's river. The terror had only started.

The Islamic State set up a *sharia* court, took over the town council, and posted guards at a hospital. It invited Derna's police, their ranks already thinned by assassinations, to atone for their sins at a "repentance station." Islamic State judges installed themselves in the city's splendorous Atiq Mosque, an ancient Sufi building with forty-two domes, after killing its shaykh and demanding a list of its members from Maryam's uncle, who handled its endowment. He refused and escaped the country.

Vice patrols from the Islamic State's *diwan al-hisbah*, or "accountability office," swept across the town and its craggy hills, prowling for offenders. Some they flogged or scolded; others they subjected to varying degrees of barbarity: cutting off thieves' hands, beheading "sorcerers," shooting homosexuals in the back. At a soccer stadium, they executed an Egyptian for murder, handing a pistol to the victim's relative to shoot him in the head.

Foreigners helmed the new order. An Iraqi named Abu Nabil al-Anbari served as the leader and military chief; he'd been an ex-policeman and confidant of the Islamic State's self-proclaimed leader or caliph, Abu Bakr al-Baghdadi. A Yemeni judge handled governance and the Islamic courts. At checkpoints across and around the city, residents encountered gunmen from Tunisia and Egypt.

Their reign was not unchallenged. Derna's homegrown militias led by the Abu Salim Martyrs Brigade opposed the intrusion on their turf. By 2014, the brigade had expanded its power, controlling banks, hotels, and several mosques. Now it faced a threat to that power. In the weeks and months that followed, the Islamic State lured some of the brigade members, along with some from Ansar al-Sharia, over to the caliphate. Salim Darbi, the leader of the Abu Salim Martyrs Brigade, vowed that he would never follow a group where foreigners ruled over Libyans.

A spat of tit-for-tat killings ensued until Salim Darbi rallied the town's jihadist militias into a new alliance, the Derna Mujahideen Shura Council. Terrified residents looked to him and the council as their savior, or at least the lesser of two evils.

"A righteous adversary against the Islamic State," a twenty-six-year-old Libyan wrote of Darbi in his diary.

Meanwhile, the Islamic State moved on to Benghazi.

Since May 2014, Hiftar and Dignity had been battling the Dawn-backed Islamists in Benghazi. By 2015 the weakened Islamist militias in the eastern city had no choice but to cooperate with the Islamic State, dividing the battlefield among their forces. Elsewhere in the country, Dawn forces had not sided with the terrorist group, but neither did they fight them—mostly because the Islamic State had not encroached on Dawn-held territory. Fighting Hiftar remained the priority, and in Benghazi an alliance with the Islamic State offered clear advantages.

"We told them, 'You take this position, we'll take this one,'" one Shura Council fighter told me. But the coalition was always fraught with suspicion; mutual animus toward Hiftar was all that held it together. "If it weren't for Hiftar, we would fight the Islamic State," he added.

Yet the cooperation with the Islamic State amounted to a Faustian pact for Benghazi Islamists, and their backers in Tripoli and Misrata. By funding and arming the Shura Council in Benghazi they were also aiding the Islamic State, since the boundary between the two had blurred. For no one was the dissonance more pronounced than for Wissam bin Hamid. In his tacit alliance with the Islamic State, some saw a rank lust for power; others, an obsession with fighting Hiftar, no matter the costs. "He found himself cornered," a fellow militia leader said.

For his part, Hiftar couldn't be happier. The arrival of the Islamic State and its foreign legions in Benghazi was a propaganda boost. He'd told me at the start of his campaign in May 2014 that he was fighting an onslaught of foreigners. Six months later it had become more of a reality, partly of his making. He'd not fulfilled his pledge to swiftly free the city, but that didn't matter. Now he had an easy pitch to the world, not just to his longtime patrons such as Egypt and the UAE, but to the United States and Europe. He wasn't just fighting a local band of militants, he told them, he was now part of a global campaign against the Islamic State.

By early 2015, the Islamic State's recruiters told Libyan and foreign aspirants to stop traveling to Syria and Iraq after Turkey had tightened its border control. Instead, jihadists were directed to Libya, to one of the three Islamic State provinces: Barqa (Cyrenaica) in the east, Fezzan in the south, and especially Tarablus (Tripolitania) in the west, where it was establishing its strongest base in the city of Qadhafi's birth.

■

SIRT IS NOW FAMOUS as a loyalist haven, the place to which Qadhafi fled in his final days and met his end. But beneath this common label the city has its own rich identity, a complex one comprising twenty-odd tribes and an ancient history. The coastline around it is scenic and unspoiled, though its shoals have long been treacherous for mariners. "Inhospita Syrtis," Virgil wrote in The Aeneid. "A large coastal city with brick walls . . . date palms and sweet-smelling springs," wrote an Andalusian geographer after a first-century visit.

In the centuries that followed, Sirt faded to the margins, a middling town linked by trade to the desert south rather than to the east or west. Qadhafi changed this, building it up as an enclave for favored tribes and elites. He erected the staggering Ouagadougou convention hall, a vanity project named for the capital of Burkina Faso.

After the revolution, Sirt fell into neglect and desperation. The Misratan-led rebels took revenge on pro-Qadhafi tribes with detentions and executions. They upset the city's social balance, disarming some tribes while favoring others. Worse, a jihadist militia from Misrata—the Faruq Brigade—moved to Sirt, training fighters for Syria and supporting a local branch of Ansar al-Sharia. By 2013, jihadists in Sirt had won locals' support for their social work efforts, which included battling drugs and mediating land disputes among quarreling tribes. Ansar al-Sharia took over security in Sirt's poorer neighborhoods after a Libyan Special Forces unit that had been patrolling the city left. All of this happened under the noses of the Misratan militias—some said with their connivance—while they were battling General Hiftar's forces for the oil ports to the east.

The Islamic State moved in slowly, dispatching military advisors, legal experts, and propagandists from Iraq and harnessing the influence of local Ansar al-Sharia leaders, whose pledges of allegiance it had won. Years later, I met one such figure, who'd been among the founders of Ansar al-Sharia in Sirt before becoming an Islamic State judge in the city. A forty-one-year-old former electrical engineer, he tilted his head when speaking to correct for a missing left eye; he'd lost it in combat, he said, and all that remained was the sutured socket. He was a committed jihadist, imprisoned by Qadhafi in 2007 for trying to go to Iraq to fight the Americans before traveling to Syria in the summer of 2014. There, the Islamic State directed him back to Libya to pave the way for the caliphate in North Africa.

He described how the Islamic State exploited Sirt's divisions. Members of some loyalist tribes welcomed the group, brutal though it was, as protection against the predations of nearby Misrata. "Better the hell of the Islamic State than the paradise of Misrata," went the saying at the time. Soon, foreigners rushed in—from Tunisia, Sudan, and the Sahel—and by the summer of 2015, after quashing a brief tribal uprising, the Islamic State's control over Sirt was complete.

■

ONE MORNING in October 2015 the Islamic State arrested a resident of Sirt named Milad Abourgheba. Forty-two and newly married with a newborn baby, he'd left school in the ninth grade but had a decent job in Sirt at the Great Man-Made River project. He liked to spearfish in his spare time, scouring the rocky seabed for octopus. This was his home. And after the Islamic State arrived, he stayed. "I don't need to escape these bastards," he told his family.

When the gunmen roused him at dawn, he was shaken, but not entirely surprised. There were six of them, foreigners mostly, who accused him of spying, for the Misratans and the Tripoli Dawn government.

By this time the Islamic State had cut off Sirt from the world. "No banks, no fuel, no clinics, no networks," a resident told me. Families traveled west of Sirt for groceries, gas, or weddings and returned, though not without raising the Islamic State's suspicion. Beyond the edges of their control, its clerics said on the radio, lies the land of disbelief. Milad risked it anyway, driving to Misrata, sometimes just for the cell phone coverage.

Months of detention followed, and no public trial. Then in January, on the second anniversary of his wedding, a crippled Tunisian shot him dead in a car market. They strung up his corpse on steel scaffolding in a roundabout. SPY FOR LIBYA DAWN, read a placard hanging from his neck.

"Three days later his brother came and cut him down," his mother told me.

She pushed me a plate of wafers. We sat in the living room of a house in Misrata where she stayed after fleeing Sirt. It had been one month since Milad's death. By this time, refugees from the city had streamed into Misrata, collecting food and blankets from a charity's warehouse. She was in her sixties, a mother of nine, but only six still lived; her husband, a son, and a daughter had died years before in a car crash. She wore the long dress favored by Libyan women of her age, the *huli*, with stripes of silver and bright magenta. It was a far cry from the full-body veil dictated by the Islamic State, "the black tent," as she called it.

She mentioned these impositions nearly as much as the torment endured by her son.

"They cut off the headstones of Sufi graves if they were too high," she told me, "and they left them as rocks." They banned incense and the Sufi practice of *dhkir*, a musical reciting of the names of God.

They professed piety, she said, but showed only greed and hypocrisy, smashing televisions as un-Islamic, while seizing the wide-screens for themselves.

I'd heard similar stories from others who'd escaped. The Islamic State levied steadily rising taxes on everyone, from shepherds to butchers to tailors, while it emptied the banks. It kept lists of attendance at mosques. Women suffered untold horrors, some of them enslaved and raped as so-called prizes of war. A Sufi biology teacher told me he'd fled the city after the banning of science, history, and English in favor of Islam and rudimentary math. He sighed at the deaths of his friends, Sufi shaykhs and healers murdered for practices such as the medicinal drinking of ink from a Qur'an or possession of a goatskin drum used in rapturous chanting. "Whatever happened to coexistence?" he asked me.

All the while, the Islamic State expanded. It moved into villages across the Sirt Basin, such as Nawfliya, where graduates of a Qur'anic school who'd fought in Iraq established a branch. It set up safe houses in Bani Walid, another town that had suffered at the hands of Misrata. It broadcast appeals to the Tabu and Tuareg in the south, speaking in their respective languages. And it started attacking across the country.

In January 2015, a team of militants stormed the Corinthia Hotel, one of the few in Tripoli that foreigners still patronized. I'd been in the capital, staying with a friend, when the assault unfolded in the morning. The assailants shot their way to the twenty-third floor after detonating a car bomb outside. Ten died, including an American security contractor, in what the Islamic State dubbed the "Battle of Abu Anas al-Libi"—a revenge attack on a "den used by the enemies of God."

In the following months, clandestine teams in Tripoli attacked checkpoints and militia bases and foreign embassies. And across Libya, the Islamic State assaulted police training centers and oil facilities. The barbarism seemed to know no limits. In February that year it released a video showing the decapitation of twenty-one Egyptian Copts on a beach near Sirt, prompting Egyptian airstrikes on Derna. And in April, it broadcast the apparently simultaneous execution—by gunshot and beheading—of Ethiopian migrants in two separate locales. Its strategy in Libya became clear: exploit the fighting between Dawn and Dignity, scare off foreigners, eliminate threats from militias and police, and, especially, sow more economic havoc by cutting off oil revenue.

By late 2015, the United Nations was warning that the Islamic State had up to three thousand fighters across Libya. It controlled a 155-mile-long stretch of territory in the center of the country's coast—about 375 miles from Europe.

■

WASHINGTON WATCHED the buildup with alarm. By now, President Obama's hopes of averting a collapse of the country had been dashed. With Dawn in Tripoli and Dignity in the east, Libya was split in two. The American embassy had evacuated and set itself up in neighboring Tunis, where many foreign embassies in Tripoli had relocated. The administration's Libyan partner, Prime Minister Ali Zeidan, had fled and the American-European project to train his army had failed. And now the world's most menacing terrorist organization was moving in.

What first caught the eye of the White House was the flow of experienced Islamic State operatives to Libya from Iraq and Syria.

"If you were going to build a business franchise," Obama's senior director for counterterrorism, Joshua Geltzer, told me, "they were sending some of their best corporate executives."

These were hardened veterans, Iraqis, Saudis, and Egyptians, with experience in military affairs and governance. Then came the foreign foot soldiers. As jihadist travel to Iraq and Syria became more difficult, they arrived in Libya in increasing numbers. Within a matter of months, Libya had become the branch of the terrorist group with the most threatening capabilities outside the Levant. And the Islamic State's leadership in Raqqa had given this branch significant operational autonomy.

That worried the White House. The Islamic State posed a threat not just to Libya's stability but to Libya's neighbors on the African continent. "Their gateway to Africa," as Geltzer called it. The Islamic State in Libya might destabilize Tunisia, and it could plot or inspire attacks against American allies in Europe.

In weighing responses, Obama ruled out ground troops. Airstrikes alone could target Islamic State leaders and supply lines but could not dislodge the terrorist group from towns it had seized. That left the option of working with Libyan forces on the ground, with the United States providing precision airstrikes and ground advisors. Obama insisted that Libyans take the lead. But which Libyans? Without a Libyan government, or a coherent military, the Americans and their allies had no choice but to work with militias. On the surface, this seemed to be a variation of the light-footprint strategy that the United States had employed in Afghanistan and during the 2011 Libyan revolution, when commandos assisted armed groups, backed by airstrikes. But now the battle lines were murkier, the militia landscape less certain. The country was caught in a multisided civil war.

"There wasn't really a great template for this," Joshua Geltzer said. The key task, then, was how to intervene against the Islamic State without inadvertently empowering militias and diminishing the prospects for unity and stability.

First the Americans needed to know with whom they were dealing. In the spring of 2015, small groups of American special operations soldiers started making clandestine trips into Libya to meet and assess the militias. In some cases they were renewing contacts they'd made during the revolution, but in many instances, they found the roster of players had changed completely. And sometimes their forays did not go as planned.

In December 2015, for instance, an American special operations team arrived at a desolate airstrip in northwest Libya, just outside Zintan, only to be turned back by a hostile militia that controlled the airfield. Photos of the flannel-clad U.S. soldiers and their vehicles flanked by militiamen quickly appeared on social media. It was yet another lesson, and a very public one, in the hazards of navigating Libya's terrain of militia and tribes.

Still, by the end of 2015, the American, British, and French special operations forces had set up two secret outposts in Libya, each in the camp of a warring faction: one at Benghazi's Banina Airport, controlled by Hiftar's men, and another at the air force academy at Misrata's airport.

Misrata was a particular focus of American and Western attention since it was closest to the Islamic State's strongest base in the country. Misratan leaders, Ambassador Jones would tell a congressional committee, were "the first to draw our attention to the growing [Islamic State] presence in Sirt." Delegations of American military officials met the Misratans in Istanbul and in Misrata itself to discuss a strategy to defeat that presence.

Yet allying with Misrata to liberate Sirt also carried risks.

First there was the bad blood between the two towns and the animus of some of Sirt's tribes toward the Misratans, whose abuses during the 2011 revolution they'd not forgotten. In the battle for Sirt, would Misratans behave as liberators or conquerors? Just as troubling, American overtures to Misrata fueled alarm in the Hiftar-aligned east, confirming a growing view that Washington was biased toward Islamists and the Misratans. Moreover, General Hiftar's forces viewed any Misratan advance on Sirt with suspicion; the city lay in the heart of Libya's oil-rich region, and moving against the Islamic State could be a useful pretext for the Misratans to grab it. To prevent this, Hiftar had pledged to move on Sirt himself.

With a collision of the two factions looming, it soon became clear that the campaign to rid Sirt of the Islamic State might very well worsen Libya's civil war. The way to avoid that, Washington believed, was to forge a national political and military coalition against the Islamic State, drawn from east and west, to avoid the risk of conflict later on. This proved exceedingly difficult.

American and British officials passed through Misrata, imploring its leaders to work with commanders from Hiftar's side in an assault on Sirt, and vice versa. But distrust remained among the armed groups. "The Americans and British tried to arrange some cooperation but failed," a Misratan militia chief told me. "The other side has a bad opinion of Misrata," he added, referring to Hiftar's Dignity commanders. Of course, the same held true for Misrata's hardliners, who continued to see Hiftar as a far greater foe than the Islamic State and refused to cooperate with him.

The last remaining avenue was the UN-sponsored peace talks that had begun in late 2014 after the eruption of the civil war. This dialogue had proceeded fitfully and slowly, aiming to produce a new government acceptable to both the Dignity and Dawn factions. Such a government, it was hoped, would not only unify the country but also provide a legitimate, centralized channel through which Western powers could work in battling the Islamic State. But whether a consensus could be reached was still unclear.

The White House waited nervously. The Islamic State's gains were outpacing the UN's glacial progress toward a peace deal between Dawn and Dignity. Some in the U.S. government, from the Pentagon and the intelligence community, wondered whether the United States shouldn't just throw its weight behind one faction—namely, Hiftar's, whom they argued was the only one fighting terrorists.

"They were saying, 'Listen, we got a ticking clock here,'" Samantha Power recalls. "'Our political investment in this shotgun marriage isn't working. We should just cut our losses.'"

As the clock ticked, Libya's factions seemed more intent on fighting each other, even if it meant ruining the country and giving space to the Islamic State. It reminded Libyans of an old joke.

A genie appears from a lamp and promises to give a man one wish, while doubling that wish for his friend.

"A blind eye," the man responds.

■

THEN THE ISLAMIC STATE overplayed its hand.

Opposition to the terrorist group had started in Libya as soon as it arrived. Towns, militias, and rival jihadists resented the Islamic State's upending of old norms and the arrogance of its foreigners.

The pushback started in Derna, the eastern coastal town long famous for its resistance to foreign encroachment. Here, the Islamic State committed a catalog of abuses, crucifying brothers from an influential tribe and opening fire on unarmed protestors. It got greedy, raising taxes on merchants and beheading the son of a fabric dealer after he failed to pay. And in the summer of 2015, it provoked open conflict with a local rival, the Derna Mujahideen Shura Council, the coalition of Islamist militias.

That June, the council declared an all-out war on the Islamic State. Derna descended into days of street battles. Among those who died was the council's chief, Salim Darbi, eulogized by Islamists and jihadists across Libya. By the fall, however, the Shura Council fighters had pushed the Islamic State to the eastern highlands outside the town, killing scores. And in November, an American airstrike killed the Islamic State's leader in Derna, Abu Nabil al-Anbari.

A Derna diarist remembers well those days of liberation. The Shura Council dragged an Islamic State leader, a young Iraqi, naked through the streets before hanging him. "I laughed until I had tears in my eyes," he wrote.

The next place where the Islamic State's fortunes fell was in the town of Sabratha, on the other side of Libya. Located some forty-five miles west of Tripoli, near the Tunisian border, Sabratha has long been famous as a beachside Roman city, second only to Leptis Magna in the grandeur of its ruins. Italian Fascists had restored the ancient site as visible proof of Rome's presence and as justification, they said, for reclaiming Libya as a possession. "Between the Rome of the past and the one of the future," Mussolini had written in Sabratha's visitors' log. In the waning years of Qadhafi's rule, the Italians returned as tourists to watch Puccini's operas in the floodlit amphitheater.

Modern Sabratha is a town of farmers, merchants, and fishermen—and smugglers. It is also a place of piety and defiance. "Derna of the west," Libyans called it. Like Derna, the sons of Sabratha had fought in Afghanistan, with some returning to join the Libyan Islamic Fighting Group. After the 2011 revolution, Ansar al-Sharia arrived. Then came the Islamic State, abetted to a large degree by Tunisians.

Tunisians had long played a disproportionate role in Sabratha's jihadist milieu, given the proximity of the border. And when the Tunisian government cracked down on Ansar al-Sharia, Tunisian jihadists in Sabratha switched to the Islamic State. Hundreds of Tunisians traveled to Sabratha for jihadist training, using the traffic of remittance workers and smuggled goods as cover. In 2015, some crossed back to launch attacks in Tunisia, including assaults on the capital's national museum in March and a popular beach in June that killed dozens of Westerners. The Tunisian government struggled to stop the carnage, closing the border for weeks and halting all flights from Libya. Still, the influx continued.

In the winter of 2015, people in Sabratha's western suburb watched the building of a high cement wall around a three-acre farmhouse. The owner was a man in his sixties, a veteran of Afghanistan who'd rented to Tunisians. This by itself was not unusual since the neighborhood was home to many Tunisians, working in Sabratha's shops and farms. Panels of zinc roofing appeared above an outdoor court. Guest rooms, a bathroom, and a kitchen soon followed. Trucks with tinted windows trickled in, until one night a month later when the neighborhood shook with a deafening boom.

The Americans had watched the buildup as well.

In the predawn darkness of February 20, two of their F-15s dropped laser-guided bombs on the farm, exposing what some had long suspected: the site had been a workshop for Islamic State members to train on explosive belts and small weapons. The strike seemed impressively precise; all I saw a week later was a crater strewn with concrete chunks, sandals, and rugs and a nervous-looking goat. More than forty Islamic State fighters, mostly Tunisians, died in the blast. Among them was a thirty-five-year-old Tunisian named Nouredinne Chouchane, whom the United States accused of masterminding the Islamic State's museum and beach attacks in Tunisia and sending hundreds of jihadists to Syria and Iraq. He and his fighters had been in Sabratha for months, enjoying support from some of the town's families.

But after the bombing, all that changed. Emboldened by the Americans' attack, Sabratha's militias hunted down the remaining cells.

One afternoon in early 2016, a few days after the strike, I flew to Sabratha from Tripoli on a militia helicopter, sitting atop boxes of bandages and ammunition in the cargo hold. Arcing over the furrows of white-capped waves, we kept far from the coast to avoid any ground fire from the fighting below. Militiamen met me at an airport in armored cars, and we drove to the center of Sabratha. This was where the battle had turned.

Acting on information from the few survivors of the airstrikes, Sabratha's militias had raided suspected safe houses a few nights before. Sensing a vacuum, the Islamic State tried to outflank them and take over the town. Hundreds of its fighters rushed by car or foot into the downtown, seizing a bank and a hospital and hoisting a black flag over the square. They stormed a police station at midnight, shooting the guard at the gate before slitting the throats of the officers inside. Then they turned on the militiamen across the street, killing scores of Sabratha's youths. By daybreak, though, the Islamic State had fled.

I met a militia leader involved in that battle, a twenty-two-year-old with a lazy eye, nicknamed al-Ammu. Hailing from a well-known tribe in the city, he was deeply involved in the trafficking of migrants. For now, however, he was among the leading fighters in Sabratha's war against the Islamic State, though for clearly self-interested motives. "This enemy," he told me, "it affects us all."

We went to a villa where al-Ammu turned the key on a gate. Inside a courtyard shaded by lemon trees, he showed me a captured arsenal: antipersonnel mines, machine-gun rounds, ten-gallon drums of explosives, and a cell phone detonator. He unfurled a black flag and showed me a pile of papers, speeches by al-Baghdadi, and a Ziploc bag of passports: Egyptian, Sudanese, Libyan, and Tunisian. I could tell he thought it was an impressive haul of booty, and it was.

I wondered, though, about the durability of his victory over the Islamic State. Sabratha's smugglers and militia bosses—not the Libyan government—were the ones who'd fought the terrorist group; each had his own reasons for seeing it leave. Al-Ammu in particular emerged more powerful than ever and would monopolize the town's illicit activities in the coming year. Moreover, Sabratha's social tolerance for the Islamic State had allowed it to arrive and flourish in the first place. And the threat it posed was far from over: many jihadists had fled to nearby farms and could very well reemerge.

I left Sabratha heading west toward the Tunisian border. Militiamen passed me off to a Libyan intelligence officer driving a beat-up Opel. Such cars are sometimes better at escaping attention than an armored Suburban, but they are just as vulnerable to an Islamic State checkpoint. My escort had brought along his four-year-old daughter, who turned and smiled from the front seat. A wall of thunderheads loomed off the coast. We stopped at a wedding in the town of Zuwara then continued west. Rain started tapping at the windshield.

At the border, I thanked the man and started to cross by foot in the dark. I always felt relief when I arrived in Tunisia from Libya, glad to see the surly custom guards in their uniforms as a sign of order. But in just six hours, at sunrise, Islamic State gunmen would attack the Tunisian town of Ben Gardane some twenty miles from the frontier, killing more than fifty. I would pass through it one hour before the assault.

The intelligence officer grabbed me before I left.

"We overthrew Qadhafi and now we don't know what do," he said excitedly. It was the clearest explanation yet I'd heard for Libya's troubles.

And then, pointing to the clouds, he added, "Even the sky is crying."

■

MEANWHILE, TRIPOLI HAD sunk to new depths due to the ongoing civil war. Oil output had plummeted and inflation soared. Food had grown scarcer, the power outages longer. As banks ran short of cash, people waited in long lines in the sun. In such despair, crime thrived and the Islamic State moved in. That winter, I went to go see the man who claimed to be fighting both, Abd al-Rauf Kara, the Salafist leader of the capital's most formidable militia.

I traveled to his base at Mitiga Airport the same way I always had, along the coastal road past the Abu Sitta racetrack. This time, a blackout had thrown the neighborhood into darkness, save for a few splotches of moonlight. A pack of feral dogs crossed a garbage-strewn park.

Kara received me in a conference room. His head was more shaven and his hirsute beard more streaked with gray than I remembered. He looked tired.

A few months before, the Islamic State had attacked his forces at Mitiga to free its prisoners. It was seven forty-five in the morning when he'd heard the explosion. There were four of them that morning—two Sudanese, a Moroccan, and a Tunisian—wearing explosive belts and carrying grenades and weapons for the prisoners they would free. They'd blown a hole in the outer wall and gotten far inside the compound, killing four of Kara's guards before they themselves were killed.

It was hardly the first of Kara's clashes with the Islamic State. "I am sitting on a volcano," he told me. But he was winning, he insisted, and he was Tripoli's last line of defense. Each arrest led to new ones, once the prisoners had been interrogated and their cell phones exploited. I wondered, though, whether Kara might be using the pretext of the Islamic State to go after local rivals in Tripoli. His arrests seemed to be happening with little or no judicial oversight, and ex-detainees complained of torture. He had also stepped up his enforcement of Salafist social mores across the city.

Yet Western powers would rely upon him in battling the Islamic State in the capital—his militia was the closest thing to a counterterrorism service. His biggest coup would come in mid-2017, when he arrested the older brother of Salman Abedi, a twenty-two-year-old Briton of Libyan descent who blew himself up in the name of the Islamic State in Manchester in May 2017, killing twenty-two people at a concert. Believing the brother to be an accomplice, British authorities have asked for his extradition to the United Kingdom. It struck me as the same sort of devil's bargain that confronted the Europeans in stanching the migrant flows: working with and through the militias against terrorists only inflated their authority. Kara, however, assured me that he was acting legally—and with humanity. The proof, he told me, was his program of prison rehabilitation.

The next morning I went to see the rehabilitation center, housed in a hangar on the northern end of Kara's prison, near a half-finished soccer field. At seven-thirty the prisoners jogged from their cells—shipping containers with narrow slits—to breakfast. Then they took classes on Islam. Some of them, my escort told me, had been brought to Kara's prison by their families, for drug use usually but also any number of behavioral problems. Then there were the jihadists. "The Islamic State guys need special treatment," he said.

Seated on a plush carpet before a cleric, they hunched over Qur'ans and pamphlets, written by religious authorities in Saudi Arabia, where similar rehabilitation programs existed. This dose of Salafist morality seemed the extent of their counseling and treatment, though Kara said he addressed more worldly needs as well. In the afternoons after lunch, the prisoners took vocational classes: cabinet making, computer literacy, baking, house painting, and electrical repair. "To rejoin society," my escort said.

I walked through the hives of activity, past the whine of buzz saws and fumes of lacquer to a small cantina where some young men were frying hamburgers.

That's where I met the Islamic State fighter named Ahmed.

In person, Ahmed is of small stature, with a patchy beard. Dressed in a cream-colored robe, he walked with a limp, the result of his capture, he said, by Kara's men months before. They'd come to his home one morning, acting on their interrogation of Islamic State prisoners who'd plotted the Corinthia Hotel attack.

In pledging fealty to the Islamic State, Ahmed said he wanted to join something bigger than himself. The recruiter told him of a borderless state, where Muslims lived peaceably, apart from the unbelievers. He marshaled an array of theological justifications for the organization's wanton brutality.

"They showed us verses from the Qur'an and the Prophet's sayings," Ahmed told me. "'You see? It's all here.'"

Now, in prison, Ahmed cooked and studied. He met with prison clerics every day who tried to purge him of what the Islamic State had told him about Islam.

Kara gave me an illustration.

"We tell the Islamic State youths that Westerners in Libya are people protected by a covenant," he said. "They are not *kuffar* [unbelievers] and you cannot kill them."

Ahmed gave me an even simpler explanation.

"I didn't know the stories behind the sayings and the verses," he said. "The Islamic State never told me the stories."

He was talking about context.

Context ultimately blocked the Islamic State's expansion in Libya. Libyans had their own stories and their own narratives, and the terrorist group found it hard to graft its sectarian and apocalyptic worldview onto the Libyan milieu. Libya's militias and social complexities were further brakes on its ambitions. In an interview just before his death, the Islamic State's emissary in Libya, Abu Nabil al-Anbari, decried "the presence of obstacles" in the North African state and its "deviant parties and divided factions."

Still, by early 2016, the Islamic State had tightened its grip on its remaining stronghold in Sirt, bolstered by fighters who'd escaped from Derna. And it could still plot attacks abroad.

THE STRONGMAN

IN DECEMBER 2015, the torturous UN-led dialogue between Dawn and Dignity factions finally bore fruit. At a seaside resort in the Moroccan town of Skhirat representatives from the two sides signed an agreement. A new "unity government," or Government of National Accord, based in Tripoli, would be the country's sole recognized authority.

That it had happened at all was due to frantic shuttle diplomacy. The United States had dispatched a special envoy from the State Department, and Secretary of State John Kerry himself had worked to broker meetings. Deploying a mix of bluffs, threats, and incentives, the UN chief in Libya, a Spanish diplomat named Bernardino León, had coaxed the opposing sides to a settlement. The Misratans came to the negotiating table motivated partly by the economic pinch of war. By early 2015, production at the city's iron and steel company had fallen by a third; container volume at the port fell as well; Misratan-owned firms in Tripoli had closed their doors. Sanctions or the threat of sanctions persuaded other, more recalcitrant figures to join the dialogue, most notably the politician Abd al-Rahman al-Suwayhli.

Support by the regional backers of Libya's factions also helped, especially from Egypt, the United Arab Emirates, and Qatar. By December 2014, León believed that the Emirates' in particular could accept a political solution in Libya. "They realized that military force can work as pressure," he told me, "but the solution will not come through the use of weapons." The Americans weighed in as well. At a May 2015 summit meeting at his Camp David retreat for the heads of the Gulf Arab states, President Obama all but scolded the leaders of Qatar and the United Arab Emirates to stop using Libya as a playground for their rivalry. Egypt soon followed the Gulf states in supporting the UN-led Libya negotiations, albeit reluctantly.

The Morocco agreement was plagued with problems from the start, rushed at the behest of outside powers, critics said. In the pursuit of consensus, it had produced a governing formula that was too unwieldy—a nine-person Presidency Council and two legislative assemblies: the House of Representatives and a new body called a State Council, mostly made up of members of the General National Congress. Moreover, the UN's selection of figures to the Presidency Council, Libyans complained, was opaque and arbitrary.

The new government was further thrown into doubt when leaked emails revealed that UN mediator León had accepted a lucrative job offer in Abu Dhabi training Emirati diplomats even as he was negotiating with the Emiratis and their Libyan allies in Dignity to end Libya's conflict. But most important, the December agreement excluded Libyans with real military clout—and the power to sabotage the deal.

Nowhere was this more apparent than in the figure of General Khalifa Hiftar.

Even though a delegation from the east had signed the peace deal, Hiftar and his military and tribal supporters opposed it. Specifically, Hiftar rejected Article Eight of the agreement, which designated the Presidency Council as the supreme commander of the Libyan armed forces. For the ambitious general, this was a nonstarter, posing a threat to the power he'd accumulated in the course of his Dignity campaign and to his aspirations for political leadership. Acting on Hiftar's behalf, the House of Representatives refused to convene and endorse the new Government of National Accord, as the December agreement required it to do.

In the coming months, the new UN-backed government in Tripoli would struggle to extend its writ in the capital, only gradually moving beyond its headquarters at a naval base to occupy a few ministries and buildings. It failed to deliver even basic services such as electricity, fuel, and water and was powerless to fix the country's worsening liquidity crisis. It got mired in disputes with the Central Bank over budgetary authority and the National Oil Corporation over the right to sell oil to foreign buyers. Lacking a police or army of its own, it depended on the goodwill of the capital's militias, some of whom tried to topple it. Disagreements among the representatives on the council led to gridlock between pro- and anti-Hiftar members. Meanwhile, Libyans who'd backed it grew impatient with its disarray.

Still, for the United States and its allies, the Tripoli government was a vital partner in Libya—especially for the campaign against the Islamic State in Sirt. American diplomats and military officials started discussing a strategy to confront the terrorist group with the new unity government soon after the signing of the Morocco agreement. Defeating the Islamic State, they also hoped, would help it gain legitimacy. To do that, though, they needed to make the campaign as national as possible, including, if possible, forces from both Misrata and from Hiftar's Libyan National Army. The figure tapped to lead this effort was Colonel Salim Joha.

Joha had returned to Libya from exile in Abu Dhabi, where he'd fled after his fellow Misratans scorned his calls for restraint during Dawn's attack on Tripoli in 2014. Now he was back on the scene, the one figure with the military expertise and respect among both eastern and western militias to lead an attack against the Islamic State. In early 2016, he'd started reaching out to military officers from across the country, including those from General Hiftar's camp to coordinate the assault. Western diplomats and military officers had supported him in this effort.

But then he pulled out. Some said it was due to the Tripoli government's lack of support or pushback from other Misratan factions. Others who knew him well attributed it to a personal quirk: he liked to exert influence behind the scenes but never out in front. Whatever the case, Joha's withdrawal eroded hopes for a national coalition to fight the Islamic State. On top of this, the Americans encountered continued rejection from General Hiftar, who still refused to join the Government of National Accord in Tripoli. "We were prepared to work with Hiftar," an American diplomat told me, "but he wouldn't cooperate."

The remaining option was for a coalition of militias led by the city of Misrata. But Misrata's leaders wanted more time to get additional support from the still-dysfunctional Tripoli government and also assurances from the Americans about airstrikes and intelligence from teams of American and British advisors. Washington, however, was still trying to work out the parameters of that support.

Eventually, as the Islamic State threatened Misrata with suicide attacks on checkpoints and tried to outflank the city by capturing Bani Walid, the Misratans could wait no longer.

On May 12, columns of their militias headed east toward Sirt. Operation Bunyan al-Marsus, or "Solid Structure," had begun.

■

THE DEAD MAN lay on his back in the shade of a eucalyptus grove not far from the sea. A large-caliber bullet had entered his eye and lodged in his forehead, its outline bulging just beneath the skin. One arm was splintered at the elbow, the other one splayed above his head. Balding and older than most Islamic State fighters, he wore a calf-length tunic and carried a bag of dates for breaking the Ramadan fast. A Casio watch had slipped off his wrist.

"Tunisian, maybe," a Misratan fighter told me.

"No, Egyptian," said another.

The Misratans had shot him the night before and would later bury his corpse in a barrow of dirt and leaves—one hand still protruded—before continuing east. It was June 2016 and the war for Sirt had only just begun.

On the eastern shores of the city, I watched a forward spotter call out corrections to mortar fire against a sniper ensconced in a hotel about four hundred meters away. Crouching on a sand dune between tufts of salt grass, he peered through binoculars for a telltale sign like a muzzle flash or the glint of a telescopic lens.

A round exploded somewhere on the beach.

"No, a little to the left," he shouted. A runner relayed the adjustment to a mortar crew in the rear.

Crawling on the sands across a tarp of scratchy burlap, I heard a low-pitched whir. I looked up.

By this time the Americans had been flying surveillance drones over Sirt and passing the intelligence to the Misratans. But this one was an off-the-shelf version, a rickety, four-rotor contraption, piloted from an iPad in a nearby truck.

"Definitely one of ours," a commander lying next to me said with a laugh. He'd not slept in days. And that afternoon, he nearly led us into a sniper's line of fire before one of his men shouted at him, "Sniper!"

I went to an Islamic State bomb workshop, seized by the Misratans only hours before, after fierce fighting. Threading my way to a villa through a reedy backyard, I heard a bulldozer punch through a breeze-block wall and bullets snapping overhead. Four or five dead Islamic State fighters lay sprawled by a puddle of seal-gray water. Inside the house the air was pungent and biting. On a shelf next to flasks, beakers, and syringes sat the bomb makers' stash of precursors: tartaric acid, acetic acid, sodium hydroxide, and sodium sulfate. In a nearby room, there were wooden crates for Russian-made rockets, whose explosives the militants extracted and repurposed for IEDs. "Lasting and Expanding," someone had scrawled on a wall—the Islamic State's motto.

By late July, the Misratans had reached an upscale western neighborhood in Sirt nicknamed the Dollar Quarter. It had been a punishing slog with heavy casualties, more than three hundred deaths so far. Early losses had come from suicide attacks with car-borne bombs, and then snipers slowed the advance, perched in high-rise housing or hiding in spider holes dug into parks or fields. On a rooftop observation post, I met Misratan fighters seated by a pigeon coop, peering across an empty lot at the Islamic State's defenses. "They are so good they can hit this," one of them said of the snipers, throwing up a small pebble. He pleaded for body armor, helmets, and binoculars.

I saw the results of the marksmen's handiwork. In a field hospital south of Sirt a doctor lamented the prevalence of head wounds. And then, as if on cue, two soldiers arrived on wheeled gurneys, with thick gauze bandages encasing their foreheads. The eyes of one of them fluttered while a clear plastic tube slurped saliva out of his mouth. The doctor rushed forward, conferring with colleagues.

"You see?" he said, turning to me. "This is one of the cases I mentioned. And this one's bad—his brain is coming out."

At three hundred meters or less, the Misratans tried to stop the snipers with a sniper of their own and a spotter. But beyond that range they took to saturating the area with mortars or artillery rounds, from batteries far to the rear. I'd spent a sleepless night with one of their crews, who sipped cardamom coffee in between salvos. I asked about civilians in the areas they were hitting. "They've all left," a colonel replied. "Anyone there we assume is with the Islamic State."

I drove through the liberated western neighborhoods. It was not hard to find evidence of the Islamic State's draconian rule. Alongside

rows of shuttered shops, I saw the stenciled logo of the Islamic State's
Office of General Services, signifying that the owner had paid his taxes.
My militia escort handed me a small pamphlet: an Islamic State driving log for military vehicles, with columns for gas expenditures and
a warning that "discrepancies will result in the application of *sharia*
punishment."

"Organizationally, they are sophisticated," the commander told me.
"Individually as fighters, they are dumb."

I asked him how long this would last.

He estimated about five hundred fighters were holed up in the city
center. And they would fight to the death.

He flicked on the truck's radio to the Islamic State's local station, still
on the air after a brief disruption. The shrill voice of the speaker taunted
the attackers: "You won't kill us, we are in Europe and America . . . and
we will go to the desert."

Life returned, slowly, in the areas freed from the Islamic State. One
afternoon, I went to a farm surrounded by desiccated fields. A sleeping
dog reared up. I sat with its owner, a middle-aged civil servant, drinking
sweet tea in the shade of an awning, next to an empty vineyard. A jet
roared overhead, and artillery thudded in the distance. The man had
stayed in Sirt during the entirety of the Islamic State's rule, caring for
two adult sons, both severely disabled. One of them, with cerebral palsy,
squatted alone on the concrete porch, glancing up briefly to salute me
before returning to swat at a buzzing fly.

The first thing the Islamic State came for, the man said, were the
records. He'd been working in Sirt's social security administration, in
the section on building registration, when a Saudi man asked him one
day to hand over the files; the Islamic State needed the data for their
bureaucracy of plunder, their so-called Office of Spoils. The man com-
plied and they fired him shortly after. Returning home, he struggled to
survive and care for his sons: food dwindled and banks and hospitals
closed.

The dog sprinted after a chicken across the field, pawing it into a frenzy of fluttering feathers. "You see, we have no food or no garbage for him and he's starving," my host said. The militiaman snatched his Kalashnikov and fired over and around the dog, kicking up small eruptions of dirt. The dog slinked off and the chicken trotted away, clucking and bleeding from its wounds.

That evening I went deeper into the front lines, to a base of a Misratan militia called the Hatin Brigade. They seemed well equipped, with T-62 tanks, clanking behemoths cursed by their sweating drivers, as well as plentiful gun trucks and mortars of assorted calibers. Setting up their command center in the garage of a villa—the former home of a loyalist professor, it seemed, from the bronze-plated plaques from Sirt's university and the studies of Qadhafi's Green Book in glass-fronted shelves—the fighters huddled by candlelight. Laundry hung across a clothesline. Some of the youths were students back in Misrata, on summer break, and they'd left their homework scattered on the floor, lined sheets of engineering formulas and economics textbooks.

The next day one of them took me to the militia's forward position, where it had been boxed in for days. From a balcony near a television building and its broken concave dishes, I watched the Islamic State "walking" their mortar rounds gradually toward us. First came the whine of a spotting round; an explosion three hundred meters away shook the building. Adjustment. The next one fell closer. What followed was house-to-house fighting with crew-served weapons. An unseen gunner fired at our car as we skirted the length of a wall.

Inside a villa, I met a commander named Ali, a former engineer at Misrata's steel works before the war. We hopped in his truck and drove past the captured bomb factory to an intersection in Dollar Quarter, the easternmost point of the Misratans' advance. It was early evening, the drawn-out time when fighting picks up, and a team of Islamic State snipers had pinned down his men.

"How far away?" I asked.

"Not far," Ali said, "just around the corner."

I watched as young men darted across the street with rocket-propelled grenades, casting long shadows in the soft light. Amid the rattle of automatic gunfire, a car stereo was playing a *nashid*, or Islamic chant, the polyphony at once elegiac and fortifying. An armored personnel carrier finally broke the impasse, lumbering to an intersection where a turret gunner fired volley after volley.

Later that night after evening prayers, back at militia's headquarters, Ali peered at a laptop with his men, plotting the next day's moves, with video from drones. Aside from correcting fires and spotting infiltrators, the drones offered a window into life and death in the enemy's camp. The Misratan fighters showed me a compilation of their favorite footage: a mortar round explodes on a parked car, and Islamic State fighters rush from a house to see what happened; a wounded Islamic fighter crawls across a road, trailing a long, dark line of blood; a projectile streaks across the screen and destroys a tank.

Now one of the men pointed at the video. The drone had revealed a group of Islamic State fighters blocking a strategic road.

"Right," the commander said, "the British told us the same thing."

It was an open secret. He meant the British soldiers from the Special Air Service (SAS) who conducted reconnaissance and on occasion, it seemed, engaged in combat. In one instance, a Misratan colonel told me, a British special forces soldier had saved countless lives by firing an antitank missile at an approaching steel-plated suicide truck. I'd gone to some frontline positions only to be told the British had been there hours before.

Ali was grateful for their assistance, and for that of the American teams who also provided intelligence from an operations room outside Sirt. What he really needed, though, was American airstrikes. That afternoon he'd unrolled a satellite map of Sirt on the hood of a truck and swept a hand across the eastern half.

"They still control most of it," he said.

Foreign media, Ali complained, had been too rosy in their reporting about the extent and speed of Misratan advances against the Islamic State. He worried that as the fighting dragged on and casualties mounted, the coalition of militias from Misrata and allied towns would fall apart. Some of them already seethed at the Tripoli government's lack of support and were ready to march on the capital. Airstrikes, he said, were the only hope.

For now, he made do. The Misratans' drone over Dollar Quarter revealed that Islamic State vehicles throughout the day always avoided a certain road, taking detours on the streets around it. "It's mined," Ali concluded. He told his mortar squad that night to fire at the area, disperse the militants, and even detonate the mines in the street if they could.

I walked outside to a sandy lot not far from the villa. The crew worked quietly, washed in moonlight, on a medium-weight variant, an 81 mm. A gunner set an angle of fire that was steep and high—the Islamic State was not far away, he said. Someone mused on the star-filled sky above. "Did you know that every one of them has already died," he said, "so we are actually looking into the past?"

They dropped a round in the tube and shouted "God is great" before the boom. The mortar whizzed into the night, its exhaust tail glowing like a floating ember.

It seemed a lifetime before it detonated.

■

THE AMERICANS finally started bombing Sirt on August 1, 2016, just days after I'd been to the front line in Dollar Quarter.

After prolonged deliberations, President Obama had approved a plan for airstrikes and ground advisors long advocated by the Pentagon. "Odyssey Lightning," they dubbed it. The option evolved out of months of consultations with the Libyan Government of National Accord, with the goal of developing protocols for the strikes and avoiding civilian casualties. "Working that out took some time," a senior American diplomat told me. "It required hundreds of hours of legwork. You can't just flip a switch."

Indeed, the delay was due in part to restrictions imposed by

Obama's Presidential Policy Guidance, a 2013 document intended to limit operations against terrorists outside declared battlefield zones such as Syria, Iraq, and Afghanistan to avoid civilian casualties. In practice, this meant that U.S. military commanders had to have "near certainty" that civilians would not be harmed or killed and that targets posed an imminent threat to U.S. persons, not just American interests. After intense discussions in the summer of 2016, Obama exempted Sirt from these rules by declaring the city and its environs "an area of active hostilities"—a practice known among staffers as a "carve-out." American military commanders now had much more latitude in conducting airstrikes without interagency vetting.

The first strikes came from American marines flying Harrier jets from an amphibious assault ship off the coast of Sirt. On the ground, American special operations teams, along with the British SAS, provided intelligence on Islamic State locations. The Pentagon predicted an end to the operation "in weeks," but the fighting dragged on. The Islamic State adapted to the strikes, camouflaging its tanks and ammunitions depots and moving its fighters through a web of tunnels. Sirt's dense residential districts naturally favored the defenders.

In late August, the marines added SuperCobras to the fight, an upgraded Vietnam-era helicopter whose loitering ability and large-caliber cannon offered more precise support than a fast-flying jet. Still, Islamic State holdouts fought back with suicide attacks, snipers, and booby traps. Some tried to escape by sea, only to drown or be nabbed by Misratan boats. Others fled to south, threading their way through the gaps in the lines of Misrata's fragmented militias, joining comrades who'd slipped out even before the attack in May. American surveillance drones circled high in the sky to track the escaping fighters.

Finally, on December 6, after weeks of house-to-house fighting, the Misratan-led forces declared victory. The struggle to free the coastal city had lasted eight months, longer than the NATO-led campaign in 2011. More than seven hundred Libyan fighters, mostly Misratans, had lost their lives, and three thousand more were wounded. The United States had flown a total of 492 sorties.

Though the victory had dealt a serious blow to the Islamic State, the aftermath in Sirt was still uncertain. One winter afternoon, a year after its liberation, I visited the city again and toured the cyclopean ruin: block after block of flattened buildings and piles of ashen debris. I spotted a rib cage poking from the rubble near a scorched car—the corpse of an Islamic State suicide bomber, someone said. Reconstruction had been slow and displaced residents were furious. "I am ready to swim to Europe," a young man told me. Some accused the Misratans of looting and others chafed at the dominance of a Salafist militia that had taken over policing and mosques.

Still, the Obama administration congratulated itself and its Libyan partners on the hard-fought battle. But a lasting solution to Libya's civil war eluded it, and the campaign against the Islamic State had possibly made that conflict worse.

■

AS THE MISRATANS were busy fighting in Sirt, Hiftar was making advances of his own in Benghazi against the Islamists, which by now included the Islamic State. In the winter of 2016, his forces captured a port south of Benghazi, a lifeline of maritime resupply for the Islamist fighters. It was a staggering blow that turned the tide of the battle in his favor, breaking months of stalemates.

Outside help had been crucial. On February 25, 2016, the Special Forces colonel Wanis Bu Khamada told foreign reporters that French military advisors were assisting Hiftar's Libyan National Army. The statement confirmed an earlier exposé by *Le Monde* that officers from the paramilitary wing of the French external intelligence service, the General Directorate for External Security (DGSE), had long been active in Benghazi, since at least early 2015, in conducting airstrikes and surveillance against the Islamic State and other militants. Official acknowledgment from the French government finally appeared in July, when a surface-to-air missile fired by Benghazi Islamists downed an LNA military helicopter outside Benghazi. On board were three DGSE officers, who died along with the Libyan crew.

What made the revelations so explosive was that European nations, along with the United States, had agreed in principle that any military assistance to Libyan forces fighting the Islamic State had to flow through the UN-backed government in Tripoli, which Hiftar and his forces openly opposed. This was certainly the publicly stated policy of the French Foreign Ministry. But the DGSE saw things differently. Determined to stop extremists from gaining a foothold in the Mediterranean or from threatening French interests in the Sahel, it backed Hiftar as a useful partner, despite his blunt-force methods. Domestic political considerations underpinned France's aggressive stance, especially after the January 2015 al-Qaeda attack on the Paris office of the *Charlie Hebdo* satirical weekly and the November 2015 Islamic State attack on the Bataclan theater. So too did France's burgeoning defense and economic ties with the United Arab Emirates, Hiftar's key Arab backer.

Despite their professed support for the UN-led negotiations for a Libyan unity government, the UAE, along with Egypt, never stopped supporting Hiftar with arms.

In the spring of 2016, the UAE delivered hundreds of armored personnel carriers to Hiftar's forces, and by the end of that year it had set up a secret air base in eastern Libya, from which it flew drones and propeller-driven attack aircraft against the general's opponents in Benghazi. All of it was in contravention of the UN arms embargo. It amounted to a two-faced policy that exasperated Washington.

"They tried to make us think they were becoming more constructive," a senior U.S. administration official confided to me, "but I'm not sure they actually were."

But it wasn't just the French and Emiratis who were backing Hiftar. Press reports trickled out that the British and the Americans also had special operations forces in Benghazi. It was said they'd been working out of an operations room with the French at Banina Airport since at least late 2015 or early 2016. A young Libyan I met in Benghazi who served as an English interpreter for the foreign soldiers confirmed this. American, French, and British military teams, he said, reconnoitered the front lines, flew drones, and passed intelligence to Hiftar's men. The Italians and Jordanians, he added, had small cadres as well, for training the Libyans. Even the Russians were there.

It was all hard to corroborate. But what was certain was that the injection of foreign assistance and military hardware, wherever it came from, had a dramatic effect in Benghazi. Emirati armored vehicles helped the Libyan National Army advance on the ground and Emirati and French airstrikes, more precise than anything Hiftar could manage, pounded the Islamists' positions and their supply boats. Foreign special operators provided intelligence that improved the accuracy of artillery. All of it combined to break the months of deadlock.

Emboldened by his victories in Benghazi and his growing national stature, Hiftar grew even more obstinate toward the UN-backed government in Tripoli. And that fall, he moved to consolidate his power.

On September 11, he sent the LNA into the Sirt Basin to wrest control of the oil ports from Ibrahim Jadhran's Petroleum Facilities Guard. After years of blockading the ports, Jadhran had finally struck a deal with the Government of National Accord and the National Oil Corporation to resume production, though actual implementation had been slow, and he'd been widely scorned. Exploiting these grievances, Hiftar mobilized local tribes against the militia boss, which, along with airpower, resulted in his quick seizure of the ports.

The United States and the Europeans condemned the brazen takeover, emphasizing that the Government of National Accord in the capital was the sole steward of Libya's oil wealth. Then, Hiftar surprised everyone by handing management of the oil facilities back to the National Oil Corporation, which was based in Tripoli. Within months, Libya's oil output had reached a three-year high, at seven hundred thousand barrels per day. It was a skillful move that recast Hiftar and his LNA as guarantors of national prosperity. Yet by placing his eastern faction in physical control of a large portion of Libya's wealth, it also decreased the chances for a political deal.

By this time, Hiftar had won recognition from European powers and the United States that he had to be part of any future political settlement. At a meeting in Abu Dhabi, American diplomats presented Hiftar an offer they thought he couldn't refuse, one that was also endorsed by the UAE: he would become commander in chief of the Libyan military under a reconfigured unity government that would include greater representation from the east. The Americans calculated that some irreconcilable Islamists in the west would oppose the arrangement, violently perhaps, but the majority of key players, including the Misratans, would not.

Hiftar rejected it out of hand, falling back on a demand he'd long stated in media interviews: he insisted on governing the country himself, through a military council, for a temporary period. He simply would not accept civilian control of the country's military. And in the weeks and months ahead, he revived his threats to march on the Libyan capital.

The end of the Obama presidency promised him even more leverage. Cheers in eastern Libya greeted the election in November of Donald J. Trump: it was a welcome change, they told themselves, from Obama and Hillary Clinton, whom they saw as too friendly to the Islamists. Trump's hard-line views on Islamism, especially his vow to declare the Muslim Brotherhood a terrorist organization, along with his warmth toward Hiftar's main patrons, the United Arab Emirates and Egypt's Abd al-Fattah al-Sisi, made him the favored candidate for many Hiftar backers.

In late November, Hiftar dispatched two of his sons and a trusted advisor to Washington to meet with Trump's transition team. In a separate meeting with State Department officials, the advisor delivered a long presentation, one that had been clearly vetted by General Hiftar. The political class of Libya is failing, the statement said, the country is facing a threat of terrorism, and the Tripoli government is impotent. What is needed is an emergency response. "General Hiftar is willing to take over," the Libyan advisor told the assembled Americans, "and hold elections in a couple of years."

The answer from the Americans was an unequivocal no. Any such action, they told the Libyan delegates, would be deemed a coup.

But such opposition, Hiftar probably calculated, was just a tenet of the outgoing administration. All he had to do was wait for Trump. And in the meantime he was basking in the attention of another superpower.

On January 11, 2017, Russian television broadcast images of General Khalifa Hiftar and his entourage touring an aging aircraft carrier, the *Admiral Kuznetsov*, anchored off Tobruk. En route home after bombing Syria, the vessel had stopped in Libya to receive an increasingly important figure. For the Libyan general, it was another boost to his prestige: Hiftar watched the catapulted launches of Sukhoi jets with white-clad Russian officers and held a videoconference with the Russian defense minister.

The visit served Russian aims as well.

Moscow had been a longtime patron of Qadhafi's Libya, with many officers of Hiftar's age training in Soviet military schools. In 2010 alone Libya accounted for 12 percent of Russian arms exports. Now, in the aftermath of the dictator's fall, Russia hoped to reenter the Libyan arms market, and it stood to gain additional billions in oil and gas exploration and other ventures. Spotting a useful ally in General Hiftar, Russia plied him with weapons, spare parts, medical care, and military training. It also provided vital assistance to his political allies in the Tobruk government by printing four billion Libyan dinars, relieving its currency crisis—a move condemned by Washington and the Europeans.

By 2017, this support had paid off. Moscow had become a major power broker in Libya, undercutting U.S. and European influence.

■

AT THE END OF JANUARY, one day before the end of his presidency, Obama intervened again in Libya. It was his last military action as commander in chief, in a country that had bedeviled him since 2011.

On January 19, 2017, two B-2 Spirit stealth bombers dropped more than one hundred bombs on two Islamic State camps southwest of Sirt, believed to be sheltering remnants of the terrorist group. More than eighty fighters died, most of them foreigners and some linked to operations outside Libya, including an Islamic State attack in Berlin in December. Misratan militias and British SAS soldiers swooped in afterward to gather intelligence.

It was an ambiguous coda to Obama's presidency. To be sure, the Sirt campaign had been a success: the Islamic State's most powerful branch outside Iraq and Syria had been ousted from its base. Yet in the coming months, fighters who'd fled south of Sirt would try to stage a comeback. After the U.S. B-2 strike, I'd sat with a Misratan intelligence officer who showed me on a satellite map where these remaining militants had gathered. "The Brothers of the Desert," they called themselves; they would soon attack Misratan patrols and even the city's courthouse. Many others would flee deeper south, across the border into Niger.

Moreover, defeating the Islamic State in Sirt did little to resolve the legacy of Obama's 2011 intervention. Politically, Libya was more divided than ever; a "shit show," the president conceded to a reporter. The failure to plan for what followed Qadhafi, he admitted, had been the "worst mistake" of his presidency.

"The degree of tribal division in Libya was greater than our analysts had expected," he said. "And our ability to have any kind of structure there that we could interact with . . . broke down very quickly."

The turmoil resulting from this failure cast a long shadow over his foreign policy: it reduced his already chastened estimation of the ability of American policy to effect changes in states devastated by conflict or dictatorship. It also arguably dissuaded him from taking action in Syria, where his demand that President Bashar al-Assad step down was never matched by commensurate efforts to make the dictator do so. "A president does not make decisions in a vacuum," Obama conceded. "He does not have a blank slate."

Perhaps this is another case of overlearning. Syria is not Libya, after all. One of Obama's former Middle East advisors agreed and was unsparing in his critique: "He invaded a country that wasn't really killing its civilians; then he called for a dictator to step down that actually was." But Samantha Power disagrees, also citing the example of Syria. Once the Libya dictator had started his violent crackdown, she told me, "once the demons had been unleashed," there was no status quo ante to which the country could return.

"How, absent our intervention," she asked me, "would Libya look much different than Syria? Much of the instability that Libya is enduring today would've come had Obama decided the other way, not to intervene."

■

I TESTIFIED ONCE AGAIN before the Senate in April 2017, concerned about the new president's policy on Libya—or lack thereof. In theory, the Trump administration still supported the UN-backed government in Tripoli and UN-led mediation, but in practice, it saw Libya primarily through the lens of countering the Islamic State. The absence of American diplomatic leadership, it seemed to me, risked ceding Libya's future to the strongest regional powers—the Emiratis and the Egyptians—as well as to the Europeans, whose approach was increasingly fragmented, and the Russians. And indeed, the first half of 2017 saw an uptick in Egyptian and Emirati military activity in Libya on Hiftar's behalf. Reinforcing these efforts was the fierce, Saudi-led blockade of Qatar, the patron of Hiftar's Libyan Islamist opponents—and President Trump's apparent encouragement of that campaign.

"The United States must avoid subcontracting its Libya policy to Egypt and the United Arab Emirates," I told the senators, "whose securitized approach [namely, backing Hiftar with weapons] will only produce more division and radicalization." I added that Hiftar's push for authoritarianism and anti-Islamism in Libya would have disastrous effects, destabilizing the country, and restocking the pool of jihadist recruits.

But most egregious perhaps was Trump's attempt to restrict Libyan visitors from entering the United States, on the basis of protecting the "homeland" against the Islamic State. The measures were especially bitter for Libyans: they had fought and defeated the Islamic State across their country—mostly on their own.

Then there was Trump's evisceration of the State Department and downgrading of support for civil society and human rights abroad. It was a poor recipe for durable peace. And it seemed a betrayal of precisely the sort of people-to-people ties that Chris Stevens had been so impassioned about during his tenure as ambassador. In the end, however, that passion outlived him and will outlive the Trump administration.

Hours after Stevens's death in 2012, friends, colleagues, family, and strangers around the world who'd been moved by his story started asking how they could preserve his legacy. His family realized quickly they should set up an endowment to receive donations, and within twenty-four hours the J. Christopher Stevens Fund was born. They didn't have the clarity of thought so soon after his death to deal in specifics, but they knew it would be about constructing bridges between youth in the United States and youth in the Middle East. They knew also it would center on education and study abroad, since these had been such a formative part of Chris's life.

Soon, the Stevens Initiative was established, growing quickly with partnerships from corporations, universities, and the State Department. The first iteration brought together youths from seventeen Middle Eastern countries, from Morocco to Iran, and students from twenty-five U.S. states in "virtual classrooms." It also expanded to include actual study in the Middle East, in Lebanon and Jordan.

"He liked the people and respected the culture," Chris's father, Jan, told me, "and we thought that a system of exchanges and fellowships and simulcast sessions seemed to be the best way to do it."

A family friend who helped start the project summed it up more briefly.

"Basically, we wanted to create more Chris Stevenses," she said.

■

ONE DAY AFTER MY TESTIMONY in April 2017, I went back to Benghazi, and found it transformed. Hiftar now controlled more than 90 percent of the city. Most Islamic State fighters had fled, and the remaining militants were confined to a couple of shorefront blocks.

In late December, an airstrike by Hiftar's forces had killed the Islamists' preeminent field commander, Wissam bin Hamid, though supporters disputed this, saying he'd been wounded and fled the city. Regardless, the removal of the charismatic leader from the scene was yet another setback to the much-diminished Benghazi Revolutionaries' Shura Council. And it seemed to bring to an end the career of one of Libya's more remarkable and polarizing revolutionaries: the former car mechanic who'd fought alongside General Hiftar against Qadhafi in 2011, assisted the Americans during the 2012 Benghazi attack, and then sided with jihadists against the Dignity campaign.

To be sure, fighting still raged in the Islamists' redoubts. But Benghazi hummed with signs of normalcy.

In the old district of Birka, once home to Ansar al-Sharia, green-checkered flags of the Nasr soccer club crisscrossed the streets, while pulsing *mirskawi* music blared from cars. Traffic police who once cowered at home for fear of assassination were back at intersections, having just switched their uniforms from winter blue to sparkling summer white. Factories and farms were creaking to life, while young entrepreneurs tried their hand at tech start-ups. The university was reopening.

Leisure had returned as well. At the Luna Mall, children played on a toy train next to ice cream parlors, candy stores, and clothing outlets. There were musical and theater troupes, poetry readings, art galleries, and rugby tournaments. On the lawn of a newly opened hotel, newly-weds smoked water pipes while a projector played Egyptian soap operas on a wall.

Preparations were under way for a celebration of the third anniversary of Operation Dignity in just a week, culminating in a lavish military parade. The Libyan National Army had declared victory and the mood was congratulatory. WE FIGHT TERRORISM FOR THE SAKE OF THE WORLD, read a billboard bearing Hiftar's visage on Dubai Street.

Yet beneath this image of recovery, Benghazi had another, darker side.

By late 2016, Hiftar's men had cornered Islamist fighters in twelve blocks of unfinished apartment buildings in the southwest neighborhood of Ganfuda. Laying siege to the area, they cut off water and electricity and refused to let males between the ages of fifteen and sixty-five evacuate. Trapped families subsisted on expired rice and contaminated water. When Hiftar's troops finally captured the area, they inflicted a string of abuses, including disinterring and posing for photos with enemy corpses and summarily executing prisoners.

One officer in particular, a Special Forces commander named Mahmud al-Warfalli, appeared time and time again in execution videos, either supervising the killings or pulling the trigger himself. When I asked the LNA spokesperson about al-Warfalli, he assured me that his case had gone to "military justice." A week or so later, however, Libyan press reported that he'd been promoted, and then more videos emerged of al-Warfalli overseeing executions. In an arrest warrant based in large part on this footage, the International Criminal Court charged him with the unlawful deaths of no fewer than thirty-three persons.

But the ultimate responsibility went higher: Hiftar himself had been filmed exhorting his troops to take no prisoners, raising the question of his own culpability.

"No mercy," he said in the fall of 2015. "Never mind the consideration of bringing a prisoner here. There is no prison here. The field is the field, end of the story."

Aside from these abuses, another by-product of Operation Dignity was a surge of conservative Islam in Benghazi and across the east. Despite his common portrayal as secular and anti-Islamist, Hiftar had co-opted and supported hard-line Salafists, the same so-called quietist Salafists who also filled the ranks of Abd al-Rauf Kara's militia-turned police in Tripoli. Supportive of the Qadhafi regime in its final years and targeted by jihadists after the revolution, these Salafists were natural allies for Hiftar's Dignity operation. One of them, a middle-aged man with a henna-dyed beard, told me he'd traveled to Saudi Arabia to seek a supportive fatwa for Hiftar from their spiritual guide, a Saudi cleric named Rabi bin Hadi al-Madkhali.

The pro-Hiftar Salafists fielded a militia that fought alongside the LNA and had a strong presence in prisons; I met one of their clerics who worked on the theological rehabilitation of captured jihadists, in the same manner as Kara's program in Tripoli. The Salafist militias also functioned as morality police, confiscating Western books, closing music clubs, and shutting down an Earth Day celebration as un-Islamic. Taken in sum, their growing authority unnerved many of Hiftar's liberal supporters, who backed the general to oust the Islamists, not anticipating that he would unleash Islamists of his own.

But even more unsettling was Hiftar's militarization of governance.

That fall, the House of Representatives had promoted Khalifa Hiftar to field marshal as his forces seized oil fields in the Sirt Basin. In tandem, Hiftar's chief of staff, by now the military governor for all of eastern Libya, dismissed the elected city council of Benghazi and installed a brigadier general as its head. In quick succession, Hiftar and his allies repeated this pattern across the east. It was all part of a broader securitization of governance: a return to the surveillance state of the old regime, justified on the basis of vague threats from "foreign intelligence" and, especially, the Muslim Brotherhood.

Many I met in Benghazi seemed not to mind the regression, given the chaos produced by the country's earlier experiment in democracy.

"I will cut off my finger before I vote in another election," a friend's mother had said.

Granted, getting at what people really thought was exceedingly hard. Libyan journalists and activists who were critical of Hiftar were silenced through intimidation. "A line of military cars showed up at my house at 2:00 a.m.," one of them told me. Others fled the country or disappeared altogether.

The restrictions grew as Hiftar tightened his grip. In February 2017, his military governor of the east issued an edict banning women under the age of sixty from traveling abroad without a male chaperone—they were easy targets for foreign intelligence, he told a Libyan television station. In the uproar that followed, he rescinded the ban but then issued another one, this time barring women *and* men ages eighteen to forty-five from traveling abroad without permission.

It was another jolt to eastern Libyans; some joked darkly that they didn't need President Trump's travel ban on Libyans when they had done it to themselves. The "deep state" was back, they admitted: Hiftar had welcomed the return of several ex-regime figures from abroad, including despised military commanders, and he'd revived the old intelligence apparatus.

By mid- and late 2017, flush from battlefield gains, Hiftar appeared to shift tack: instead of insisting on running the country through a military council, he hinted he'd accept a position in a reconstituted Presidency Council or run as a candidate in presidential elections. I found signs of this attempted rebranding in another, newly erected billboard: Hiftar is wearing a gray suit and tie and surrounded by adoring crowds. THE POPULAR AUTHORIZATION MOVEMENT FOR SAVING THE COUNTRY, reads the wording beneath him. Inside a tent, in Benghazi's main square, the movement's organizers explained its goal: to obtain hundreds of thousands of signatures "authorizing" Hiftar to govern the country.

In the coming months, however, I realized that this transformation was a ploy, an effort to bolster his position as a sort of plebiscitary populist. Though he nominally supported elections, he had still not abandoned his threats to conquer Tripoli by force, and indeed the tempo of those threats was quickening. And meanwhile, a spate of car bombings shook Benghazi, belying his claim to have pacified the city.

Even Hiftar's onetime supporters seemed weighed down with buyer's remorse. For them, the saga of his comeback from obscurity and his rise to national dominance carried all the makings of a personality cult.

"We've come to regard him as a mini-god," a Benghazi activist confided to me, "and that's dangerous. That's what we did with Qadhafi."

■

AND YET for all the analogies to the late dictator, what is happening in eastern Libya heralds something newer: a type of upgraded authoritarianism that is spreading across the Arab world, in a time of unprecedented conflict. It is a bleak vista, akin to what George Orwell must've seen gazing from the precipice of the Spanish civil war onto what another writer called the "dark valley" of 1930s Europe. It also carries echoes of the antiliberalism and nativism sweeping the globe and even the States. At the same time, Tripoli and the west of Libya aren't much better. Here, fractious militias hold sway, sometimes using the support of the internationally recognized government to enrich themselves through smuggling and other illicit activities.

The dissolution in the capital and across the country parallels a collapse and renegotiation of political order under way across much of the Middle East. Yet the impact of recent Western policies in this fracturing should not be overinflated. As much as anything, the disorder is the consequence of decades of dictatorship. It is no accident that the most violent aftershocks of the 2011 Arab uprisings took place in the states that had the most brutal despots. In Libya's case, the chaos has been aggravated by Qadhafi's ruinous reign of "statelessness," which worsened the already parlous condition of the country under the monarchy, the British, and the Italians.

There are no easy fixes. It is likely that Libya will simmer with violence and instability. A formal redrawing of Libya's boundaries, as some have suggested, is unworkable and will only lead to more war, since the rival factions do not lend themselves to a neat geographical separation.

What is needed instead is a new social contract, drawn up by Libyans themselves, which devolves some degree of power to the local level and which is supported by outside states that must cease their harmful meddling. Whether and when this will happen is still uncertain. What is clear is that the old order, in Libya and across the Arab world, has been irrevocably shaken and with it old notions of sovereignty and nationhood.

The effects will be felt by generations.

EPILOGUE:

BENGHAZI, 2017

ONE AFTERNOON IN MAY 2017 I drove to see the deserted house of Salwa Bugaighis. A stately two-story building with a Spanish tiled roof, it sits on a quiet side street in the farmlands of Hawari, not far from grain silos, power lines, and a cement factory. There is a weathered sign for the now-closed International School. Farther down the highway sits the abandoned base of an Islamist militia, the Rafallah al-Sahati Companies, named for an ex–political prisoner Salwa once defended as a lawyer.

I glanced through the wrought-iron gate flanked by tumbling bougainvillea for a half-obscured view of the house. I thought of Salwa and her family and the brave decision they made that fateful day in February 2011—and the meetings they'd had since in the living room.

Her three sons are all that remain of that family now. The eldest, Wail, had won a Fulbright scholarship shortly after her death, fulfilling one of his mother's dreams: she'd been badgering him constantly, he said, to apply. Studying engineering in Florida, he was among the last group of Libyan students to receive a Fulbright before their country's program was canceled. He did not intend to return to Benghazi.

That same day I drove to the site of the U.S. diplomatic mission in the Fwayhat neighborhood. The greensward villa compound has a placid feel as well, bearing few exterior scars of what happened that September night. Its frosted-glass gate is slightly smashed, but otherwise secured and locked. I resisted the temptation to see too much of what happened in Libya as stemming from the tragedy. And yet Benghazi had been changed because of it, as had the lives of countless Libyans.

A few weeks later, I met one of them.

Fathi al-Obeidi, who'd helped the American rescue team the night of the attacks, had recently fled Benghazi to a location he didn't want mentioned. After Hiftar had attacked Benghazi in 2014, al-Obeidi fought back, joining the forces of his old militia commander Wissam bin Hamid. He helped build a jetty at a Benghazi port controlled by militias so they could receive heavy weapons and vehicles ferried by boat from Misrata. Now, his two daughters were trapped by Hiftar's siege in western Benghazi.

He met me for coffee one evening dressed in a white prayer gown, tinted wire glasses perched over a face spangled with liver spots. A beard was a recent addition, he said, to disguise his identity, since extremists had threatened him for working with the Americans.

He seemed to me then an emissary of Libya's morass and an emblem of the tangled loyalties that had confounded America's policy. Hiftar had claimed to the Americans that he was fighting those who'd killed Chris Stevens, and yet his adversaries included this man, who'd actually helped. On the other hand, al-Obeidi had later fought with militants who'd shared the front lines with the Islamic State.

Did the Americans misplace their trust that night in September 2012? Perhaps. But they had no other choice. There was no black and white here, only shades of gray.

Al-Obeidi pleaded with me for help.

"We helped you and now you've abandoned us," he said.

And then to underscore his point, he showed me a scan of a certificate that American diplomats had given him shortly after the 2012 attack, in a ceremony at Tripoli's Rixos hotel.

CERTIFICATE
The United States of America
Would like to recognize
FAHTI Al-OBEIDI
Captain First Libya Shield
For heroic achievement on the night of 11 September 2012.

On the evening of the death of the U.S. Ambassador and three other Americans during the attack on the U.S. consulate in Benghazi, Fahti went above and beyond in order to provide security and facilitate movement for the American Rescue forces sent to evacuate all U.S. personnel in Benghazi. Fahti was committed and professional in every way, he continually risked his life and the life of his men to ensure our safety. Fahti was also instrumental in the repatriation of the U.S. Ambassador's remains. Fahti's actions reflect great credit upon himself and his country and are in keeping with the highest standards of military duty and service.

(*Signed*) Lieutenant Colonel Phillips, *defense attaché*
(*Signed*) Lawrence Pope USEMB, Tripoli *Chargé d'affaires*,
USEMB, Tripoli

NOTES

Unless otherwise noted below, material in this book is drawn from interviews and field observations in Libya from 2009 to 2017 and interviews with current and former U.S. and European officials and personnel from the United Nations. In some cases, sources are anonymous to protect their identity; in others, pseudonyms have been used.

PROLOGUE

3 *Tariq felt an unbearable pain*: Pseudonym used to protect identity.

1. "THE TENT CONQUERED THE CASTLE"

10 *"Libya is the world's third part"*: Lucan, *Civil War*, trans. Matthew Fox (New York: Penguin Books, 2012), 264.

11 *their principalities never fully controlled it*: Anna Baldinetti, *The Origins of the Libyan Nation* (New York: Routledge, 2010), 27–29; Lisa Anderson, "'They Defeated Us All': International Interests, Local Politics, and

Contested Sovereignty in Libya," *Middle East Journal* 71, no. 2 (Spring 2017): 232–33.

11 *The Italians arrived in 1911*: Claudio G. Segre, *Fourth Shore: The Italian Colonization of Libya* (Chicago: University of Chicago Press, 1974).

11 *luring Italian settlers to emigrate*: Ibid., 147.

11 *imprisoned two-thirds of the population*: Ronald Bruce St John, *Libya: Continuity and Change* (New York: Routledge, 2011), 17. For a rare Western description of the camps, see the contemporary account of the Danish traveler Knud Holmboe, *Desert Encounter: An Adventurous Journey Through Italian Africa* (London: George Harrap, 1936), 90.

11 *one out of every five persons in the country*: Dirk Vandewalle, *A History of Modern Libya* (New York: Cambridge University Press, 2006), 31.

11 *gave rise to one of Libya's great legends*: Hala Khamis Naser and Marco Boggero, "Omar al-Mukhtar: The Formation of Cultural Memory and the Case of the Militant Group That Bears His Name," *Journal of North African Studies* 13, no. 2 (2008), 201–17.

11 *with the exception of a Sufi revivalist movement*: Ali Abdullatif Ahmida, *The Making of Modern Libya: State Formation, Colonization, and Resistance* (Albany: State University of New York Press, 2009), 73–102.

12 *The literacy rate barely rose*: St John, *Libya: Continuity and Change*, 38.

12 *"I wish your people had discovered water"*: Quoted in Wolfgang Saxon, "John Paul Barringer, 93, Envoy Who Owned a Meteorite Crater," *New York Times*, August 25, 1996, http://www.nytimes.com/1996/08/25/world/john-paul-barringer-93-envoy-who-owned-a-meteorite-crater.html?mcubz=3.

12 *"The king offers Libya no inspiring leadership"*: Central Intelligence Agency, *Libya Threatened with Disintegration*, June 24, 1953, released April 13, 2005, CIA FOIA Reading Room; https://www.cia.gov/library/readingroom/document/cia-rdp79r00890a000100050010-0.

12 *Urbanization and education exposed*: Ali Abdullatif Ahmida, *Forgotten Voices: Power and Agency in Postcolonial Libya* (New York: Routledge, 2005), 79.

12 *buoyed by the quadrupling*: Vandewalle, *History of Modern Libya*, 97–138.

13 *literacy rose to 82 percent*: St John, *Libya: Continuity and Change*, 65.

13 *Women's status improved as well*: Ibid., 63–64.

13 *renting was a form of tyranny*: Mary Fitzgerald and Tarek Megerisi, *Libya: Whose Land Is It?*, Legatum Institute, April 2015, https://lif.blob.core.windows.net/lif/docs/default-source/publications/libya—whose-land-is-it-2015-transitions-forum.pdf?sfvrsn=8.

13 *he used Libya to project that ideology*: St John, *Libya: Continuity and Change*, 125–27; CIA Directorate for Intelligence, *Libyan Activities in the South Pacific*, May 4, 1987, CIA FOIA Reading Room, https://www.cia.gov/library/readingroom/document/cia-rdp90t00114r000200270001-7.

13 *a disastrous nine-year war with neighboring Chad*: John Wright, *Libya, Chad, and the Central Sahara* (London: Hurst, 1989).

13 *"mad dog of the Middle East"*: Tom Bowman, "For Reagan, Gadhafi Was a Frustrating 'Mad Dog,'" *Morning Edition*, National Public Radio, March 4, 2011, http://www.npr.org/2011/03/04/134228864/for-reagan -gadhafi-was-a-frustrating-mad-dog.

13 *In 1986, citing evidence of Qadhafi's complicity*: Judy G. Endicott, "Raid on Libya: Operation El Dorado Canyon," U.S. Department of Defense, n.d., https://media.defense.gov/2012/Aug/23/2001330097/-1/-1/0/Op %20El%20Dorado%20Canyon.pdf.

14 *a kleptocratic elite*: Luis Martinez, *The Libyan Paradox* (London: Hurst, 2007), 97.

14 *Unemployment was rising*: Tim Niblock, *Pariah States & Sanctions in the Middle East: Iraq, Libya, Sudan* (Boulder, CO: Lynne Rienner, 2001), 68; Martinez, *Libyan Paradox*, 3.

14 *leaned on tribes even more*: Martinez, *Libyan Paradox*, 98–101.

14 *useful counterterror partner*: Ibid., 43–80.

14 *dismantle its nascent nuclear weapons program*: Målfrid Braut-Hegghammer, "Libya's Nuclear Turnaround: Perspectives from Tripoli," *Middle East Journal* 62, no. 1 (Winter 2008), 55–72.

15 *America and Libya restored full diplomatic relations*: St John, *Libya: Continuity and Change*, 139–42.

15 *a seeming tug-of-war*: Alison Pargeter, "Reform in Libya: Chimera or Reality?," Mediterranean Paper Series 2010, German Marshall Fund of the United States, October 2010, http://www.gmfus.org/publications/reform -libya-chimera-or-reality.

17 *"sink like a stone"*: U.S. Embassy Tripoli Cable, "The Frogman Who Couldn't Swim: A Cooperation Cautionary Tale," WikiLeaks, February 17, 2009, http://www.telegraph.co.uk/news/wikileaks-files/libya -wikileaks/8294936/THE-FROGMAN-WHO-COULDNT-SWIM -A-COOPERATION-CAUTIONARY-TALE-TRIPOLI-00000155 -001.2-OF-002.html.

18 *"wanted a vacation in Rome"*: Ibid.

18 *One unit in particular*: Brian E. Linvill, "Retaking the Lead from Behind: A New Role for America in Libya," U.S. Army War College, 2003, 9, www.dtic.mil/get-tr-doc/pdf?AD=ADA592903.

18 *Hannibal, the most notorious*: Hwaida Saad and Rick Gladstone, "Qaddafi Son Arrested by Lebanon in New Twist on Missing Imam Mystery," *New York Times*, December 14, 2015, https://www.nytimes.com/2015 /12/15/world/middleeast/qaddafi-son-arrested-by-lebanon-in-new-twist -on-missing-imam-mystery.html.

18 *Muatassim had hired the pop singers*: Matthew Perpetua, "Beyoncé, Mariah Carey, and Usher Performed at Qaddafi Family Parties," *Rolling*

Stone, February 24, 2011, http://www.rollingstone.com/music/news /beyonce-mariah-carey-and-usher-performed-at-qaddafi-family-parties -20110224.

18 *soccer-crazed Saadi had been suspended:* John Foot, "A Qaddafi Son, Italian Soccer, and the Power of Money," *New York Times*, February 25, 2011, https://goal.blogs.nytimes.com/2011/02/25/a-qaddafi-son-italian -soccer-and-the-power-of-money/.

18 *"Anyone intent on assuming power":* U.S. Embassy in Tripoli Cable, "Saif al-Islam's Staff Reaches Out on Pol-Mil Issues," December 14, 2009, WikiLeaks, http://www.telegraph.co.uk/news/wikileaks-files/libya -wikileaks/8294701/SAIF-AL-ISLAMS-STAFF-REACHES-OUT -ON-POL-MIL-ISSUES.html.

19 *General Dynamics signed an £85 million deal:* Alexander Dziadosz, "Exclusive: Documents Detail Western Arms Firm's Libya Deal," Reuters, September 7, 2011.

19 *"Little Bird" helicopters:* U.S. Embassy in Tripoli Cable, "Saif al-Islam's Staff Reaches Out on Pol-Mil Issues."

19 *Qadhafi had freed many jihadists:* Omar Ashour, "Post-Jihadism: Libya and the Global Transformations of Armed Islamist Movements," *Terrorism and Political Violence* 23, no. 3 (2011): 377–97.

19 *Qadhafi had hired the Monitor Group:* Ed Pilkington, "US Firm Monitor Group Admits Mistakes over $3M Gaddafi Deal," *Guardian*, March 3, 2011; Paul M. Barrett, "The Professors and Qaddafi's Extreme Makeover," *Bloomberg Businessweek*, April 6, 2011, https://www.bloomberg.com/news /articles/2011-04-06/the-professors-and-qaddafis-extreme-makeover.

20 *"A laid-back autocrat":* Benjamin R. Barber, "Gaddafi's Libya: An Ally for America?," *Washington Post*, August 15, 2007.

20 *"If Gadafy is sincere about reform":* Anthony Giddens, "My Chat with the Colonel," *Guardian*, March 8, 2007.

21 *reform project under Saif al-Islam:* Roula Khalaf, "Gaddafi Family Tensions Keep Son in Check," *Financial Times*, December 20, 2010; Reuters, "Son of Libya's Gaddafi Denies Family Feud," December 24, 2010.

21 *one of his cables leaked by WikiLeaks:* U.S. Embassy Tripoli Cable, "A Glimpse into Libyan Leader Qadhafi's Eccentricities," September 29, 2009, WikiLeaks, https://www.theguardian.com/world/us-embassy-cables -documents/227491.

21 *"how business is conducted":* Joby Warrick, "U.S. Officials Assisted Visit by Gaddafi Son," *Washington Post*, March 25, 2011, https://www.washington post.com/world/us-officials-assisted-visit-by-gaddafi-son/2011/03/25 /AFT017YB_story.html?utm_term=.625cadb11769.

21 *"engagement breakthrough":* Linvill, "Retaking the Lead from Behind," 12.

22 *ten people had died:* BBC, "Ten Die in Libya Cartoon Clash," February 18, 2006, http://news.bbc.co.uk/2/hi/africa/4726204.stm.

22 *concerned with preserving*: Nick Hopkins, "The Libya Papers: A Glimpse into the World of 21st-Century Espionage," *Guardian*, September 9, 2011.

2. UPRISING

25 *It began in the fifth century B.C.*: Hadi M. Bulugma, *Benghazi Through the Ages* (n.p., 1972), 37–49; Al-Tahir Ahmad al-Zawi, *Mu'jam al-buldan al-Libiya* [Encyclopedia of Libyan towns] (Tripoli: Al-Nur, 1968), 63–65.

25 *"the river of forgetfulness"*: Virgil, *The Aeneid*, trans. Robert Fitzgerald (New York: Random House, 2013), 185.

25 *By the time of the Ottomans*: Bulugma, *Benghazi Through the Ages*, 55–60.

25 *"The Italian authorities would never manage"*: Alessandro Spina (pen name of Basili Shafik Khouzam), *The Confines of the Shadow* (London: Darf, 2013), 201.

25 *Benghazi changed hands*: al-Zawi, *Mu'jam al-buldan al-Libiya*, 65.

26 *After Libya's independence*: Bulugma, *Benghazi Through the Ages*, 61–75.

27 *On June 28, 1996, at around four-thirty*: This account of the massacre is reconstructed from my interviews with former prisoners and from the following sources: Human Rights Watch, "Libya: June 1996 Killings at Abu Salim Prison," June 27, 2006; Human Rights Watch, "Libya: Abu Salim Prison Massacre Remembered," June 27, 2012; Amnesty International, "Rising from the Shadows of Abu Salim Prison," June 26, 2014, https://www.amnesty.org/en/latest/news/2014/06/rising-shadows-abu-salim-prison/; Stuart Franklin, "Abu Salim: Walls That Talk," *Guardian*, September 30, 2011.

28 *The next three days changed everything*: Muhammad Muhammad al-Mufti, *Dhākirat al-nār: Yawmīyāt thawrat Fabrāyir al-majīdah: Lībiyā, Fabrāyir-Uktūbar 2011* [Memory of fire: Diary of the glorious February revolution: Libya, February–October 2011] (Tripoli: Dar al-Fergiani, 2012), 29–57.

29 *One of the protestors, a diabetic middle-aged manager*: Robert Worth, "On Libya's Revolutionary Road," *New York Times Magazine*, March 30, 2011, http://www.nytimes.com/2011/04/03/magazine/mag-03Libya-t.html?mcubz=3.

29 *The next tipping point*: "Qaddafi Alone," *Atlantic*, February 22, 2011, https://www.theatlantic.com/daily-dish/archive/2011/02/qaddafi-alone/175417/; speech translated by Sultan Al Qassemi.

30 *Sabri, for decades a beachfront shanty*: Bulugma, *Benghazi Through the Ages*, 87–90.

31 *the February 17 Brigade*: Bu Katif later became head of an eastern militia coalition called the Gathering of Revolutionary Companies.

32 *Born in 1943 in Ajdabiya*: Jean-Louis Tremblais, "Khalifa Haftar, un maréchal face au chaos libyen," *Le Figaro*, January 5, 2018, http://www.lefigaro.fr/international/2018/01/05/01003-20180105ARTFIG00035-khalifa-haftar-un-marechal-face-au-chaos-libyen.php.

34 *Saif gave an impromptu televised address*: Available at https://www.youtube
.com/watch?v=Wsy1QWbnCKg.

34 *Qadhafi the father gave his now-famous diatribe*: Available at https://www
.youtube.com/watch?v=69wBG6ULNzQ.

3. INTERVENTION

38 *"Tens of thousands of Africans"*: Samantha Power, "Remember Rwanda
but Take Action in Sudan," *New York Times*, April 6, 2004.

39 *"we will find you in your closets"*: David Kirkpatrick and Karim Fahim,
"Qaddafi Warns of Assault on Benghazi as U.N. Vote Nears," *New York
Times*, March 17, 2011.

41 *Intervention, he argued*: David E. Sanger and Thom Shanker, "Gates
Warns of Risks of a No-Flight Zone," *New York Times*, March 2, 2011,
http://www.nytimes.com/2011/03/03/world/africa/03military.html
?pagewanted=all.

41 *Gates also worried*: Robert M. Gates, *Duty: Memoirs of a Secretary at War*
(New York: Alfred A. Knopf, 2014), 511–13.

42 *with its views of a luminous Eiffel Tower*: Hillary Rodham Clinton, *Hard
Choices* (New York: Simon & Schuster, 2014), 364.

43 *Abstentions by China and Russia*: Ann Karin Larssen, "Russia: The Prin-
ciple of Non-Intervention and the Libya Case," and Sheng Ding, "The
Political Rationale of China's Deliberately Limited Role in the Libyan
Civil War," in *Political Rationale and International Consequences of the
War in Libya*, eds. Dag Henriksen and Ann Karin Larssen (Oxford:
Oxford University Press, 2016), 67–85; 86–101.

44 *American, British, and French strikes*: Frederic Wehrey, "NATO's Intervention," in *The Libyan Revolution and Its Aftermath*, ed. Peter Cole and
Brian McQuinn (London: Hurst, 2015), 105–25.

45 *"If we tried to overthrow Qadhafi"*: White House Office of the Press Secretary, Remarks by the President in Address to the Nation on Libya,
National Defense University, Washington, DC, March 28, 2011, https://
obamawhitehouse.archives.gov/the-press-office/2011/03/28/remarks
-president-address-nation-libya.

47 *the CIA had sent officers*: "CIA Operatives Gathering Intelligence
in Libya," National Public Radio, March 31, 2011, https://www.npr
.org/2011/03/31/135005728/cia-operatives-gathering-intelligence-in
-libya.

48 *"Theater teaches empathy"*: Austin Tichenor, "Ambassador Chris Stevens,"
October 21, 2012, episode 307, Reduced Shakespeare Company podcast,
http://www.reducedshakespeare.com/2012/10/episode-307-ambassador
-chris-stevens/.

49 *People in Ouaouizerth recalled*: Malanie Kodrat, "Remembering Chris

Stevens: My Journey to Ouaouizerth," Peace Corps Worldwide, October 8, 2012, http://peacecorpsworldwide.org/remembering-3/.

51 *On the night of April 5*: Mario Montoya, "Mission to a Revolution," *State*, December 2011, 20, https://www.state.gov/documents/organization /178204.pdf.

51 *"My mandate was to go out"*: Ibid.

51 *"They behaved like children"*: Kareem Fahim, "Rebel Leadership in Libya Shows Strain," *New York Times*, April 3, 2011, http://www .nytimes.com/2011/04/04/world/africa/04rebels.html?pagewanted =all&mcubz=3.

51 *"I want NATO to defend my front line"*: Rod Nordland, "As British Help Libyan Rebels, Aid Goes to a Divided Force," *New York Times*, April 19, 2011.

57 *"A man of god and technology"*: Anne Barnard, "A Man of God and Technology, Trying to Steady Libya," *New York Times*, September 17, 2011, http://www.nytimes.com/2011/09/17/world/africa/aref-nayed-man-of -god-and-technology-tries-to-steady-libya.html?mcubz=3.

57 *"We are creating a contingent of forces"*: Briefing provided to the author.

60 *His badly burned body was found*: Al-Mufti, *Dhākirat al-nār*, 469–76.

61 *Already, acts of sabotage in Tripoli*: Ibid., 537–52.

63 *"The previous regime no longer rules Libya"*: Author's observation of a pamphlet on display at the Misrata military museum, July 2012.

64 *"What is this? What are you doing?"*: Martin Chulov, "Gaddafi's Last Moments: 'I Saw the Hand Holding the Gun and I Saw It Fire,'" *Guardian*, October 20, 2012.

64 *Hillary Clinton learned of his death*: Corbett Daly, "Clinton on Qaddafi: 'We Came, We Saw, He Died,'" CBS News, October 20, 2011, https:// www.cbsnews.com/news/clinton-on-qaddafi-we-came-we-saw-he-died/.

4. FALSE HOPES

67 *an international team of postconflict experts*: International Stabilisation Resource Team (ISRT), 20 May to 30 June 2011, 27; report provided to the author.

69 *What would happen now*: Frederic Wehrey, "Libya's Terra Incognita: Who and What Will Follow Qaddafi," *Foreign Affairs*, February 28, 2011.

70 *"Nobody knows now what the political fabric"*: Tara Bahrampour, "Battles in Libya Raise Specter of Insurgency," *Washington Post*, September 22, 2011, https://www.washingtonpost.com/world/battles-in-libya-raise -specter-of-insurgency/2011/09/21/gIQAneT0oK_story.html?utm _term=.45e6a5719007.

71 *Early elections also risked*: Larry Diamond, "Promoting Democracy in Post-conflict and Failed States: Lessons and Challenges," *Taiwan Journal of Democracy*, December 2006, 93–116.

71 *One authoritative survey of civil wars*: Dawn Brancati and Jack L. Snyder, "The Libyan Rebels and Electoral Democracy," *Foreign Affairs*, September 2, 2011, https://www.foreignaffairs.com/articles/libya/2011-09-02/libyan-rebels-and-electoral-democracy.

72 *tried to nourish*: Mieczysław P. Boduszyński, "The External Dimension of Libya's Troubled Transition: The International Community and 'Democratic Knowledge' Transfer," *Journal of North African Studies* 20, no. 5 (2015): 735–53.

74 *"Armageddon predictions [are] a bit overstated"*: Gene Cretz to Jacob Sullivan and Jeffrey Feldman, email, February 24, 2012, https://foia.state.gov/searchapp/DOCUMENTS/HRCEmail_Jan7thWeb/O-2015-08636-JAN7/DOC_0C05790705/C05790705.pdf.

75 *"would serve as a powerful example"*: Statement of John Christopher Stevens, Ambassador-Designate to Libya Before the Senate Committee on Foreign Relations, March 20, 2012; https://www.foreign.senate.gov/imo/media/doc/Stevens.pdf.

75 *he'd cemented that trust*: Michael Lewis, "Obama's Way," *Vanity Fair*, October 2012.

78 *"frame of reference"*: Barbara Slavin, "Jibril: Libya Is a 'Stateless Society,'" *Al-Monitor*, November 8, 2012, http://www.al-monitor.com/pulse/originals/2012/al-monitor/libyajibrilinterview.html.

79 *While urban centers grew*: Emrys L. Peters, *The Bedouin of Cyrenaica: Studies in Personal and Corporate Power* (Cambridge: Cambridge University Press, 1990), 29–39.

79 *traced their lineage back to Egypt*: E. E. Evans-Pritchard, *The Sanusi of Cyrenaica* (London: Oxford University Press, 1968), 43–51.

79 *Cyrenaican identity was further bound*: Ali Abdullatif Ahmida, *The Making of Modern Libya: State Formation, Colonization, and Resistance* (Albany: State University of New York Press, 2009), 73–102; Faraj Najem, *Tribe, Islam, and State in Libya: Analytical Study of the Roots of Libyan Tribal Society and Evolution up to the Qaramanli Reign (1781–1835)* (Benghazi: Center for Africa Research, 2017), 130–39.

79 *a period of self-governance*: Salaheddin Salem Hasan, "The Genesis of the Political Leadership of Libya, 1952–1969: Historical Origins and Development of Its Component Elements" (PhD diss., George Washington University, 1973), 119–91.

79 *True, the constitution of 1951*: Ronald Bruce St John, *Libya: Continuity and Change* (New York: Routledge, 2011), 39–41.

79 *a three-way alliance*: Dirk Vandewalle, *A History of Modern Libya* (New York: Cambridge University Press, 2006), 152.

81 *The Carter Center rated 98 percent*: Carter Center, "Carter Center Congratulates Libyans for Holding Historic Elections," July 9, 2012, https://www.cartercenter.org/news/pr/libya-070912.html.

82 *"another milestone on their extraordinary transition"*: White House, Office of the Press Secretary, "Statement by the President on Libya," July 7, 2012, https://obamawhitehouse.archives.gov/the-press-office/2012/07/07 /statement-president-libya.

5. YOUNG MEN WITH GUNS

85 *"Little America"*: Quoted in "Opening Statement by US Ambassador-Retired Deborah K. Jones," U.S. Senate Committee on Foreign Relations, "The Crisis in Libya: Next Steps and U.S. Policy Options," April 25, 2017, https://www.foreign.senate.gov/imo/media/doc/042517_Jones _Testimony.pdf.

87 *"McDonald's, Kentucky Fried Chicken"*: U.S. Agency for International Development (USAID), "Disarmament, Demobilization, and Reintegration (DDR) Scoping Mission in Libya," August 2012, 18.

88 *"security dilemma"*: Véronique Dudouet, "Nonstate Armed Groups and the Politics of Postwar Security Governance," in *Monopoly of Force: The Nexus of DDR and SSR*, ed. Melanne A. Civic and Michael Miklaucic (Washington, DC: National Defense University Press, 2011), 7.

88 *a kind of Catch-22 ensued*: Macartan Humphreys and Jeremy M. Weinstein, "Demobilization and Reintegration," *Journal of Conflict Resolution* 51, no. 4 (August 2007): 531–67.

88 *At stake was what the sociologist*: Max Weber, "Politics as a Vocation" (1919), available at http://anthropos-lab.net/wp/wp-content/uploads/2011 /12/Weber-Politics-as-a-Vocation.pdf.

88 *inhabitants had been farmers*: Al-Tahir Ahmad al-Zawi, *Mu'jam al-buldan al-Libiya* [Encyclopedia of Libyan towns] (Tripoli: Al-Nur, 1968), 197.

91 *the Nafusa was haven to an array of sects*: Hadi Bulugma, "Ethnic Elements in the Western Coastal Zone of Tripolitania," in *Field Studies in Libya*, ed. S. G. Willimott and J. I. Clarke (Durham, UK: University of Durham), Research Paper Series 4 (1960), 111–19.

95 *"Our most important goal"*: BBC Monitoring World Media, "Libya's Military Commanders Meet to Unify Anti-Qadhafi Brigades," quoting Al Jazeera TV, Doha, in Arabic, 2130 GMT, September 22, 2011, available at WikiLeaks, https://wikileaks.org/gifiles/docs/12/126759_re-fwd-s3 -libya-libyan-rebels-form-united-front-.html.

95 *It traded wood, olive oil, and dates*: G. H. Blake, *Misurata: A Market Town in Tripolitania* (Durham, UK: University of Durham), Research Paper Series 9 (1968), 11.

95 *"The inhabitants are rich"*: Leo Africanus, *The History and Description of Africa and of the Notable Things Contained Therein* (London: Hakluyt Society, 1846), 775.

96 *The city's influence waxed and waned*: Ibid., 11–21.

96 *"Patients were brought to us"*: Quoted in Reuters, "MSF Quits Prisons in

Libya City over 'Torture,'" January 26, 2012, http://www.reuters.com/article/us-libya-torture/msf-quits-prisons-in-libya-city-over-torture-idUSTRE80P1KN20120126.

97 *The most brutalized of Misrata's victims*: Human Rights Watch, "Libya Ensure Safe Return of Displaced Tawerghans," June 20, 2017, http://www.hrw.org/news/2017/06/20/libya-ensure-safe-return-displaced-tawerghans.

98 *Freud's thesis*: Sigmund Freud, *Totem and Taboo* (New York: W. W. Norton, 1990).

98 *Ramadan al-Suwayhli, who fought the Italians*: Lisa Anderson, "Ramadan al-Suwayhli: Hero of the Libyan Resistance," in *Struggle and Survival in the Modern Middle East*, ed. Edmund Burke III (Berkeley: University of California Press, 1993), 114–28.

98 *with German U-boats docking at Misrata's port*: Ali Abdullatif Ahmida, *The Making of Modern Libya: State Formation, Colonization, and Resistance* (Albany: State University of New York Press, 2009), 129.

98 *an autonomous "Republic of Tripolitania"*: Lisa Anderson, "The Tripoli Republic, 1918–1922," in *Social and Economic Development of Libya*, ed. George Joffe and Keith MacLachlan (Wisbech, UK: Menas Press, 1982), 43–66.

98 *In 2011, Misratans carried portraits*: Brian McQuinn, "History's Warriors: The Emergence of Revolutionary Battalions in Misrata," in *The Libyan Revolution and Its Aftermath*, ed. Peter Cole and Brian McQuinn (London: Hurst, 2015), 230.

102 *destroy a quarter of the country's*: Agence France Presse, "US-Libyan Experts Dispose of 5,000 Surface-to-Air Missiles," December 13, 2011.

103 *"Libya lacks an alternative"*: Brian E. Linvill, "Retaking the Lead from Behind: A New Role for America in Libya," U.S. Army War College, 2003, 6.

6. "WE DON'T KNOW WHO'S WHO"

106 *"Our situation is fine"*: Quoted in *Al-Hayat* (Arabic), June 8, 2012, http://www.alhayat.com/Details/409278.

106 *"Libya is not Afghanistan!"*: Quoted in *New Quryna* (Arabic), June 14, 2012 (website no longer active).

106 *"This group comes here"*: Al Aan Television (Arabic), June 12, 2012, https://www.youtube.com/watch?v=pxD8OWAFa6E.

106 *details of al-Zahawi's life were sketchy*: Ansar al-Sharia's Facebook page, http://www.facebook.com/anssarelsharieah, accessed on July 25, 2012 (no longer available).

107 *Al-Zahawi's group derived its deeper ideology*: Cole Bunzel, "Toward an Islamic Spring: Abu Muhammad al-Maqdisi's Prison Production,"

Jihadica (blog), June 11, 2013, http://www.jihadica.com/toward-an
-islamic-spring-abu-muhammad-al-maqdisi%E2%80%99s-prison
-production/; Aaron Y. Zelin, "Maqdisi's Disciples in Libya and Tunisia," *Foreign Policy* Middle East Channel, November 14, 2012, http://
foreignpolicy.com/2012/11/14/maqdisis-disciples-in-libya-and-tunisia/.

110 *violence in Benghazi surged*: U.S. House of Representatives, *Final Report
of the Select Committee on the Events Surrounding the 2012 Terrorist Attack
in Benghazi* (Washington, DC: U.S. Government Printing Office, 2016),
263–352, https://www.gpo.gov/fdsys/pkg/CRPT-114hrpt848/pdf/CRPT
-114hrpt848.pdf. See also U.S. Department of State, *Accountability Review Board Report*, December 19, 2012, https://2009-2017.state.gov
/documents/organization/202446.pdf.

111 *Chris Stevens sent a cable*: U.S. Embassy Tripoli Cable, "Libya's Fragile
Security Deteriorates as Tribal Rivalries, Power Plays, and Extremism Intensify," June 25, 2012, http://oversight.house.gov/wp-content/uploads
/2012/10/DEI-to-BHO-10-19-2012-attachments.pdf.

112 *fifty-four assessments*: U.S. House of Representatives, Select Committee
on Benghazi, *Honoring Courage, Improving Security, and Fighting the Exploitation of a Tragedy: Report of the Democratic Members*, June 2016, 169,
https://democrats-benghazi.house.gov/sites/democrats.benghazi.house
.gov/files/documents/Report_of_the_Benghazi_Select_Committee
_Democratic_Members-Honoring_Courage_Improving_Security
_and_Fighting_the_Exploitation_of_a_Tragedy.pdf.

112 *reports by other intelligence agencies*: U.S. Senate Select Committee on Intelligence, *Review of the Terrorist Attacks on U.S. Facilities in Benghazi,
Libya, September 11–12, 2012*, January 15, 2014, 9–11, https://www
.intelligence.senate.gov/sites/default/files/publications/113134.pdf.

113 *irrigation canals, orchards*: Muhammad Muhammad al-Mufti, *Sahari Derna:
Tarikh ijtima'i al-Madina* (Benghazi: Dar Kutub al-Wataniya, 2008), 34,
available at https://www.scribd.com/doc/183911908/%D8%B3%D9%8
0%D9%87%D8%A7%D8%B1%D9%8A-%D8%AF%D8%B1%D9%86%
D9%80%D8%A9.

114 *Refugees from Andalusia*: Al-Tahir Ahmad al-Zawi, *Mu'jam al-buldan al-
Libiya* [Encyclopedia of Libyan towns] (Tripoli: Al-Nur, 1968), 130.

114 *Derna's history collided*: This account of the 1805 war is taken from *Naval
Documents Related to the United States Wars with the Barbary Powers*
(Washington, DC: U.S. Government Printing Office, 1939–1944), vols.
5 and 6, available at http://www.ibiblio.org/anrs/barbary.html; Frank
Lambert, *The Barbary Wars: American Independence in the Atlantic World*
(New York: Hill and Wang, 2005), 123–56. For an Arabic account, see
al-Mufti, *Sahari Derna*, 53–56.

115 *It became a center of culture*: Al-Mufti, *Sahari Derna*, 157–71.

116 *"Fighting against U.S. and coalition forces"*: U.S. Embassy Tripoli Cable, "Diehard in Derna," June 6, 2008, http://www.telegraph.co.uk/news /wikileaks-files/libya-wikileaks/8294818/DIE-HARD-IN-DERNA .html.

117 *Breaking with Darbi and al-Hasadi*: Wolfram Lacher, "Libya: A Jihadist Growth Market," in *Jihadism in Africa: Local Causes, Regional Expansion, International Alliances*, ed. Guido Steinberg and Annette Weber, Stiftung Wissenschaft und Politik, German Institute for International and Security Affairs, June 2015, 40, https://www.swp-berlin.org/fileadmin /contents/products/research_papers/2015_RP05_sbg_web.pdf.

118 *The nighttime meeting in Benghazi*: This account of the September 9 meeting is drawn from interviews with two Libyan attendees; the meeting has also been reported in *The New York Times*. David D. Kirkpatrick, "A Deadly Mix in Benghazi," *New York Times*, December 28, 2013.

120 *"If there is a real mission"*: U.S. Senate Select Committee on Intelligence, *Review of the Terrorist Attacks on U.S. Facilities in Benghazi, Libya, September 11–12, 2012*, 17.

120 *Then, in July, the State Department*: U.S. House of Representatives, Select Committee on Benghazi, *Honoring Courage, Improving Security, and Fighting the Exploitation of a Tragedy*, 113.

120 *On August 15, diplomats in Benghazi*: U.S. House of Representatives, *Final Report of the Select Committee on the Events Surrounding the 2012 Terrorist Attack in Benghazi*, 473.

120 *"evaluate [the diplomatic mission's] tripwires"*: Select Committee on Benghazi, *Honoring Courage, Improving Security, and Fighting the Exploitation of a Tragedy*, 130.

120 *"new normal"*: U.S. Senate Select Committee on Intelligence, *Review of the Terrorist Attacks on U.S. Facilities in Benghazi, Libya, September 11–12, 2012*, 15.

120 *A CIA officer then gave a briefing*: Ibid.

120 *"coordinated attack due to limited manpower"*: Ibid., 16.

120 *called Chris Stevens after seeing it*: Ibid., 20.

121 *"included a weak and very extended perimeter"*: Ibid., 17.

122 *In May and again in June, the ranking diplomat*: "Memos Recovered from Benghazi Compound Detail Staff Security Worries," *Washington Times*, October 19, 2015, https://www.washingtontimes.com/news/2015/oct /19/benghazi-memos-recovered-from-compound-detail-staf/.

122 *a cable from Stevens warned*: U.S. House of Representatives, *Final Report of the Select Committee on the Events Surrounding the 2012 Terrorist Attack in Benghazi*, 21.

122 *was provided by the February 17 Brigade*: The full name of this militia is the February 17 Martyrs Brigade.

123 *his militiamen had responded promptly*: Ibid., 336.

123 *they refused to augment their numbers*: Ibid., 337.

123 *"we should be in line with the [Libyan government] policy/law"*: Ibid.

123 *On September 8, the February 17 militiamen*: Ibid.

123 *American policy, he told the commanders*: Ibid., 14.

123 *"What's your role?"*: Ibid., 15.

124 *McFarland found the mixed signals exasperating*: Ibid.

7. THE ATTACK ON THE AMERICANS

125 *"Call everybody on my cell phone"*: U.S. House of Representatives, *Final Report of the Select Committee on the Events Surrounding the 2012 Terrorist Attack in Benghazi* (Washington, DC: U.S. Government Printing Office, 2016), 138.

126 *"I'm going to start shooting"*: United States of America v. Ahmed Salim Faraj Abu Khattalah, 1:14-cr-00141-CRC-1, October 2, 2017, afternoon session.

126 *"White ties and tails"*: Shane Harris, "Chris Stevens' Benghazi Diary Reveals His Brooding, Hopeful Final Days," *Foreign Policy*, June 26, 2013, http://foreignpolicy.com/2013/06/26/chris-stevens-benghazi-diary-reveals-his-brooding-hopeful-final-days/.

126 *he had a number of goals*: U.S. Department of State, *Accountability Review Board Report*, December 19, 2012, 18, https://2009-2017.state.gov/documents/organization/202446.pdf.

127 *"I didn't [like] the idea"*: U.S. House of Representatives, *Final Report of the Select Committee on the Events Surrounding the 2012 Terrorist Attack in Benghazi*, 12.

127 *Stevens traveled to the CIA annex*: Ibid., 17.

127 *"a sourness about why it has taken so long"*: Ibid., 18.

127 *"Hey are you watching TV?"*: Ibid., 24.

128 *"It's so nice to be back in Benghazi"*: Jack Murphy and Brandon Webb, "Breaking: The Benghazi Diary, a Hero Ambassador's Final Thoughts," *SOFREP*, June 26, 2013, https://sofrep.com/22460/ambassador-chris-stevens-benghazi-diary/.

128 *thickets of silphium*: Zaria Gorvett, "The Mystery of the Lost Roman Herb," *BBC*, September 7, 2017, http://www.bbc.com/future/story/20170907-the-mystery-of-the-lost-roman-herb.

129 *plan that had been rehearsed*: U.S. House of Representatives, *Final Report of the Select Committee on the Events Surrounding the 2012 Terrorist Attack in Benghazi*, 335.

130 *Libyan guards briefly traded fire*: Ibid., 32.

130 *"This is not a drill"*: Ibid., 31.

130 *Banging on the ambassador's door*: United States of America v. Ahmed Salim Faraj Abu Khattalah, 1:14-cr-00141-CRC-1, October 2, 2017, afternoon session.

130 *"A jail cell door"*: U.S. House of Representatives, *Final Report of the Select*

Committee on the Events Surrounding the 2012 Terrorist Attack in Benghazi, 138.

130 *he heard gunfire and explosions*: United States of America v. *Ahmed Salim Faraj Abu Khattalah*, 1:14-cr-00141-CRC-1, October 2, 2017, afternoon session.

130 *Could they contact the February 17 Brigade*: U.S. House of Representatives, Select Committee on Benghazi, *Honoring Courage, Improving Security, and Fighting the Exploitation of a Tragedy: Report of the Democratic Members*, June 2016, 26, https://democrats-benghazi.house.gov/sites/democrats .benghazi.house.gov/files/documents/Report_of_the_Benghazi _Select_Committee_Democratic_Members-Honoring_Courage _Improving_Security_and_Fighting_the_Exploitation_of_a_Tragedy .pdf.

131 *"they weren't actually very helpful"*: U.S. House of Representatives, *Final Report of the Select Committee on the Events Surrounding the 2012 Terrorist Attack in Benghazi*, 39.

131 *He asked the February 17 Brigade for a gun truck*: Ibid., 40.

131 *the former navy rescue swimmer*: United States of America v. *Ahmed Salim Faraj Abu Khattalah*, 1:14-cr-00141-CRC-1, October 2, 2017, afternoon session.

131 *There were about forty of them*: Ibid.

131 *He glanced to his left*: Ibid.

131 *It was just eight meters away*: Ibid.

132 *"on fire"*: U.S. House of Representatives, *Final Report of the Select Committee on the Events Surrounding the 2012 Terrorist Attack in Benghazi*, 139.

132 *"seconds left of life"*: Ibid., 140.

132 *"Come on, guys"*: Ibid., 139.

132 *annex team climbed out of their vehicles*: Ibid., 50.

132 *They identified themselves*: U.S. Department of State, *Accountability Review Board Report*, 35.

133 *"Gunfire, gunfire, I am subjected to gunfire!"*: United States of America v. *Ahmed Salim Farraj Abu Khattalah*, 1:14-cr-00141-CRC-1, October 18, 2017, morning session.

133 *Americans from the annex pulled up*: United States of America v. *Ahmed Salim Faraj Abu Khattalah*, 1:14-cr-00141-CRC-1, October 24, 2017, morning session.

133 *"When is our reaction force coming"*: U.S. House of Representatives, Select Committee on Benghazi, *Honoring Courage, Improving Security, and Fighting the Exploitation of a Tragedy*, 26.

133 *the agents donned SCape hoods*: United States of America v. *Ahmed Salim Faraj Abu Khattalah*, 1:14-cr-00141-CRC-1, October 5, 2017, afternoon session.

133 *when he came across a motionless body*: U.S. House of Representatives, *Final Report of the Select Committee on the Events Surrounding the 2012 Terrorist Attack in Benghazi*, 53.

133 *an avid and accomplished participant*: Robert Beckhusen, "Diplomat Killed in Libya Told Fellow Gamers: I Hope I 'Don't Die Tonight,'" *Wired*, September 12, 2012.

133 *Tethering themselves to avoid getting lost*: U.S. House of Representatives, Select Committee on Benghazi, *Honoring Courage, Improving Security, and Fighting the Exploitation of a Tragedy*, 28.

133 *"You guys have got to get the fuck out of here"*: United States of America v. Ahmed Salim Faraj Abu Khattalah, 1:14-cr-00141-CRC-1, October 5, 2017, afternoon session.

134 *Overhead drones had spotted armed men*: United States of America v. Ahmed Salim Faraj Abu Khattalah, 1:14-cr-00141-CRC-1, October 24, 2017, morning session.

134 *DS agents turned right*: U.S. House of Representatives, *Final Report of the Select Committee on the Events Surrounding the 2012 Terrorist Attack in Benghazi*, 72.

134 *someone they believed to be a February 17 militiaman*: Ibid.

134 *Three hundred meters later*: U.S. Department of State, *Accountability Review Board Report*, 24.

134 *Now they too drove away*: U.S. House of Representatives, *Final Report of the Select Committee on the Events Surrounding the 2012 Terrorist Attack in Benghazi*, 567.

135 *went off-line for twenty-eight minutes*: Ibid., 568.

135 *With a ninth-grade education*: United States of America v. Ahmed Salim Faraj Abu Khattalah, 1:14-cr-00141-CRC-1, October 31, 2017, afternoon session.

135 *In July 2011, the Abu Obeida Brigade*: ibid.

135 *a stash of heavy weapons*: United States of America v. Ahmed Salim Faraj Abu Khattalah, 1:14-cr-00141-CRC-1, November 6, 2017, afternoon session.

135 *"going to do something about the facility"*: Eyder Peralta, "Benghazi Suspect, Ahmed Abu Khattala, Is Indicted on 17 New Charges," NPR, October 14, 2014, http://www.npr.org/sections/thetwo-way/2014/10/14/356196973/benghazi-suspect-ahmed-abu-khattala-is-indicted-on-17-new-charges.

136 *a front for intelligence gathering*: United States of America v. Ahmed Salim Faraj Abu Khattalah, 1:14-cr-00141-CRC-1, October 31, 2017, afternoon session.

136 *"Jamaica"*: United States of America v. Ahmed Salim Faraj Abu Khattalah, 1:14-cr-00141-CRC-1, October 18, 2017, morning session.

136 *"like a chimpanzee"*: United States of America v. Ahmed Salim Faraj Abu Khattalah, 1:14-cr-00141-CRC-1, October 30, 2017, morning session.

136 *a religious authority with Ansar al-Sharia*: United States of America v. Ahmed Salim Faraj Abu Khattalah, 1:14-cr-00141-CRC-1, October 18, 2017, afternoon session.

136 *"If you kill one of us"*: United States of America v. Ahmed Salim Faraj Abu Khattalah, 1:14-cr-00141-CRC-1, October 31, 2017, afternoon session.

136 *a cooperative commander obliged*: United States of America v. Ahmed Salim Faraj Abu Khattalah, 1:14-cr-00141-CRC-1, November 6, 2017, afternoon session.

136 *The murky landscape*: United States of America v. Ahmed Salim Faraj Abu Khattalah, 1:14-cr-00141-CRC-1, October 30, 2017, morning session.

137 *Relocated to the United States with his family*: United States of America v. Ahmed Salim Faraj Abu Khattalah, 1:14-cr-00141-CRC-1, October 18, 2017, morning session.

137 *citing his demand for $10 million*: United States of America v. Ahmed Salim Faraj Abu Khattalah, 1:14-cr-00141-CRC-1, October 17, 2017, afternoon session.

137 *a forty-year-old Benghazi businessman*: United States of America v. Ahmed Salim Faraj Abu Khattalah, 1:14-cr-00141-CRC-1, November 6, 2017, morning session.

137 *prosecutors allege*: Peralta, "Benghazi Suspect."

137 *Libyan guard emerged on the tarmac*: U.S. House of Representatives, *Final Report of the Select Committee on the Events Surrounding the 2012 Terrorist Attack in Benghazi*, 78.

138 *"It was completely dead"*: Ibid.

138 *the American defense attaché*: U.S. House of Representatives Permanent Select Committee on Intelligence, *Investigative Report on the Terrorist Attacks on U.S. Facilities in Benghazi, Libya, September 11–12, 2012*, November 21, 2014, 10, https://intelligence.house.gov/sites/intelligence.house.gov/files/documents/benghazi%20report.pdf. Abd al-Salam Hasi is referred to in this report as "General Hasani." A U.S. official present at the embassy that night confirmed to the author that this was in fact Abd al-Salam al-Hasi.

138 *"Okay, I will look into it"*: U.S. House of Representatives, Committee on Oversight and Government Reform and Committee on Armed Services, interview of U.S. Defense Attaché, January 31, 2014, Washington, DC, https://democrats-benghazi.house.gov/sites/democrats.benghazi.house.gov/files/documents/2014-01-31%20LTC%2C%20Defense%20Attache%20OCR.pdf, 92.

138 *after 2:00 a.m., they received the news*: U.S. House of Representatives, *Final Report of the Select Committee on the Events Surrounding the 2012 Terrorist Attack in Benghazi*, 569.

139 *retrieved the ambassador's cell phone*: U.S. Department of State, *Accountability Review Board Report*, 26.

139 *"a lot of the hallmarks"*: U.S. House of Representatives, *Final Report of the Select Committee on the Events Surrounding the 2012 Terrorist Attack in Benghazi*, 79.

139 *that Ansar al-Sharia was guarding*: U.S. House of Representatives Permanent Select Committee on Intelligence, *Investigative Report*, 10–11.

140 *according to what Abu Khattala tola a witness*: United States of America v. Ahmed Salim Faraj Abu Khattala, 1:14-cr-00141-CRC-1, November 6, 2017, afternoon session.

141 *in the words of one special operator*: U.S. House of Representatives, *Final Report of the Select Committee on the Events Surrounding the 2012 Terrorist Attack in Benghazi*, 81.

141 *someone had thrown down a glow stick*: Ibid., 69.

141 *one of the special operators insisted*: U.S. House of Representatives, Select Committee on Benghazi, *Honoring Courage, Improving Security, and Fighting the Exploitation of a Tragedy*, 44.

141 *car alarms*: U.S. House of Representatives, *Final Report of the Select Committee on the Events Surrounding the 2012 Terrorist Attack in Benghazi*, 570.

141 *six 81 mm mortar rounds arrived*: Ibid., 108.

142 *the attackers were more precise*: Ibid., 181.

142 *"by just skin and some muscle"*: United States of America v. Ahmed Salim Faraj Abu Khattalah, 1:14-cr-00141-CRC-1, October 5, 2017, morning session.

142 *"grapefruit-size chunk"*: United States of America v. Ahmed Salim Faraj Abu Khattalah, 1:14-cr-00141-CRC-1, October 4, 2017, morning session.

142 *"thousand bees"*: Ibid.

142 *the larger Shield convoy*: Based on the author's interview with Fathi al-Obeidi and another militia member present at the annex during the evacuation. Also, *United States of America v. Ahmed Salim Faraj Abu Khattalah*, 1:14-cr-00141-CRC-1, October 24, 2017, morning session.

142 *Abu Baker Habib, Stevens's close friend and aide*: Bubaker Habib, "I Was Working with Chris Stevens Before He Died. Honor Him with Truth, Not Lies," *Washington Post*, July 6, 2016, https://www.washingtonpost .com/opinions/global-opinions/i-was-working-with-chris-stevens-before -he-died-honor-him-with-truth-not-lies/2016/07/06/efc8714c-3ef4-11e6 -84e8-1580c7db5275_story.html.

8. THE REVOLUTION DEVOURS ITS OWN

145 *eighth American ambassador to die*: U.S. State Department, Office of the Historian, https://history.state.gov/about/faq/ambassadors-killed.

145 *similar incident in Benghazi in the summer of 1967*: Library of Congress interview with John G. Kormann, Association for Diplomatic Studies and Training Foreign Affairs Oral History Project, February 7, 1996, https:// cdn.loc.gov/service/mss/mfdip/2004/2004kor02/2004kor02.pdf.

147 *The Political Isolation Law*: Human Rights Watch, "Libya: Reject 'Political Isolation Law,'" May 4, 2013, https://www.hrw.org/news/2013/05/04 /libya-reject-political-isolation-law.

151 *"Confusion is hard to report"*: Christopher Massie, "Libya, a Country Under-Covered," *Columbia Journalism Review*, August 27, 2013.

151 *a retrograde theocracy*: For an argument against this myth of an Islamist conspiracy in Libya, see Karim Mezran, "Conspiracism in and Around Libya," *International Spectator* 51 (2016): 113–18.

152 *"This squalid brawl in a distant city"*: George Orwell, *Homage to Catalonia* (London: Penguin Books, 2000), 222.

154 *It was to be a basic infantry force*: This account of the "general purpose force" is taken from interviews with Libyan and American officials involved in the effort. See also Frederic Wehrey, "Modest Mission? The U.S. Plan to Build a Libyan Army," *Foreign Affairs*, November 4, 2013, https://www .foreignaffairs.com/articles/libya/2013-11-04/modest-mission; and Frederic Wehrey, "Libya Doesn't Need More Militias," *New York Times*, June 10, 2013.

158 *The Libyan trainees roamed intoxicated*: Lizzie Dearden, "Libyan Soldiers Convicted for Raping Man in Cambridge After Tracking Him Like 'Hunting Dogs,'" *Independent*, May 15, 2015.

158 *the Americans had opened another front*: Eric Schmitt, "U.S. Training Elite Antiterror Troops in Four African Nations," *New York Times*, May 26, 2014.

159 *Zeidan held a press conference*: "Zeidan Condemns the Attack and Pillage of 'Barracks 27,'" *Libya Herald*, August 5, 2013, https://www .libyaherald.com/2013/08/05/zeidan-condems-the-attack-and-pillage-of -barracks-22/.

160 *he'd grabbed six hundred thousand barrels*: Ghaith Shennib and Julia Payne, "Armed Groups in Libya Are Selling the Oil They Seized," Reuters, January 8, 2014.

160 *On October 5, 2013, U.S. Delta Force commandos*: Adam Goldman, "Video Shows U.S. Abduction of Accused Al-Qaeda Terrorist on Trial for Embassy Bombings," *Washington Post*, February 10, 2014.

162 *two thousand protestors organized by Tripoli's city council*: Umar Khan, "The Gharghour Tragedy: An Eyewitness Account," *Libya Herald*, November 16, 2013, https://www.libyaherald.com/2013/11/16/the-ghar ghour-tragedy-an-eyewitness-account/.

163 *violence rattled the city*: Frederic Wehrey, "The Battle for Benghazi," *Atlantic*, February 28, 2014, https://www.theatlantic.com/international/archive /2014/02/the-battle-for-benghazi/284102/.

165 *when it was all over, thirty-one people*: "Libyan Army Chief Quits After Deadly Clashes," *Al Jazeera*, June 9, 2013, http://www.aljazeera.com /news/africa/2013/06/20136916201458523.html.

167 *"Public patience with the militias"*: Frederic Wehrey, Senate Foreign Relations Committee testimony, Subcommittee on Near Eastern and South and Central Asian Affairs, November 21, 2013, https://www.foreign.senate.gov/imo/media/doc/Wehrey_Testimony.pdf.

167 *before a precursor to that committee*: Full House Committee on Oversight and Government, "Reform, Benghazi, Instability, and a New Government: Successes and Failures of U.S. Intervention in Libya," May 1, 2014, https://oversight.house.gov/hearing/benghazi-instability-new-government-successes-failures-u-s-intervention-libya/.

168 *millions of dollars investigating*: Glenn Kessler, "Have Republicans Really Spent $7 Million on the Benghazi Committee?" *Washington Post*, May 17, 2016, https://www.washingtonpost.com/news/fact-checker/wp/2016/05/17/have-republicans-really-spent-7-million-on-the-benghazi-committee/?utm_term=.1c8336eab50b.

168 *the FBI director had testified*: U.S. Senate Select Committee on Intelligence, *Review of the Terrorist Attacks on U.S. Facilities in Benghazi, Libya, September 11–12, 2012*, January 15, 2014, 41, https://www.intelligence.senate.gov/sites/default/files/publications/113134.pdf.

9. "THIS IS DIGNITY"

172 *Dressed in his army uniform*: Tshrafi Abdul-Wahab, "General Haftar Announces Coup; Politicians React with Scorn, Order His Arrest," *Libya Herald*, February 14, 2014.

173 *Dubbed "No Extension"*: Rafaa Tabib, "Mobilized Publics in Post-Qadhafi Libya: The Emergence of New Modes of Popular Protest in Tripoli and Ubari," *Mediterranean Politics* 21, no. 1 (2016): 87.

174 *shelled the convention center*: Associated Press, "Tripoli Tense After Attack on Libyan Parliament," May 19, 2014.

174 *Zeidan had publicly denounced*: Quoted in David Kirkpatrick, "In Libya, a Coup. Or Perhaps Not," *New York Times*, February 14, 2014.

174 *A team of U.S. Navy Seals swooped in*: Fred Barbash, "Navy SEALs Board Mystery Tanker Morning Glory Near Cyprus. No One Hurt, Pentagon Says," *Washington Post*, March 17, 2014.

178 *There were nearly twenty gunshots*: Libyan Ministry of Justice investigation and autopsy report (in Arabic), December 2, 2014, provided to the author.

180 *"I am not going to come out"*: Barbara Slavin, "US Ambassador Says Libyan General Is Going After 'Terrorists,'" Al-Monitor, May 14, 2014, http://www.al-monitor.com/pulse/originals/2014/05/us-ambassador-libya-Hifter-terrorists-attack.html.

181 *After the Americans snatched al-Libi*: United States of America v. Ahmed Salim Faraj Abu Khattalah, 1:14-cr-00141-CRC-1, November 6, 2017, afternoon session.

181 *just after midnight on June 15*: Spencer S. Hsu, "Thirteen Days in the History of the Accused Leader of the Benghazi Attacks," *Washington Post*, June 9, 2016.

181 *Code-naming him Greenbrier River*: United States of America v. Ahmed Salim Faraj Abu Khattalah, 1:14-cr-00141-CRC-1, November 8, 2017, morning session.

181 *jurors' doubts about the motivation*: Spencer S. Hsu, "Benghazi Juror: Prosecutors Overplayed Emotional Appeal, Lacked Proof Abu Khattala Killed Americans," *Washington Post*, December 8, 2017.

181 *A tribal militia leader named Salah Bu Lighib*: United States of America v. Ahmed Salim Faraj Abu Khattalah, 1:14-cr-00141-CRC-1, October 12, 2017, afternoon session. Bu Lighib, who hails from the Awaqir tribe, is identified as the leader of the Military Intelligence Security Support Brigade, a pro-LNA militia. See also Spencer S. Hsu, "Libyan Is First Witness to Directly Implicate Benghazi Suspect at Trial in Washington," *Washington Post*, October 16, 2017. For reporting on his secret prison, see *Libya al-Akhbar* (Arabic), August 1, 2017, https://www.noonpost.org/content /19158.

183 *Zintani militias had threatened*: Ghaith Shennib and Ulf Laessing, "Libyan Militias Threaten Parliament, Deploy Forces in Tripoli," Reuters, February 18, 2014.

183 *weapons flowed*: UN Security Council, *Final Report of the Panel of Experts on Libya Established Pursuant to Resolution 1973 (2011)*, June 1, 2017, 24–25.

10. CIVIL WAR

188 *American, British, and United Nations diplomats*: Tariq Mitri, *Masālik waʿirah: Sanatān fī Lībiyā wa-min ajlihā* [Rugged paths: Two years in Libya, for its sake] (Beirut: Riyāḍ al-Rayyis, 2015), 236–42; "Opening Statement by US Ambassador-Retired Deborah K. Jones," U.S. Senate Committee on Foreign Relations, "The Crisis in Libya: Next Steps and U.S. Policy Options," April 25, 2017; https://www.foreign.senate.gov /imo/media/doc/042517_Jones_Testimony.pdf.

193 *Al-Sisi started a pipeline*: UN Security Council, *Final Report of the Panel of Experts on Libya Established Pursuant to Resolution 1973 (2011)*, February 23, 2015, 39.

193 *Egyptian troops joined an Emirati*: David D. Kirkpatrick and Eric Schmitt, "Arab Nations Strike in Libya, Surprising U.S.," *New York Times*, August 25, 2014.

193 *On the other side, backing the Dawn forces*: *Final Report of the Panel of Experts on Libya Established Pursuant to Resolution 1973 (2011)*, February 23, 2015, 43–45.

194 *"I think we should be slightly careful"*: UN Security Council, *Final Report of the Panel of Experts on Libya Established Pursuant to Resolution 1973 (2011)*, March 9, 2016, annex 30, 146.

194 *Emirati security forces rounded up ten Libyans*: Human Rights Watch, "UAE: Reveal Whereabouts of 'Disappeared' Libyans," October 5, 2014, https://www.hrw.org/news/2014/10/05/uae-reveal-whereabouts-disappeared-libyans.

195 *UN reported that the clashes had displaced*: UN High Commissioner for Refugees, "Over 100,000 People Displaced in Libya over the Past Three Weeks," October 10, 2014, http://www.unhcr.org/en-us/news/briefing/2014/10/5437b1a3746/100000-people-displaced-libya-past-three-weeks.html.

195 *Anyone affiliated with Dignity*: Letter dated February 23, 2015, from the Panel of Experts established pursuant to resolution 1973 (2011) addressed to the President of the Security Council, 18–22.

196 *I traveled to the Dawn-held front*: Frederic Wehrey, "The Battle for Libya's Oil," *The Atlantic*, February 9, 2015.

200 *And the Misratans had been an inseparable part*: Faraj Najem, *Tribe, Islam, and State in Libya: Analytical Study of the Roots of Libyan Tribal Society and Evolution up to the Qaramanli Reign (1781–1835)* (Benghazi: Center for Africa Research, 2017), 163.

200 *"The Misratans founded in Benghazi"*: Ibid.

202 *the source for the mythical Garden of the Hesperides*: Anthony Thwaite, *The Deserts of Hesperides: An Experience of Libya* (London: Martin Secker & Warburg, 1969), 62.

204 *saving "Libyan social fabric"*: Amnesty International, "Benghazi's Descent into Chaos: Abductions, Summary Killings, and Other Abuses," January 28, 2015, 17, https://www.amnesty.org/en/documents/mde19/0001/2015/en/.

11. EUROPE'S AFRICAN SHORES

208 *French colonialists were both terrified and enchanted*: Baz Lecocq, "Unemployed Intellectuals in the Sahara: The *Teshumara* Nationalist Movement and the Revolutions in Tuareg Society," *International Review of Social History* 49, no. S12 (December 2004): 89.

208 National Geographic *visited the Sahara's Tuareg regions*: Donovan Webster, "Journey to the Heart of the Sahara," *National Geographic*, March 1999, 6–33, quoted in ibid., 87.

209 *younger Tuareg entered a remittance economy*: Delphine Perrin, "Tuaregs and Citizenship: The Last Camp of Nomadism," *Middle East Law and Governance* 6 (2014): 299.

209 *had a name: ishumar*: Ines Kohl, "Libya, the 'Europe of Ishumar': Between

Losing and Reinventing Tradition," in *Tuareg Society Within a Globalized World*, ed. Anja Fischer and Ines Kohl (London: I. B. Tauris, 2010), 143–54.

209 *In 1980 he set up a camp*: Lecocq, "Unemployed Intellectuals in the Sahara," 102.

209 *half-crescent barchan dunes*: Gus H. Goudarzi, "Geology and Mineral Resources of Libya—a Survey," Geological Survey Professional Paper 660 (Washington, DC: U.S. Government Printing Office, 1970), 18–19.

210 *according to the Greek historian Herodotus*: Robert B. Strassler, ed., *The Landmark Herodotus: The Histories* (New York: Anchor Books, 2009), 357.

210 *They shipped this human chattel*: Kyle Harper, *Slavery in the Late Roman World, AD 275–425* (Cambridge: Cambridge University Press, 2011), 88.

211 *"His body was thrust*: Ibrahim al-Koni, *The Bleeding of the Stone*, trans. May Jayyusi and Christopher Tingley (Northampton, MA: Interlink Books, 2013), 134.

211 *they drew inspiration from the solos*: Lecocq, "Unemployed Intellectuals in the Sahara," 96.

211 *"Voice of the Beasts"*: Lyrics quoted in Nadia Belalimat, "Qui sait danser sur cette chanson, nous lui donnerons de la cadence: Musique, poésie et politique chez les Touaregs," *Terrain* 41 (2003), http://terrain.revues.org /1660; translated by author.

212 *The Tabu are a dark-skinned African people*: For background on the Tabu, see Philip Martin and Christina Weber, "Ethnic Conflict in Libya: Toubou," Norman Paterson School of International Affairs, Carleton University, June 21, 2012, https://carleton.ca/cifp/wp-content/uploads/1393-1 .pdf; Christophe Boisbouvier, "Libye: Quand les Toubous se réveillent" [Libya: When the Tabu awaken], *Jeune Afrique*, May 5, 2012, http:// www.jeuneafrique.com/141629/politique/libye-quand-les-toubous-se-r -veillent/; and Rebecca Murray, "Libya's Tebu: Living on the Margins," in *The Libyan Revolution and Its Aftermath*, ed. Peter Cole and Brian McQuinn (London: Hurst, 2015), 303–19.

213 *In towns across the south*: Frederic Wehrey, *Insecurity and Governance Challenges in Southern Libya* (Washington, DC: Carnegie Endowment for International Peace, 2017), http://carnegieendowment.org/2017/03 /30/insecurity-and-governance-challenges-in-southern-libya-pub -68451.

215 *340,000 barrels of oil*: Ulf Laessing, "Struggle for Libyan Oilfield Reflects Fractured Nation's Conflict," Reuters, November 12, 2014.

217 *Ghat had been a center of Saharan trade*: Amal Mohammed Hassan Jamal, "The Kel Azjer Tuareg Culture: Public and Private Space in Ghat" (PhD diss., McGill University, 2008), 228, 229.

218 *seven hundred thousand to one million migrants*: International Organization for Migration (IOM), "Libya," https://www.iom.int/countries/libya.

218 *Just over 50 percent are believed*: Associated Press, "UN Agency: Most Migrants in Libya Don't Want to Reach Europe," November 22, 2016, https://apnews.com/c3ffe75904dd413993ce896a1fd3b5da/un-agency-most-migrants-libya-dont-want-reach-europe.

219 *In 2016 alone, nearly five thousand died*: Ben Quinn, "Migrant Death Toll Passes 5,000 After Two Boats Capsize off Italy," *Guardian*, December 23, 2016.

219 *Libya has long existed as a portal*: Alex De Waal, "African Roles in the Libyan Conflict of 2011," *International Affairs* 89 (2013): 365.

219 *when a number African states*: James Kirchick, "South Africa Stands with Qaddafi," *Atlantic*, September 6, 2011, https://www.theatlantic.com/international/archive/2011/09/south-africa-stands-with-qaddafi/244584/.

220 *170,000 migrants passing through it*: Lucas Destrijcker, "Welcome to Agadez, Smuggling Capital of Africa," *Politico*, October 17, 2016, http://www.politico.eu/article/the-smuggling-capital-of-africa-agadez-niger/.

224 *Outside sources including the United Nations*: Mark Micallef, "UN Libya Mission Calls for Inquiry into Zawiya Detention Centre Probe," Xchange: Research on Migration, April 8, 2016, http://xchange.org/un-libya-mission-calls-inquiry-zawiya-detention-centre-probe/.

224 *"vegetable peeler applied to someone's buttocks"*: Sarah Giles, "Fuel Burns," Médecins Sans Frontières, December 6, 2016, http://blogs.msf.org/en/staff/blogs/moving-stories/fuel-burns.

225 *started training and equipping*: UN Security Council, *Final Report of the Panel of Experts on Libya Established Pursuant to Resolution 1973 (2011)*, June 1, 2017, 41.

226 *Then Italy began paying the traffickers*: Declan Walsh and Jason Horowitz, "Italy, Going It Alone, Stalls the Flow of Migrants. But at What Cost?," *New York Times*, September 17, 2017; see also http://uk.reuters.com/article/uk-europe-migrants-libya/armed-group-seeks-legitimacy-with-tripoli-migrant-deal-source-says-idUKKCN1BW0HO.

226 *"reconversion" of smugglers*: Patrick Wintour, "Italian Minister Defends Methods That Led to 87% Drop in Migrants from Libya," *The Guardian*, September 17, 2017.

226 *like the smuggling of subsidized fuel*: Frederic Wehrey, "Bleeding Fuel," *Diwan* (blog), Carnegie Middle East Center, June 14, 2017, http://carnegie-mec.org/diwan/71223.

226 *A video surfaced*: Bel Trew, "Video Shows Libyan Coastguard Whipping Rescued Migrants," *Times* (London), February 14, 2017, https://www

.thetimes.co.uk/article/video-shows-libyan-coastguard-whipping -rescued-migrants-6d8g2jgz6.

227 *set themselves up*: UN Security Council, *Final Report of the Panel of Experts on Libya Established Pursuant to Resolution 1973 (2011)*, June 1, 2017, 61.

227 *complicit in the trafficking trade*: Ibid., 103, 133.

12. THE ISLAMIC STATE'S AFRICAN HOME

230 *thousands of Libyans left to fight*: UN Security Council, *Report of the Analytical Support and Sanctions Monitoring Team Submitted Pursuant to Paragraph 13 of Security Council Resolution 2214 (2015) Concerning the Terrorism Threat in Libya Posed by the Islamic State in Iraq and the Levant, Ansar al Charia, and All Other Al-Qaida Associates*, November 19, 2015, 24.

231 *U.S. government estimates put the death toll of civilians*: Joby Warrick, "More Than 1,400 Killed in Syrian Chemical Weapons Attack, U.S. Says," *Washington Post*, August 30, 2013, https://www.washingtonpost.com/world /national-security/nearly-1500-killed-in-syrian-chemical-weapons-attack -us-says/2013/08/30/b2864662-1196-11e3-85b6-d27422650fd5_story .html?utm_term=.8b39c16d46c7.

232 *STRETCH FORTH THE HANDS*: Aymenn Jawad Al-Tamimi, "The Emergence of the Islamic State's 'Cyrenaica Province' (Wilayat Barqa) in Libya," *Pundicity* (blog), November 17, 2014, http://www.aymennjawad .org/2014/11/the-emergence-of-the-islamic-state-cyrenaica.

233 *At a soccer stadium*: Amnesty International, "'Public Execution' in Football Stadium Shows Libya's Descent into Lawlessness," August 22, 2014, https://www.amnesty.org/en/press-releases/2014/08/public-execution -football-stadium-shows-libya-s-descent-lawlessness/.

233 *Foreigners helmed the new order*: UN Security Council, *Report of the Analytical Support and Sanctions Monitoring Team*, 9.

234 *"A righteous adversary against the Islamic State"*: Quoted in "The Islamic State Diary: A Chronicle of Life in Libyan Purgatory," *Spiegel Online*, September 4, 2015, http://www.spiegel.de/international/world/the -islamic-state-diary-a-chronical-of-life-in-libyan-purgatory-a-1051422 .html.

235 *"Inhospita Syrtis"*: Virgil, *The Aeneid*, book 4, line 41, http://www .thelatinlibrary.com/vergil/aen4.shtml.

235 *"A large coastal city with brick walls"*: Quoted in Al-Tahir Ahmad al-Zawi, *Mu'jam al-buldan al-Libiya* [Encyclopedia of Libyan towns] (Tripoli: Al-Nur, 1968), 188.

236 *The Islamic State moved in slowly*: Frederic Wehrey and Ala' Alrababa'ah, "Taking on Operation Dawn: The Creeping Advance of the Islamic State in Western Libya," *Diwan* (blog), Carnegie Middle East Center, June 24, 2015, http://carnegie-mec.org/diwan/60490.

238 *"Battle of Abu Anas al-Libi"*: SITE Intelligence Group, January 27, 2015, https://news.siteintelgroup.com/Jihadist-News/is-division-in-tripoli -libya-claims-attack-on-corinthia-hotel-as-battle-of-abu-anas-al-libi .html.

239 *up to three thousand fighters across Libya*: UN Security Council, *Report of the Analytical Support and Sanctions Monitoring Team*, 9.

240 *In December 2015, for instance*: Jack Moore, "Libya Air Force Reveals Failed U.S. Special Forces Mission," *Newsweek*, December 18, 2015.

240 *two secret outposts in Libya*: Missy Ryan, "U.S. Establishes Libyan Outposts with Eye Toward Offensive Against Islamic State," *Washington Post*, March 12, 2016.

241 *"the first to draw our attention"*: "Opening Statement by US Ambassador-Retired Deborah K. Jones," U.S. Senate Committee on Foreign Relations, "The Crisis in Libya: Next Steps and U.S. Policy Options," April 25, 2017, https://www.foreign.senate.gov/imo/media/doc/042517_Jones _Testimony.pdf.

242 *pushback started in Derna*: Frederic Wehrey and Ala' Alrababa'ah, "Splitting the Islamists: The Islamic State's Creeping Advance in Libya," *Diwan* (blog), Carnegie Middle East Center, June 19, 2015, http://carnegie -mec.org/diwan/60447.

243 *"I laughed until I had tears in my eyes"*: Quoted in "Islamic State Diary."

243 *a beachside Roman city*: Al-Zawi, *Mu'jam al-buldan al-Libiya*, 211.

243 *"Between the Rome of the past"*: Massimiliano Munzi, "Italian Archaeology in Libya from Colonial Romanità to Decolonization of the Past," in *Archaeology Under Dictatorship*, ed. Michael L. Galaty and Charles Watkinson (New York: Springer, 2004), 85.

249 *In an interview just before his death*: *Dabiq* (Islamic State English-language magazine), September 9, 2015; available at https://kyleorton1991.word press.com/2015/09/10/an-interview-with-the-islamic-states-leader-in -libya/.

13. THE STRONGMAN

252 *motivated partly by the economic pinch*: Frederic Wehrey, "Libya's War-Weary Make Peace? Letter from Misrata," *Foreign Affairs*, February 2, 2015.

252 *leaked emails revealed*: David D. Kirkpatrick, "Leaked Emirati Emails Could Threaten Peace Talks in Libya," *New York Times*, November 12, 2015.

261 *The first strikes came from American marines*: Sam LaGrone, "Marine Harriers Strike ISIS Targets in Libya from USS Wasp," *United States Naval Institute News*, August 3, 2016.

261 *the marines added SuperCobras to the fight*: Thomas Gibbons-Neff, "Marine Gunships Enter the Fight Against the Islamic State in Libya," *Washington Post*, August 22, 2016.

262 *exposé by Le Monde*: Nathalie Guibert, "La guerre secrète de la France en Libye," *Le Monde*, February 24, 2016, http://www.lemonde.fr /international/article/2016/02/24/la-guerre-secrete-de-la-france-en -libye_4870603_3210.html.

262 *Official acknowledgment from the French government*: Cyril Bensimon, Frédéric Bobin, and Madjid Zerrouky, "Trois membres de la DGSE tués en Libye, le gouvernement libyen proteste," *Le Monde*, July 20, 2016.

263 *UAE, along with Egypt, never stopped supporting*: UN Security Council, *Final Report of the Panel of Experts on Libya Established Pursuant to Resolution 1973 (2011)*, June 1, 2017, 24–35.

263 *In the spring of 2016, the UAE delivered hundreds*: Ibid., 43–44.

263 *Press reports trickled out*: Karim El-Bar, "UK Troops 'Operating from French-Led Libyan Base Aiding Renegade General," *Middle East Eye*, June 23, 2016.

264 *Emirati armored vehicles helped the Libyan National Army*: Aidan Lewis, "Covert Emirati Support Gave East Libyan Air Power Key Boost: U.N. Report," Reuters, June 9, 2017.

266 *Russian television broadcast images*: Reuters, "East Libya Strongman Visits Russian Aircraft Carrier in Mediterranean: RIA," January 11, 2017.

266 *12 percent of Russian arms exports*: Alexei Anishchuk, "Gaddafi Fall Cost Russia Tens of Blns in Arms Deals," Reuters, November 2, 2011.

266 *Spotting a useful ally*: Jo Becker and Eric Schmitt, "As Trump Wavers on Libya, an ISIS Haven, Russia Presses On," *New York Times*, February 7, 2018, https://www.nytimes.com/2018/02/07/world/africa/trump-libya -policy-russia.html.

266 *It also provided vital assistance*: Rami Musa, "Defying Critics, Libya's Eastern Bank Prints Its Own Money," Associated Press, May 27, 2016.

266 *By 2017, this support*: Phil Stewart, Idrees Ali, and Lin Noueihed, "Exclusive: Russia Appears to Deploy Forces in Egypt, Eyes on Libya Role— Sources," Reuters, March 18, 2017.

267 *two B-2 Spirit stealth bombers*: Joe Pappalardo, "To Libya and Back: Inside a Stealth Bomber Strike Against ISIS," *Popular Mechanics*, February 8, 2017.

267 *"shit show"*: Jeffrey Goldberg, "The Obama Doctrine," *Atlantic*, April 2016, https://www.theatlantic.com/magazine/archive/2016/04/the-obama -doctrine/471525/.

267 *"worst mistake" of his presidency*: Fox News, "Exclusive: President Barack Obama on 'Fox News Sunday,'" April 10, 2016, http://www.foxnews .com/transcript/2016/04/10/exclusive-president-barack-obama-on-fox -news-sunday.html.

267 *"The degree of tribal division"*: Goldberg, "Obama Doctrine."

267 *"A president does not make decisions in a vacuum"*: Ibid.

271 *they inflicted a string of abuses*: Human Rights Watch, "Libya: War Crimes as Benghazi Residents Flee," March 22, 2017, https://www.hrw.org/news /2017/03/22/libya-war-crimes-benghazi-residents-flee.

271 *the International Criminal Court charged him*: International Criminal Court, Request to Libya for cooperation in the arrest and surrender of Mahmoud Mustafa Busayf al-Werfalli, August 21, 2017, https://www.icc -cpi.int/Pages/record.aspx?docNo=ICC-01/11-01/17-3.

271 *"No mercy," he said in the fall of 2015*: Media Office, General Command of the Libyan Armed Forces (Arabic), October 10, 2015, https://www .youtube.com/watch?v=PlBWhuMsdW4.

272 *Hiftar had co-opted*: Frederic Wehrey, "Quiet No More," *Diwan* (blog), Carnegie Middle East Center, October 13, 2016, http://carnegie-mec .org/diwan/64846.

272 *dismissed the elected city council*: Maha Sulaiman and Ajnadin Mustafa, "Benghazi Municipal Council Suspended by Nazhuri," *Libya Herald*, August 11, 2016.

273 *issued an edict*: "Nazhuri Bans Women Flying from Labraq Without Male Guardian," *Libya Herald*, February 19, 2012.

274 *onto what another writer called*: Piers Brendon, *The Dark Valley: A Panorama of the 1930s* (New York: Alfred A. Knopf, 2000).

ACKNOWLEDGMENTS

I incurred countless debts in writing this book, but above all to the many Libyans who shared their insights with me, who sheltered me, and who protected me. Many did so at risk to themselves. Those who can be named here include Emad Ben Matoug, a cherished companion and guide, and Faraj Najem, an esteemed Libyan historian, who both assisted during multiple trips. I also learned a great deal from Abd al-Rahman al-Agily, Rami Musa, Abd al-Karim Bazama, Fathi Bashaaga, Kamal Showaia, Abu Bakr al-Khaty, Younis Essa, Hashim Bishr, Mustafa al-Siqizly, and Serageldin Ben Ali. I thank Iman Bugaighis, Wail Gheriani, Laila Bugaighis, Wafa Bugaighis, and Tamim Baiou for sharing their memories of the late Salwa Bugaighis.

Though this book is mostly concerned with Libyan narratives, it also explores the experiences of Americans, especially those who were on the ground. I am grateful to Jan Stevens and Anne Stevens for speaking with me about their son and brother, the late Chris Stevens, as well as Austin Tichenor for his recollections of a dear friend. A number of current and former officials and diplomats discussed their roles in America's Libya policy: Susan Rice, Samantha Power, Derek Chollet, Michael McFaul, Jake Sullivan, Ben Fishman, Alex Bick, Steve Simon, Joshua Geltzer, Deborah Jones, Brian Linvill, Jonathan Winer, Gene Cretz, Lydia Sizer, Lawrence Pope, Mietek Boduszyński, and Erica Kaster.

From the United Nations, I extend my thanks to Ian Martin, Tarek Mitri, Bernardino Léon, Michael Smith, and Salim Raad.

Several keen observers of Libya were kind enough to read chapter drafts: Karim Mezran, Wolfram Lacher, Rebecca Murray, Peter Bartu, Frank Revuelto-Lanao, Jalel Harchaoui, and Ariel Ahram. In researching Libya the past decade, I've profited from the work of other scholars of the country, both established and up-and-coming, including Ronald Bruce St John, Lisa Anderson, Dirk Vandewalle, Muhammad al-Mufti, Ali Abduallatif Ahmida, Amal Obeidi, Peter Cole, Geoffrey Howard, Mary Fitzgerald, and Mattia Toaldo.

For more than five years, the Carnegie Endowment for International Peace has been my professional home, blessed with an elusive combination of independence, intellectual excellence, and collegiality. I would not have traveled to Libya were it not for the Endowment's sustained support. I wish to thank the past and current presidents of this unique institution—Jessica Mathews and William J. Burns—for their principled leadership, as well as Marwan Muasher, Katherine Wilkens, and Michele Dunne for helming the Middle East Program. The inimitable Sarah Chayes rallied me at the starting line and a legion of talented junior fellows at Carnegie carried me through the finish: Ala' Alrababa'h, Varsha Kodavayur, Caroline Zullo, and Katherine Pollock all provided invaluable help in ferreting out Arabic sources, reading drafts, and fact-checking. The resourceful staff of Carnegie's library—Kathleen Higgs, Christopher Lao-Scott, and Alexander Dodd—tracked down hard-to-find historical works.

I owe so much to my agent, Bridget Matzie, who believed that Libya's story was worth telling on its own terms, and I am equally indebted to the team at Farrar, Straus and Giroux: Jonathan Galassi, Jeff Seroy, Steven Pfau, Sarita Varma, Dominique Lear, and Katie Hurley. I am most grateful for the efforts of Alex Star, my superb editor, whose felicitous counsel helped me to grow as a writer and improved the book significantly.

This journey would not have been the same without Nakisa Karimian, whose warmth and encouragement made all the difference.

Finally, this book is dedicated to my parents, whose own curiosity about the world and affinity for the written word has been inspiring in more ways than they know.

INDEX

A NOTE ABOUT THE AUTHOR

Frederic Wehrey is a senior fellow at the Carnegie Endowment for International Peace. His writing on Libya has appeared in *The New Yorker, The Atlantic, The New York Times,* and other publications. A U.S. military veteran who served across the Middle East, he holds a doctorate in international relations from Oxford University. His first book, *Sectarian Politics in the Gulf,* was chosen as a Best Book on the Middle East by *Foreign Affairs* magazine. Born and raised in Southern California, he now lives in Washington, D.C.